AFTER THE
COLD WAR

Studies on Contemporary China

Studies on Contemporary China

AFTER THE
COLD WAR

Domestic Factors and U.S.-China Relations

ROBERT S. ROSS

Editor

Barry Naughton   Robert S. Ross
Marcus Noland   Robert G. Sutter
Steven M. Teles

AN EAST GATE BOOK

M.E. Sharpe
Armonk, New York
London, England

An East Gate Book

Library of Congress Cataloging-in-Publication Data

After the Cold War : domestic factors and U.S.–China relations /
Robert S. Ross, editor.
p.   cm. — (Studies on contemporary China)
"An East gate book."
Includes index.
ISBN 0-7656-0291-1 (c : alk. paper). —
ISBN 0-7656-0292-X (p : alk. paper)
1. United States—Foreign relations—China.   2. China—Foreign
relations—United States.   3. United States—Foreign relations—1989–
4. United States—Politics and government—1989–
5. United States—Foreign relations—China—Public opinion.
6. China—Foreign relations—United States—Public opinion.
7. Public opinion—United States.   I. Ross, Robert S., 1954–
II. Series.
E183.C5A637   1998
327.73051′09′049—dc21   98-16762
CIP

Printed in the United States of America

The paper used in this publication meets the minimum requirements of
American National Standard for Information Sciences—
Permanence of Paper for Printed Library Materials,
ANSI Z 39.48-1984.

MV (c)   10   9   8   7   6   5   4   3   2   1
MV (p)   10   9   8   7   6   5   4   3   2   1

Contents

Foreword

Robert S. Ross

From the historic visits to Beijing by Henry Kissinger and Richard Nixon in the early 1970s to the demise of the Warsaw Pact and the end of the Cold War in 1989, the United States and China developed a very successful cooperative relationship. Despite the previous twenty years of animosity and numerous crises, Washington and Beijing rapidly joined forces to deal with their common Soviet adversary. They normalized diplomatic relations, conducted high-level strategic dialogues, engaged in bilateral arms transfers, and developed and expanded economic and cultural relations. They also coordinated policies to contend with Soviet policy in Indochina and Afghanistan. Simultaneously, they negotiated compromise solutions to serious conflicts of interests, including that over U.S. policy toward Taiwan, and shelved more intractable issues, such as ideological differences over human rights. In the context of common vital interests, American and Chinese leaders were able to forge a mutually beneficial relationship.

The era of U.S.-China cooperation reflected the unique dynamics of the latter half of the Cold War. It is now widely understood that in the aftermath of the Cold War, common strategic concerns, such as those that promoted U.S.-China cooperation, no longer compel nations to accommodate each other's interests and that absent any strategic imperative, domestic factors have become an increasingly important factor in foreign policy-making. This transformation is readily apparent in U.S. foreign policy. In the absence of the overriding Soviet threat, public opinion, interest groups, policy debates, and bureaucratic politics have all developed significant influence in the policy-making process and in shaping policy toward both allies and adversaries. The result has been a less coherent and less consistent American foreign policy toward a wide range of countries and issues.

The premise of this volume is that the post–Cold War importance of domestic factors in foreign policy-making is especially pronounced in U.S. policy toward China and that China, as well, has experienced a similar change in its foreign policy and that its policy toward the United States is equally influenced by Chinese domestic factors. The result is that the course of U.S.-China relations will be fundamentally affected by the evolution of each country's domestic system and that understanding the impact of domestic factors on U.S. and Chinese policy-making is crucial to understanding U.S.-China relations and the prospects for stability in both East Asia and in global politics.

U.S.-China cooperation during the 1970s and 1980s was different than other cooperative great-power relationships during the Cold War. Unlike relations between the United States and the other NATO countries, between the United States and Japan, and between China and the Soviet Union during the 1950s, China and the United States did not possess a common ideology, or similar political or economic systems, or shared cultural traditions. They were drawn together almost exclusively for strategic necessity. This strategic complementarity provided the basis for twenty years of cooperation, but it did not create shared traditions or common economic and political systems that could sustain cooperation in the absence of strategic imperatives. Common strategic interests allowed for compromises over the Taiwan issue and encouraged the two sides to minimize their ideological differences, but they did not allow for resolution of these important differences. To the extent that common U.S.-China economic and cultural interests developed, the importance of these interests in the overall relationship were minimal compared to their importance in relations between the United States and its other Cold War partners.

For the United States, the relationship with China was consistently viewed as part of a Cold War strategy of coping with Soviet power. Nixon and Kissinger did not possess any romantic illusions about traditional U.S.-China friendship or the prospects for developing an enduring friendship between democratic America and totalitarian China. They viewed the demise of the Sino-Soviet alliance as an opportunity for the United States to open relations with China to contend with the growth of Soviet power during a period of U.S. retrenchment. The relatively idealistic Carter administration chose to meet the People's Republic of China's (PRC) demands for normalization of relations only when it saw the benefit of improved U.S.-China relations to contending with Soviet expansionism. Even during the latter years of the relationship, when economic and cultural ties expanded, American policymakers primarily viewed these new relationships as efforts to develop domestic institutions that would contribute to greater stability in the strategic relationship. Ultimately, these institutions proved very important. They established the minimal foundation necessary to prevent open-ended U.S. hostility toward China after the Cold War. But they could not enable the United States to sustain cooperation with China at Cold War levels. Thus, in the absence of strategic necessity and possessing little else in common with China, domestic interests have often prevailed in the making of China policy.

For the United States, the dilemma of China policy has been an especially pronounced facet of America's well-understood search for a post–Cold War foreign policy. But this post–Cold War dynamic is just as true for China as for the United States. Mao Zedong's turn to the United States in the early 1970s reflected his heightened concern for the Soviet threat following the 1969 Sino-Soviet border war and his understanding that the United States was withdrawing from the war in Vietnam. Deng Xiaoping continued and consolidated Mao's U.S. policy for similar reasons. In the context of Soviet expansionism into Asia and on the Chinese periphery in the 1980s, he, too, sought strengthened U.S.-China strategic and economic cooperation. China's accommodation to the Reagan administration's insistence that it would maintain extensive security ties with Taiwan reflected China's immediate preoccupation in preserving U.S.-China cooperation against Soviet power. China's open door economic policy and expanded U.S.-China economic relations were also partly seen in this context. China needed to modernize its economy to enhance national security, and economic and educational ties with the United States served this purpose.

At no time during the 1970s and 1980s did China's senior policymakers believe that the U.S.-China relationship was anything but a marriage of strategic convenience. Throughout this period China's Communist leaders viewed the United States as the ideological adversary of Chinese communism. Nonetheless, cooperation with American "imperialism" was preferable to contending with Soviet power alone. Thus, for China, as well as for the United States, the end of the Cold War and the demise of the Soviet threat eliminated the primary foundation of close cooperation with the United States. And, similar to the post–Cold War changes in U.S. policy-making, in China the domestic sources of policy toward the United States expanded as parochial political and economic interests, rather than solely strategic considerations, influenced the policy-making process.

At the end of the Cold War, China and the United States could draw considerable satisfaction from the retreat of Soviet power, yet the very success of U.S.-China strategic cooperation has also removed the foundation for cooperative relations for the post–Cold War era. That relations between two large countries with little in common except for temporal strategic interests would drift apart and experience greater tension was perhaps inevitable. But it was also likely that in normal circumstances this would be a gradual devolution that could be managed by policy-making elites so as to avoid dramatic reversals. Policy would be more complex as domestic factors intruded into the policy-making process, but in the absence of immediate bilateral conflicts over vital interests Chinese and American leaders could sustain cooperation in secondary arenas. But this was not to be the case. On the contrary, coinciding with the demise of the Warsaw Pact in 1989, U.S.-China cooperation plummeted. Rather than focus on developing new forms of cooperation in post–Cold War relations, policymakers in both Beijing and Washington became preoccupied with damage limitation.

Relations plummeted because of the reaction in both China and the United States to the development of and the Chinese leadership's crackdown on the 1989 Beijing democracy movement. It is difficult to overemphasize the importance of this development for policy-making in both countries. In the United States, China's democracy movement and the ultimate crackdown on the demonstrators occurred as Communist governments were falling in Eastern Europe. The demonstrations in Beijing, viewed on television sets throughout America, gave rise to unrealistic expectations that communism might fall in China, thereby bringing greater freedom to the largest country in the world. The violent crackdown on the demonstrators, also viewed on America's televisions, not only produced widespread disappointment and hostility toward Chinese leaders, but in the view of many Americans also set Chinese leaders apart from the "civilized world," insofar as they refused to conform to a global trend of democratization. Chinese leaders had become Communist pariahs; they had developed the reputation as the world's most repressive leadership and had become the focus of Americans concerned with the fate of human rights around the world.

Overnight, in the view of the American public, Chinese leaders had turned from strategic partners promoting economic and political liberalization to authoritarian dictators pursuing policies inimical to core American values. Although the reality was far more complex—China was both authoritarian and liberalizing; it was no longer a strategic partner, but there were American interests that required cooperation with China—widespread American acceptance of the one-dimensional image of China as a retrograde communist state had transformed the policy-making process. Without the restraints of the strategic imperative of managing the Soviet threat, politicians developed parochial interests in promoting a hard-line China policy to appeal to domestic constituencies and to prove their foreign policy toughness. Interest groups opposed to a wide range of Chinese policies affecting the U.S. economy, weapons proliferation, the global environment, and various human rights issues gained a larger national audience and greater political clout as Americans and their elected officials were now more sympathetic to criticisms of the Chinese leadership. This trend assumed even greater salience after the fall of the Communist Party of the Soviet Union in 1991.

In this transformed political environment, American policymakers could no longer make China policy without responding to the pressures of public opinion, narrow economic interests, special interest groups, and members of Congress. Equally important, White House efforts to ease U.S.-China tensions would necessarily entail risks for the White House, which would be criticized for ignoring China's human rights abuses and compromising American values. Maintaining U.S.-China cooperation had become a complex and politically costly enterprise for any American administration.

China's foreign policy-making process experienced an equally profound response to the 1989 democracy demonstrations. Whereas Americans viewed the Chinese democracy demonstrations with unmitigated enthusiasm, Chinese leaders viewed the democracy movement as an unequivocal challenge to their political leadership and to the survival of the Chinese Communist Party. That hundreds of thousands of Chinese dared to congregate without government permission in China's most important public place reflected a significant degradation of central authority. That such independent political activity occurred while communism was collapsing in Eastern Europe made the Chinese elite insecurity especially acute. Continued unchecked, Chinese leaders feared that the Chinese Communist Party might suffer the fate of its East European counterparts. They had both the determination and the ability to make sure that did not happen.

The democracy demonstrations and their aftermath held particular significance for the Chinese leadership's view of the United States. They understood that a major cause of the demonstrations was the exposure of Chinese youth to Western values, in particular to American values because more Chinese have visited that United States than any other Western country and American cultural influence in China exceeded that of any other foreign country. During the demonstrations, Voice of America played a role in encouraging student activism and the Cable News Network (CNN) was instrumental in arousing international support for the movement. After the crackdown, the United States took the lead in organizing international economic and diplomatic sanctions against the Chinese leadership, trying to coerce the Chinese leadership into allowing the very activities that they had identified as threats to their survival, and the United States pressed China to allow Voice of America to broadcast information into China regarding international support for the Chinese democracy movement and stories critical of the Chinese leadership.

Just as the democracy movement and Beijing's response transformed America's understanding of China, the Chinese leadership assessment of the U.S. role in the democracy demonstrations transformed Beijing's appraisal of the United States. In April 1989 China's dominant image of the United States was that of an economic and strategic partner. Two months later the United States had become the foremost ideological and political adversary of the Chinese Communist Party. The implications for Chinese policy-making were profound. Freed from the constraints imposed by the Soviet threat, opposition Chinese elites now used China's U.S. policy as a political instrument in intraleadership struggles. In this context, cooperative PRC initiatives, regardless of their intrinsic benefit to Chinese economic and security interests, now carried political risk, for ideological conservatives could portray compromises as accommodation to American "hegemony." Domestic actors that had lost out from the open door economic policy could portray economic compromises with the United States as cooperation with U.S. subversion and continued Chinese economic reform as risking political instability. Much like American policymakers, China's policy-making elite now encountered often irresistible pressure to distort policy to accommodate parochial domestic interests.

This was the domestic and international context in which the United States and China addressed their bilateral relationship at the onset of the post–Cold War period. Expected post–Cold War policy management problems were exacerbated by the weakness of nonstrategic ties between the two countries and the mutual ideological animosity and the ensuing politicization of policy in both countries that developed in the aftermath of the June 1989 Chinese democracy movement. Conflicts over human rights issues (including imprisoned political dissidents, the status of Tibet, and China's population planning policies), competing economic interests, weapons proliferation, and the Taiwan issue came to dominate the bilateral agenda while cooperation become increasingly marginal and tenuous.

Recognition that domestic factors have assumed heightened importance in U.S.-China relations is the first step toward understanding the sources of post–Cold War U.S.-China relations. Full understanding requires analysis of the post–Cold War international context of U.S.-China relations. China and the United States may no longer be security partners, but what is the dominant character of their international relationship and how does this contribute to the importance of domestic factors in each country's foreign policy? Comprehensive understanding also requires analysis of why certain issues and not other issues reach the attention of the political elites in both countries and the circumstances in which these issues assume heightened importance on the bilateral agenda. It also requires understanding of how the combination of domestic and international factors contribute to the outcome of domestically derived bilateral disputes. Understanding contemporary U.S.-China relations requires a close analysis of each country's domestic condition in different arenas.

To address these issues, with the generous support of the Asia Foundation and the encouragement of Allen Choate, the Asia Foundation's director of program development, the Fairbank Center for East Asian Research at Harvard University, and the Research Center for Contemporary China at Peking University carried out a joint research project. The two institutes organized research teams to analyze the international context and the domestic factors that shape post–

Cold War U.S.-China relations. After presentation of their papers at a workshop at the Fairbank Center, the American participants met with their Chinese counterparts at a joint research conference at Peking University. This was a very productive and rewarding meeting. The exchange of research about the importance of each country's political, economic, and societal conditions in their respective foreign policies proved to be highly informative to all the participants, offering new insights into U.S.-China relations and suggesting important directions for additional research.

The Peking University research team was led by Professor Zhao Baoxu, director of the Research Center for Contemporary China. The other members of the Chinese research team were professors Sun Liping (Peking University), Wang Jisi (Chinese Academy of Social Sciences), and Zhu Shanli (Guanghua School of Management, Peking University). The proceedings in Beijing benefited from the insightful comments of the conference discussants. The Chinese discussants were professors Li Qingyuan (Peking University), Lu Jianhua (Chinese Academy of Social Sciences), Song Yimin (Institute of International Studies), Xin Qi (Center for Peace and Development), and Zi Zhongyun (Chinese Academy of Social Sciences). The American research team included the chapter authors for this volume, as well as professors Michael Mandelbaum (School of Advanced International Studies, Johns Hopkins University) and Joseph Massey (Dartmouth University).

The chapters in this volume reflect the rich dialogue among the Chinese and American scholars that took place in Beijing. The American authors revised their papers after both the Cambridge workshop and the collaborative conference in Beijing. The authors also benefited from helpful comments and suggestions provided by Ezra F. Vogel and Allen S. Whiting. The result is that the final product reflects the insights of both Chinese and American perspectives on the importance of domestic factors in U.S.-China relations.

AFTER THE
COLD WAR

1

The Strategic and Bilateral Context of Policy-Making in China and the United States

Why Domestic Factors Matter

Robert S. Ross

Successful management of U.S.-China relations is of central importance to the interests of both countries and to the interests of their neighbors throughout East Asia. It is no exaggeration to say that the two countries' ability to maintain cooperative relations and avoid escalated conflict and hostilities will determine the prospects for peace in East Asia in the next century. Nonetheless, the most prominent characteristic of post–Cold War U.S.-China relations, despite summitry and periodic improvement in relations, is persistent animosity and friction and constant threats to continued cooperation. Despite recent U.S.-China summitry and greater cooperation, the relationship remains turbulent and subject to recurring conflict, with implications for regional peace and stability.

The underlying sources of instability in U.S.-China relations are numerous. As subsequent chapters reveal, instability arises from such factors as historical legacies, elite and societal ideological differences, interest groups, and domestic economic and political interests. But the bilateral and regional contexts affect the changing salience of such factors. International sources of conflict and cooperation and bilateral negotiating dynamics create the parameters in which statesmen first address what policy *should* be and provide the expanding or contracting opportunities for other factors to affect ultimate policy choices.

The major dilemma in contemporary international relations is the diplomatic management of formerly minor issues that have assumed greater importance in the absence of any imperative for strategic cooperation. This is particularly the case for U.S.-China relations. The rapid disappearance of the Soviet threat led to escalated U.S.-China conflict over a wide range of issues and the emergence of a new bilateral bargaining relationship reflecting new dependencies and new sources of negotiating leverage. In this context, domestic factors have assumed greater importance in U.S.-China relations than at any time since the late 1960s. The post–Cold War foreign policy challenge for American and Chinese leaders is to build a new foundation for a cooperative relationship in the absence of important common interests and despite difficult negotiating dynamics.

The United States and China in East Asia

U.S.-China interactions in East Asia are characterized by minimal common security interests. Rather, Washington and Beijing frequently find themselves on opposite sides of regional security issues. But the resulting U.S.-China conflicts of interest do not entail immediate challenges to either side's non-negotiable vital interests. Rather, U.S.-China regional conflicts concern interests over which Washington and Beijing can reach a modus vivendi which preserves both their respective interests and stable U.S.-China relations. Their conflicts of interest are amenable to great-power management.

It is difficult to establish what common security interest the United States and China have in East Asia. Perhaps the most widely heard statement is that the two countries share an interest in regional stability. Chinese and American diplomats frequently insist that this common interest provides the foundation for cooperation across a wide range of areas and the basis for resolving conflicts of interest. In his banquet toast in the United States, Jiang Zemin argued that the United States and China "share broad common interests in ... the maintenance of world peace and security, the promotion of global economic growth and prosperity, and the protection of the living environment of mankind." China's Ambassador to the United States Li Daoyu argues that the foundations of the relationship are the U.S.-China common interests in peace and stability in East Asia.[1]

Yet peace and stability are not common interests. They are merely the environment in which nations pursue objectives. Although it is far less expensive to achieve objectives with peaceful means, nations often opt for conflictual methods when peace is not conducive to their interests. Conflict over the terms of peace is not unusual. Such was the case in Sino-Vietnamese relations, when Hanoi sought peaceful relations with China while it occupied Cambodia. Similarly, the Soviet Union and the United States both insisted that they wanted a stable international order; they simply could not agree on what that order should look like.

This is the dilemma faced by the United States and China. Both would prefer to achieve their international objectives without incurring the costs of instability and heightened conflict. But whether they can do so depends on whether or not they can develop a peaceful order that can accommodate each of their respective interests.

Are there common regionwide interests that might bring the United States and China together so that conflicts of interests are negotiated within a stable framework? Such interests clearly existed during the latter half of the Cold War. Common U.S. and Chinese interests in resisting Soviet power compelled the two countries to reach compromise solutions to fundamental conflicts of interests, including the volatile Taiwan issue.[2] It is also clear that such a compelling vital strategic interest does not exist today. Both U.S. and Chinese analysts stress that in the emerging East Asian balance of power, crosscutting relationships exist in various policy arenas, so that competition and cooperation coexist in the bilateral relationships among all of the great powers.[3] There has not emerged a great power whose capabilities and ambitions have galvanized any of the great powers, including the United States and China, into developing common comprehensive security policies based on immediate security threats.

It is also clear that neither China nor the United States has identified the other as posing an immediate threat to their respective vital interests or to the stability of the regional balance of power. Beijing is pleased that China's borders are more secure now than at any time in the last 150 years and that the United States does not have significant strategic or political influence with any of China's immediate neighbors. The United States is secure in its status as the world's sole superpower and in its overwhelming superiority in strategic missiles. China is secure with the conventional balance of power on the mainland of East Asia, and the United States enjoys uncontested supremacy in maritime East

Asia. Washington carefully observes China's rise in power, but still assesses China as a "potential" threat.[4]

Because Beijing and Washington do not identify each other as an immediate threat to vital interests, their foreign policy interactions focus on the long-term implications of regional and third-party issues. Consideration of such issues inherently allows governments greater flexibility to incorporate domestic factors into foreign policy-making. This flexibility is compounded because the United States and China have so little in common regarding policy toward regional issues and third parties. Indeed, to the extent that Beijing and Washington consider likely sources of future threat in the regional balance of power, their estimates are wildly different. Chinese and American policymakers also have conflicts of interests regarding regional disputes and territorial conflicts.

Contrasting Chinese and American perspectives regarding Russia reflect these differences. Chinese leaders consider Russia the least likely of the great powers to threaten Chinese interests. They consider Russian domestic political and economic turmoil as impediments to Russian ability to challenge Chinese interests. In contrast, American leaders remain apprehensive over Russia's nuclear arsenal, oppose its proliferation practices, and consider Russian military and political presence in Eastern Europe as a major security concern. They also are wary of Russian objectives in the Persian Gulf region. Washington is thus alarmed by the prospects of heightened Russian domestic instability and the potential for increased foreign policy nationalism.

These differing perspectives translate into conflicts of interest over contemporary Sino-Russian relations. Sino-Russian security cooperation reflects the combination of the absence of strategic conflicts of interests and the presence of complementary economic and even political interests. Denied access to Western weaponry in the aftermath of its repression of the June 1989 democracy movement, China turned to Russia for advanced military equipment to upgrade its antiquated armed forces, in return offering Moscow the hard currency it needs to acquire Western goods. China also provides the Soviet Far East with inexpensive consumer goods, plentiful manpower, and investment capital, all of which are important elements in Moscow's effort to maintain stability in that region. In this context, the Russian ambassador to China considered the problems associated with Chinese migration into the Russian Far East a minor issue. Even more important, China and

Russia have made extensive efforts to control Chinese migration into the Russian Far East, so that from 1995 to 1997 Chinese border violations had been reduced by over 80 percent.[5] Sino-Russia cooperation also reflects their mutual interest in resolving conflicts that could lead to heightened tension in the future. Their success in negotiating their territorial dispute and completing the demarcation of the eastern border in 1997 reduces the likelihood that their long border could once again become a source of military conflict.[6]

Equally important, the two sides find reassurance in their common difficulty in dealing with the United States. In particular, American efforts to expand the North Atlantic Treaty Organization (NATO) alliance into Eastern Europe arouses Russian concern just as improving U.S.-Japan security relations arouse Chinese concern.[7] Chinese and Russian "resolve" at the April 1996 Beijing summit to establish a "strategic partnership of equality, mutual confidence and mutual coordination toward the twenty-first century" reflected the wide range of common bilateral interests and their mutual concern for the direction of U.S. foreign policy.[8] Their support during the November 1997 Beijing summit for a multipolar world reflected an effort to accentuate their ability to counteract U.S. policies in Europe and East Asia.[9]

From Washington's perspective, Sino-Russian cooperation not only assists Beijing's effort to modernize its military but also creates the option of strategic cooperation should U.S. relations with either or both deteriorate. Russian transfer of Su-27s, Sovremennyy-class destroyers, surface-to-air missiles, Kilo-class submarines, and other equipment to China creates security concerns among America's strategic partners in East Asia. Although U.S. officials remain unruffled by current Chinese-Russian cooperation, the prospect of Russian transfer of SS-18 long-range ballistic missile technology to China prompted Secretary of Defense William Perry to warn Moscow that such a transfer would be a "big mistake."[10] Further Sino-Russian strategic cooperation could thus become an issue in both U.S.-Russian and U.S.-Chinese relations.

United States and Chinese estimates of Japan are equally divergent but are mirror images of their views of relations with Russia. Washington considers Japan a force for strategic stability in East Asia and an ally in U.S. efforts to maintain a favorable regional balance of power. As President Clinton explained during his April 1996 visit to Japan, the U.S.-Japanese security alliance is "key to maintaining a Pacific at peace." Similarly, Secretary of Defense Perry argued that the U.S.-

Japan security relationship is a "linchpin" for "all of the security issues in East Asia."[11] Thus, U.S. concern for alliance cohesiveness after the demise of the Soviet Union and for Japanese readiness to cooperate in military crises has encouraged the United States to enhance U.S.-Japan strategic cooperation. In addition, Washington has sought expanded cooperation with Japan to enhance U.S. ability to contend with growing Chinese power as well as American leverage over China regarding U.S.-China conflicts of interest.[12] These concerns led the United States to initiate negotiations with Japan over revised guidelines for security cooperation, resulting in the September 1997 U.S.-Japan revisions of the "Guidelines of U.S.-Japan Defense Cooperation." The revised guidelines call for the extension of security cooperation "in the areas surrounding Japan," including greater Japanese naval activities throughout the region, and greater U.S. reliance on the Japanese military in maintaining regional stability.[13]

Common interests with Japan, including concern for the development of Chinese power and for alliance stability in the post–Cold War period, also encourages Washington to cooperate with Japanese military modernization, confident that Japan will use expanded capabilities and regional authority in ways compatible with American interests. Washington has helped Japan develop the advanced F-2 fighter and, despite Japanese reluctance, has promoted U.S.-Japan cooperation in developing theater missile defense and deployment of such a system in Japan.[14] In this strategic context, U.S.-Japan economic conflict is problematic for the United States only insofar as it interferes with consolidation of strategic cooperation.

China, on the other hand, considers Japan a major regional competitor and a potential security threat. Beijing opposes Japanese defense acquisitions, which it characterizes as signs of resurgent "militarism" and intentions to become a strategic power. It is apprehensive over Japan's current military capabilities as well as its financial and technological ability to develop sophisticated power-projection capabilities on very short notice. Chinese analysts focus on Japanese development of nuclear capabilities, missile technologies, and military aircraft. They conclude that Japan is now developing sufficient military capability so that it will become a player in the regional balance of power and a potential source of regional instability.[15]

Apprehension over Japanese capabilities and intentions shape Beijing's assessment of U.S.-Japan relations. Although Beijing shares with the United States an interest in a demilitarized Japanese foreign policy and it values U.S.-Japanese security cooperation as a restraint on excessive Japanese rearmament, it is concerned that U.S.-Japanese cooperation contributes to Japanese military expansion and that the security alliance might actively focus on China should China's relations with Japan and/or the United States further deteriorate. In 1996 *People's Daily* explained that U.S.-Japan security cooperation "gives the feeling" that the two countries "work hand-in-hand to dominate the Asia-Pacific region." Another report explained that the April 1996 U.S.-Japan Joint Declaration on Security issued a "dangerous signal" that Japan has been "brought into the U.S. global military strategy."[16] In 1997, as the United States and Japan moved toward finalizing the treaty revisions, Chinese analysts explained that simultaneous expansion of NATO and U.S.-Japan security cooperation was part of U.S. global expansion. In East Asia, the United States was using U.S.-Japan cooperation to contain China.[17] Beijing is wary of U.S.-Japanese discussions of deploying a theater missile defense system in Japan, which would degrade China's second-strike nuclear retaliatory capability. It is especially suspicious that the guideline's ambiguity regarding the scope of the treaty obscures U.S. and Japanese intent to cooperate on the Taiwan issue. In 1998, for example, as Japan considered legislation to implement the revised guidelines, Chinese leaders repeatedly warned that the alliance should not interfere in China's domestic affairs and that the course of Sino-Japanese relations depended on this issue.[18]

Chinese and American interests also diverge over issues involving local powers. The most disruptive of such conflicts is the Taiwan issue. The domestic and historical aspects of the Taiwan issue are addressed in later chapters. Here it is important to note that the U.S.-China conflict over Taiwan also reflects conflicting strategic interests. For the United States, Chinese pressure on Taiwan challenges U.S. credibility as an East Asian power. Seeking to reassure the region that the United States will continue to participate actively in the regional balance of power, Washington has an interest in strongly signaling its opposition to mainland use of force against Taiwan. Assistant Secretary of State Winston Lord explained that the presence of a U.S. aircraft carrier near Taiwan during China's March 1996 military exercises in the Taiwan Strait aimed to "reassure our friends . . . that we have a big stake in the stability and peace of that region."[19]

Equally important, Taiwan has geostrategic significance in U.S. security policy. Chinese accuse the United States of opposing unification because it wants to retain access to its "unsinkable aircraft carrier."

Beijing is right—Taiwan is a strategic asset to the United States and that partially explains U.S. interest in maintaining Taiwan's independence. It is reassuring for the United States to have the option of cooperating with Taiwan should the United States and China become adversaries. But it is exactly Taiwan's strategic significance that contributes to Beijing's insistent claim to sovereignty over Taiwan and its efforts to weaken U.S.-Taiwan relations. Taiwan is too small to independently threaten China, but in collaboration with a great power Taiwan can contribute to Chinese insecurity. In strategic matters, Taiwan is to China as Cuba is to the United States. Beijing seeks to isolate and control Taiwan's international posture, trying to minimize the likelihood that Taiwan will once again serve as an "unsinkable aircraft carrier" for any great power.[20] This perspective helps to explain China's concern over the geographic scope of the U.S.-Japan security treaty.

During the Cold War, Washington compromised U.S.-Taiwan relations in order to develop cooperative security relations with the mainland, and China was relatively tolerant of ongoing U.S.-Taiwan economic and military relations. But in the absence of common U.S. and Chinese threat perceptions, the trend in U.S. policy toward Taiwan has been toward greater cooperation, including more liberal arms export policies and improved protocol treatment of Taiwan officials, which, Chinese leaders believe, have enhanced Taiwan's ability to resist mainland pressures. Simultaneously, Beijing has been less tolerant of U.S. challenges to its security regarding Taiwan. Although both China and the United States have no interest in seeing the outbreak of hostilities in the Taiwan Strait, and since 1996 Washington has adopted a more cautious Taiwan policy, in the more complex strategic and diplomatic circumstances of post-1989 U.S.-China relations, in conjunction with changing political developments on Taiwan and in Taiwan's foreign policy, it is far from clear that U.S.-China conflict of interests over Taiwan can be contained.

The United States interest in maritime Southeast Asia also compels it to support Malaysia and the Philippines in their territorial disputes with China over the Spratly Islands. The islands have little strategic significance and the exploration of the surrounding waters has yet to reveal significant deposits of natural resources, so that Chinese claims to the island do not affect U.S. economic interests or its interests in the security of the sea lanes of communication. But the United States does have an interest in reassuring the maritime countries of Southeast Asia of its regional presence so that they do not accommodate themselves to Chinese power in the regional balance. This requires Washington to signal opposition to any effort by the People's Republic of China (PRC) to expand its occupation of the islands. Although U.S. policy statements on the dispute have suggested neutrality on sovereignty over the islands, it was Chinese actions on Philippine-claimed islands that elicited U.S. statements regarding its interest in regional stability. It is also widely acknowledged that the United States has looked the other way when other claimants have tried to consolidate their own positions. Beijing cannot but view U.S. policy, no matter how tactful it may be, as siding with the other claimants against China's claim.[21]

Perhaps the only issue on which the United States and China have significant common interests concerns the Korean peninsula. Washington and Beijing have a strong interest in preventing North Korean acquisition of nuclear weapons. Not only would a nuclear-armed North Korea make a North-South war far more dangerous, but it might also encourage South Korean and Japanese acquisition of nuclear weapons and cause a nuclear arms race in Northeast Asia. Thus, at times Beijing has applied economic pressure on North Korean rulers, assisting U.S. efforts to compel Pyongyang to curtail its nuclear program.[22] Indeed, Chinese policy toward nuclear proliferation into North Korea is one Chinese policy that consistently draws praise from Washington for having "concerns similar" to America's and for playing "an important cooperative role" and providing "critical cooperation" in U.S. efforts to freeze North Korea's nuclear program.[23] China has also been supportive of U.S. efforts to bring about North Korean participation in the four-party peace talks involving the two Koreas, China, and the United States.[24]

The United States and China also share an interest in preventing economic and political instability in North Korea from leading to war between the two Koreas. China has contributed to this common objective of a "soft" rather than a "crash landing" of the North Korean government by encouraging Pyongyang to open its economy to foreign trade and investment and by supplying it with subsidized energy resources. As the North Korean economy rapidly deteriorated in 1995–96, Beijing supplied Pyongyang with emergency food and clothing supplies.[25] Since then, Beijing has continued to provide North Korea with food, consumer goods, and energy assistance.

But even U.S.-China relations on this relatively cooperative issue has tensions. Whereas Washington's policy toward North Korea is primarily focused on preventing nuclear proliferation, Beijing's policy attaches equal weight to its vital interest in preserving its significant influence in a border state located at the intersection of all of the great powers. Moreover, Beijing has even greater interest than Washington in preventing war on the Korean peninsula, insofar as it would be waged on China's border and could spill over into Chinese territory. U.S.-China friction results from Washington's frustration when Chinese caution inhibits Beijing from applying greater pressure on the North Korean leadership. Thus far, U.S.-China common interests in regional stability have prevailed, but should the U.S.-North Korean agreement collapse, U.S.-China tension over North Korea could intensify.

The two sides also have divergent interests in Korean unification. Washington understands that unification would likely lead to expanded U.S. influence in Northeast Asia. Because South Korea is a U.S. ally and would continue to have an interest in strategic cooperation with the United States after unification, even should it demand that U.S. ground forces leave the peninsula, American political influence would extend throughout the peninsula. China, on the other hand, not only would resist greater U.S. influence on its border, but it would also lose North Korea as a dependent security ally and buffer state. Instead of bordering North Korea, China would border a more powerful and independent unified Korea aligned with the United States. A unified Korea under the control of Seoul might also be closer to Japan than is now the case for South Korea and it would possibly possess nuclear weapons. These conflicting U.S. and Chinese interests may be future oriented, but they nonetheless influence policy toward contemporary issues.

Finally, the two sides have a conflict over the value and role of regionwide multilateral institutions in maintaining stability in East Asia. The United States, as a beneficiary of the regional status quo and the region's dominant military power, believes that its leadership in multilateral institutions promotes stability, insofar as U.S.-supported multilateral approaches to regional problems may be more conducive to bringing about negotiated solutions than reliance on bilateral methods. It also believes that multilateral institutions can reinforce its cooperative bilateral relationships, thus enhancing the foundation of stability and U.S. regional presence. China, on the other hand, is distrustful of U.S. leadership in multilateral institutions. It understands that international organizations can be used as foreign policy instruments of dominant powers. Such was the case when the United States used the United Nations in its involvement in the Korean War. Because China lacks the ability to dominate East Asian institutions and because it lacks confidence in the course of U.S.-China relations, it is often distrustful of regional institutions. It seeks to enter such institutions in order to avoid isolation and to influence their agenda, but it has tended to use its influence to keep the institution weak and ineffectual.

China's policy agenda in regional multilateral institutions also differs from that of the United States. China has worked with like-minded countries, including Malaysia, to resist U.S. pressure to use Asia Pacific Economic Cooperation (APEC) to expand trade liberalization in East Asia.[26] It has resisted efforts to use the Association of Southeast Asian Nations (ASEAN) Regional Forum (ARF) to address regional disputes involving the PRC, preferring that the ARF focus on dialogue and confidence-building measures. On the other hand, it has tried to use multilateral diplomacy within the ARF to oppose and weaken regional support for the U.S.-Japan alliance, and its proposals for confidence-building measures has elicited U.S. opposition. Thus, whereas the United States had presumed that regional institutions would complement U.S. bilateral diplomacy, it now finds that these institutions can be instruments of Chinese diplomacy and can undermine U.S. objectives, so that it has reconsidered its initial enthusiasm for the ARF.[27]

The United States and China have a wide range of conflicts in East Asia that necessarily undermine stable and cooperative relations. Nonetheless, none of these conflicts entails fundamental vital interests. Rather, each of the conflicts is manageable through national policies. China can exercise restraint in its Russia policy, thus minimizing fears of Sino-Russian strategic cooperation. Similarly, the United States can temper its Japan policy to mitigate Chinese fears of U.S.-Japan strategic cooperation. U.S.-China conflict over disputed territories in the South China Sea should also be containable. Because neither Washington nor Beijing has important strategic or economic interests in the islands, they should be able to avoid conflict. But because the dispute entails sensitive sovereignty issues, to avoid escalating land-grabbing among the claimants Chinese policy must exercise restraint and the United States must counsel restraint on the other claimants, while reassuring them of U.S. strategic support. Finally, given their significant common interests in the Korean peninsula, Washington and Beijing should be able to manage the collapse of the North Korean economy and promote nuclear nonproliferation on the Korean peninsula, despite differences over long-term North-South relations.

Conflict over the Taiwan issue, the most difficult issue in U.S.-China relations, is also manageable. U.S. strategic and economic interests are not affected by the legal status of Taiwan so that U.S. policy toward Taiwan can simultaneously respond to Chinese interests while not undermining American interests. This was the case throughout the 1970s and 1980s, when U.S. policy enabled Taiwan to achieve its most vital interests in security, democracy, and economic prosperity and enabled the United States to maintain cooperation with the mainland. This formula remains available to leaders in Washington and Beijing. Indeed, since Lee Teng-hui's May 1995 high-profile visit to the United States and Chinese missile tests in the Taiwan Strait in March 1996, Beijing and Washington seemed to have worked out a new modus vivendi regarding Taiwan. The White House has reassured Beijing that future visits to the United States by senior Taiwan leaders will only be considered on a case-by-case basis and that they will be rare, personal, and unofficial. Washington has also reassured Beijing of the so-called three-nos—that Washington does not support a two-China policy, Taiwan independence, and Taiwan membership in the United Nations and other international organizations requiring sovereignty for membership. For its part, China has tolerated routine transit visits to the United States by senior Taiwan officials.[28]

There are many important U.S.-China conflicts of interests in East Asia, but thus far there are no irreconcilable conflicts over vital interests, only the potential for such conflicts to develop. Given the stake both sides have in finding less costly ways to manage these conflicts and to avoid escalated conflict and regional instability, these conflicts should be amenable to diplomatic management.

U.S.-China Bilateral Conflicts of Interests

The United States and China also have a wide range of bilateral relationships that affect each country's interests. These relationships are characterized by a complex combination of common and conflictual interests. Similar to the dynamics of U.S.-China relations in East Asia, the issue is to what extent bilateral conflicts so challenge important interests of either China or the United States that conflict management or negotiated solutions are not possible. Following the pattern of security interactions in East Asia, bilateral U.S.-China relations are riddled with conflict, but none of these conflicts involve the vital interests of either party. Mutual adjustment of interests should allow for conflict management and continued cooperation.

U.S.-China Conflict over Proliferation

U.S.-China conflict over weapons proliferation is perhaps the most serious of the bilateral conflicts of interests. U.S. nonproliferation policies reflect three distinct sets of interests. The first concerns controlling proliferation of medium-range missiles to Third World countries in regions in which the United States has vital interests and in which it seeks to maintain a favorable status quo. America is concerned that possession of missiles and other destabilizing weaponry by such countries as Iran, Iraq, Libya, and Syria could undermine the regional balance, thereby jeopardizing the Arab-Israeli peace process and U.S. access to the region's oil reserves, and could lead to military conflict requiring U.S. intervention.

America's second reason for opposing proliferation reflects its world-order interest in establishing a global regime controlling exports of "weapons of mass destruction." Seeking to take advantage of its overwhelming global authority in the post–Cold War era, Washington attempts to minimize the destructiveness of war, while focusing on those weapons that it cannot defend against, such as missiles, chemical and biological weapons, and nuclear weapons. Thus, the United States not only opposes missile exports to "rogue states" in sensitive regions, through enforcement of the Missile Technology Control Regime (MTCR), it seeks a blanket global prohibition on medium-range missiles sales and related technology by any missile-producing country to any Third World country. For similar reasons, the United States has been a major proponent of the Nuclear Non-Proliferation Treaty, the Comprehensive Nuclear Test-Ban Treaty, and the Chemical Weapons Convention.

Because of its interest in ending proliferation, the United States perceives every case of proliferation as a challenge to its credibility to uphold global antiproliferation regimes. It thus feels compelled to sanction every violation. This undermines America's ability to consider regional security dynamics and develop arms control policies promoting stable deterrence relationships. It also interferes with U.S.

ability to develop negotiated solutions to conflicts of interests by obstructing its capacity to accommodate other states' security interests, thus contributing to escalated tension over unresolvable conflicts. This has been a source of U.S.-China conflict over China's assistance to Pakistan's nuclear program.

Washington's third set of interests concerning proliferation reflects its willingness to make exceptions to international regimes when its narrow national interests conflict with world-order interests. Thus, the United States has acquiesced to Israeli development of a nuclear-weapons capability. During the Cold War, the United States decided that rather than risk participating in a war to defend Israel against the Soviet-aided Arab bloc or deploy troops in Israel to deter such a war, which would undermine its relationship with the oil-producing Arab states, it would acquiesce to Israeli development of nuclear weapons, enabling Israel to deter war. A nuclear-armed Israel has the advantage of deterring an Arab attack on Israel at little cost to other U.S. interests in the Middle East. Confident in the stability of the U.S.-Japan alliance and not willing to disrupt ties with Tokyo, Washington also acquiesced to Japanese acquisition of nuclear-weapons capability. After the end of the Cold War it continued to provide Japan with technologies for the development of advanced missile systems and with the technology to refine bomb-grade plutonium from its breeder reactors.[29] In the 1990s Washington also sold Trident strategic missiles to Great Britain.

As a regional power with a more pragmatic approach to security, China does not share America's capabilities, its global interests, nor its interests in the efficacy of global institutions. It thus lacks a commitment to developing and imposing global regimes to control proliferation of missiles or other types of advanced weaponry. But it does have an interest in preventing proliferation into regions in which it has vital interests and in which there is a beneficial status quo. This is the situation in Northeast Asia. China opposes proliferation into Northeast Asia of missile systems and nuclear capabilities. In this respect, Beijing shares with the United States opposition to North Korean acquisition of nuclear weapons and their delivery vehicles. But China's concern for the regional balance of power also leads it to oppose proliferation of nuclear weapons and ballistic missiles to Japan. Japan is considered a potential great power rival and its possession of nuclear weapons would pose a grave threat to Chinese security.[30]

China also opposes the sale of advanced weaponry to Taiwan. This may not entail nuclear or missile proliferation, but its consequences are the same for China. Transfer to Taiwan of weaponry that Beijing cannot defeat, such as U.S. F-16s and French Mirage fighter aircraft, undermines Beijing's position in the cross-Strait balance. When Washington presses China to control proliferation of "weapons of mass destruction" and to adhere to the MTCR, Beijing frequently responds that the most pressing proliferation issue is U.S. arms sales to Taiwan and that Washington must abide by the U.S.-China August 17, 1982, joint communiqué. In the negotiations leading to the June 1998 summit in Beijing, Washington proposed to China PRC membership in the MTCR, but Beijing declined.[31] The implication for the regional balance and Chinese security, not the weapon *per se*, determines Beijing's assessment of proliferation practices.

China's second set of interests affecting proliferation, like the United States, leads it to make exceptions to nonproliferation principles when narrow national interests would be served. This is the explanation for China's contribution to Pakistan's nuclear weapons program and its transfer to Pakistan of medium-range M-11 missiles. Pakistan is Beijing's strategic ally in Southern Asia, a region of vital concern to Chinese security. The region abuts Chinese borders and is dominated by India, with whom China has fought a war and has an unresolved territorial conflict. Pakistan confronts in India a far greater power that has exploded a nuclear device, is developing ballistic missiles, refuses to support the Comprehensive Nuclear Test-Ban Treaty, and is close to establishing regional hegemony. Rather than risk having to defend Pakistan in a war with India or deploy troops in Pakistan to deter such a war, which would complicate China's improving relationship with India, Beijing has chosen to assist Pakistan deter India by helping it to develop nuclear weapons capability and delivery systems. In many respects, with regard to proliferation, Pakistan is to China as Israel is to the United States.

China's third interest in proliferation is profit for its munitions industries. The United States also has this interest, particularly because the Pentagon has cut back on weapons acquisition since the end of the Cold War. But because of its global power, Washington must balance the economics of exports with its interests in regional balances of power. This helps to constrain exports for profit. China, on the other hand, has limited national interests outside of its neighboring regions and can discount the implications of exports for regional balances of power. In these circumstances, China's interests in profits for its weapons manufacturers can be a major concern. This helps to explain Beijing's sales of conventional arms to Iran and Iraq during the late 1980s, its CSS-2 missile sale to Saudi Arabia in 1988, its interest in the early 1990s in selling the M-9 missile to Syria, and its ongoing interest in transferring to Iran nuclear energy technologies and short-range missiles.[32]

Thus far, the arms sales record of both countries suggests that mutual restraint can form the basis for managing the proliferation issue. After having elicited U.S. sanctions following the CSS-2 missile sale to Saudi Arabia and the threat of sanctions over the planned M-9 missile sale to Syria, China has accommodated itself to U.S. interest in controlling proliferation of nuclear weapons and medium-range missiles, with the important exception of its military relationship with Pakistan. In 1992 Beijing canceled its agreement to provide Syria with M-9 missiles, and in 1995 it "suspended" its 1992 agreement to provide Iran with two nuclear reactors. In 1997 it agreed to end all nuclear cooperation with Iran, enabling the White House to license for export to China nuclear energy equipment.[33] Although Beijing has sold Iran short-range C-802 and C-801K cruise missiles, these are relatively backward missiles that do not affect U.S. operations in the Persian Gulf. Former Secretary of Defense William Perry compared these missiles to German World War II V-2 rockets and minimized their military significance.[34]

For its part, the United States has shown less restraint in accommodating Chinese interests in controlling proliferation. U.S.-Japan strategic cooperation is a serious issue to Chinese leaders. But Beijing has been most adamant that the United States moderate its arms sales to Taiwan. This was a major issue in U.S.-China relations during the 1980s and could destabilize future relations. China transferred M-11 missiles to Pakistan, reversing its February 1992 decision to cancel the sale, and it agreed to aid Iran's nuclear energy program in retaliation against President George Bush's decision in September 1992 to sell F-16 aircraft to Pakistan.[35] The United States has also provided Taiwan such sophisticated weaponry as E-2T Hawkeye II early warning and command aircraft, Perry-class frigates, sidewinder missiles, antisubmarine aircraft, and Patriot air-defense missiles.[36]

Complete resolution of the proliferation issues may prove impossible. In 1998 Washington proposed PRC membership in the MTCR, thus removing a PRC pretext to withhold cooperation. Resolution of the issue now requires PRC policy change. But China is reluctant to join the MTCR or to commit to abide by the guidelines and parameters of the regime because the threat of missile proliferation is one of the few sources of leverage it has over the United States. Thus far, Beijing has only agreed not to export weapons proscribed by MTCR as of October 1994. It has not agreed to curtail export of missile-related technologies covered by MTCR or to end transfers to Iran of other categories of missiles.[37] By keeping its options open, Beijing maintains some negotiating leverage and cautions the United States from disregarding Chinese interests in nonproliferation—U.S. arms sales to Taiwan. Upgraded U.S. arms exports to Taiwan could lead to Chinese proliferation into the Middle East.

An additional obstacle to resolving conflict over proliferation is the inability of the Chinese central government to control exports of dual-use technologies. The fragmentation of political authority and the absence of an effective legal system have given rise to corruption throughout the government, the party, and the military. Self-interested dual-use technology manufacturers, including government enterprises, export proscribed products for personal gain, such as missile technologies and chemicals that can be used to make chemical weapons. In addition, the technological and regulatory sophistication of establishing and enforcing an export-control system for dual-use technologies has been beyond China's grasp.

Washington's recognition of China's domestic problems persuaded it not to impose sanctions against China's 1996 export of ring magnets to Pakistan. Instead, in May 1996 the Clinton administration agreed to provide technical assistance to aid Chinese development of a more effective nuclear technology export-control system. This program culminated in Chinese institution of comprehensive nuclear export-control regulations. The issuance of these regulations contributed to the October 1997 White House certification of China as a nuclear nonproliferator, enabling U.S. licensing of exports to China of nuclear energy facilities. Similar U.S.-China cooperation may lead to improved Chinese controls over missile exports.[38]

The United States and China are dissatisfied with each other's arms export policies. China assists Pakistan's nuclear deterrent and it will not commit to end proliferation of MTCR-proscribed technologies. Its dual-use technology manufacturers elude state control to export proscribed products. The United States assists Japan and Taiwan improve their capabilities vis-à-vis China. It may well be that none of these conflicts are susceptible to negotiated solutions. But they can be managed so as to prevent escalation in tension. Southern Asia is not vital to U.S. security—Chinese proliferation to Pakistan infringes primarily on American credibility to uphold world-order rules—and Washington can maintain Taiwan's security without selling it provocative weaponry. The 1997 U.S.-China summit and the associated agreements on nonproliferation and China's accession to the Nuclear Non-Proliferation Treaty in 1992, its signing of the Comprehensive Test-Ban Treaty in 1996, and its 1997 decision to join the Zangger Committee suggest that conflict can be reduced and that China and the United States can cooperate on nuclear nonproliferation. Indeed, despite different interests, their response to the 1998 Indian and Pakistani nuclear tests suggests that they may be able to develop complementary positions toward a South Asian arms race. President Clinton was pleased with China's reaction to the tests and its role in chairing the meeting of the five nucler powers to discuss South Asia and he observed that "China must be a part of any ultimate resolution of this matter."[39]

U.S.-China Economic Conflicts

The second major issue concerns economic relations—the U.S. trade deficit with China and the associated problems of Chinese protectionism and Chinese membership in the World Trade Organization (WTO) and Chinese infringement of the intellectual property rights of American corporations. Although neither of these issues has the strategic importance of proliferation issues, they can lead to considerable conflict and to aggravate conflict over other issues.

There is no question that China has a large and growing trade surplus with the United States. According to U.S. statistics, in 1997 the United States had a $49.7 billion trade deficit with China, second only to the U.S. trade deficit with Japan. Moreover, China's 1996 exports to the United States increased by 21.4 percent over the previous year and will likely continue to grow at a rapid pace insofar as U.S. imports from China are growing significantly faster than U.S. exports to China.[40] It is especially important that a portion of this deficit results from Chinese protectionism and that American access to the Chinese market is more difficult than is Chinese access to the U.S. market.

Nevertheless, it is not clear that the trade deficit with China significantly affects U.S. interests. Former American officials acknowledge that U.S. statistics inflate the size of the deficit with China by 25 percent (as Barry Naughton explains in Chapter 5).[41] More important, it is not clear that the trade deficit has had a significant impact on the U.S. labor force or primarily reflects unfair Chinese trade practices. First, for the most part, the United States no longer produces in quantity most of the products that China exports to the United States, such as textiles, shoes, toys, and inexpensive electronic goods. Exports from Japan, South Korea, and Taiwan replaced American production of these goods over twenty years ago. Growing Chinese exports to the United States have taken jobs away from these countries, not from the United States.

Second, as Barry Naughton explains in Chapter 5, the growth in Chinese exports to the United States reflects investment in China by more developed East Asian countries. As labor costs in these countries increased, their businesses have moved their production facilities to China. In so doing, they have also moved to China their trade surpluses with the United States. Adjusted for inflation, the size of the American deficit with China is approximately the same as the combined U.S. deficit with Taiwan, Hong Kong, Japan, and South Korea in the late 1980s, indicating that the growth of the U.S. deficit with China has had little impact on the U.S. economy.

Finally, it is not clear that if China liberalized foreign access to its market there would be a significant increase in U.S. exports. The United States runs a trade deficit with many countries. This is partly because many U.S. exports are not competitive in foreign markets. To some extent, this also explains the U.S. deficit with China. In those areas in which U.S. exports can compete in international markets, they have also done well in the Chinese market. America is the largest exporter to China of civilian aircraft (Boeing), personal computers (AST, Compaq, and IBM), cellular telephones (Motorola), other high-technology consumer goods, agricultural goods, and fertilizer, and it is one of the largest providers to China of industrial and power-generating equipment. But because these are expensive goods that face limited domestic competition and have finite demand, liberalization of the Chinese market would not necessarily lead to improved exports. Most of the benefit of a more open Chinese market would go to producers of inexpensive consumer goods—Japan and the newly industrialized economies of East Asia.

These trends in U.S.-China trade suggest that the American trade deficit with China primarily reflects structural economic conditions rather than unfair Chinese trade practices. Economists argue that the

U.S. trade deficit with China reflects the problems associated with the general U.S. difficulty in competing in foreign markets—American export goods tend to be expensive. Moreover, Americans have a low savings rate compared to the savings rate in many other countries, including China. They thus spend a greater share of their income and purchase more consumer goods than workers in other countries.[42]

On the other hand, the United States does benefit from exports to China. Access to the Chinese civilian aircraft market is fundamental to the health of Boeing and to the Greater Seattle area. Chinese purchases of such goods as grain, industrial equipment, fertilizer plants, pharmaceuticals, and automobiles make important contributions to growth in each of these industries and to the work force in these industries. The U.S. government estimates that trade with China creates 170,000 jobs. Moreover, U.S. exports are increasing dramatically. U.S. exports to China in 1996 grew by 27 percent over 1995 exports.[43] China also benefits from bilateral trade. Chinese access to the American consumer market makes a significant contribution to China's consumer-goods industries, which export such low-technology goods as textiles, toys, and inexpensive electronic products. It also provides China with much of the hard currency it needs to purchase advanced Western technology.

Nevertheless, mutual benefit does not guarantee conflict-free cooperation. Although economic conditions may make a U.S. trade deficit with China inevitable, it is in the U.S. interest to narrow the deficit, if only because Chinese protectionism limits the ability of American businesses and workers to benefit fully from the Chinese market. In particular, U.S. service and entertainment industries would profit from enhanced access to the Chinese market. But it is in China's interest to maintain protectionist policies in these and other areas. Just as during the early stages of their economic development Japan, South Korea, and Taiwan used protectionism to allow infant industries to become established, China uses trade policy to protect its nascent industries and inefficient state enterprises from the challenges posed by foreign competition. There exists a clear U.S.-China conflict over trade. The United States pressures China to widen its market to foreign competition while China seeks to slow the pace of liberalization.

This conflict of economic interests informs the ongoing negotiations over Chinese entry into the WTO.[44] On the one hand, the United States and many other developed countries, coping with large trade deficits with China and seeking greater access to the lucrative Chinese market, want Beijing's trade practices to comply quickly with the WTO regulations applicable to the advanced industrial countries. On the other hand, China wants entry into the WTO on terms that would enable it to maintain for an extended period the same trading privileges that South Korea and Singapore had when they first acceded to the General Agreement on Tariffs and Trade.[45]

Thus, whereas the U.S. trade deficit in itself is not cause for serious conflict, there is a conflict between U.S. demands for greater access to the Chinese market and China's interest in maintaining trade barriers. Without compromise, this conflict will endure. Nonetheless, the status quo does not adversely affect either side's vital interests. It is not imperative for the United States that it have greater access to the Chinese market, insofar as the status quo does not significantly disadvantage the U.S. economy, and it is not imperative for China that it be admitted into the WTO. While maintaining protectionist policies, Chinese access to foreign markets is protected by the leverage it derives from granting access to its market to other countries and from its most favored nation (MFN) trading rights.

U.S.-China economic conflict also reflects China's failure to protect the intellectual property rights (IPR) of American corporations. Chinese entrepreneurs copy and sell bootleg versions of American pop music, computer software, and Hollywood movies. The result is the loss of the profits that these corporations would make if Chinese consumers bought legally licensed products. According to U.S. industry estimates, American manufacturers lose approximately $2 billion per year from IPR piracy in China, a considerable portion of which is from Chinese exports to Hong Kong and Southeast Asia.[46] The United States has a strong interest in ending these practices. Nonetheless, it is not clear how significant the damage is to U.S. interests and whether or not the issue is resolvable, suggesting potential for management and damage limitation.

The primary cause of Chinese IPR violations has been the political and economic decentralization in post-Mao China and the lack of an effective Chinese legal system and customs control to enforce government regulations. Similar to the domestic causes of Chinese weapons proliferation, the central Chinese government has lacked the full ability to control the behavior of politicians and entrepreneurs at local levels. Indeed, by all appearances, the Chinese government would like to end IPR piracy—its own software and entertainment industries suffer considerable financial losses from copyright infringements and experience negative incentives to increase investment—but it has simply lacked the authority.

Moreover, there seems little the United States can do to change Chinese society—economic sanctions will not expand central Chinese government authority at local levels. The United States has been negotiating IPR violations with China since 1991, and three times China agreed to make far-reaching changes. The economics of piracy guarantee that such agreements and subsequent Chinese government efforts will not end piracy. It is profitable for Chinese firms shut down by the central government to purchase new software and video copying equipment and reopen elsewhere in connivance with local officials or to sell pirated software produced elsewhere. Thus, American pressure often encourages Chinese leaders to sign agreements calling for local economic changes that are not susceptible to central government policy, creating periodic crises when such agreements are not fulfilled. The result is increased U.S.-China acrimony, as ongoing Chinese IPR violations lead to frustrated U.S. expectations and to charges that China negotiates in bad faith.

Equally important, as Marcus Noland explains in Chapter 4, the actual total loss to the U.S. economy from Chinese IPR piracy is far less than the industry estimate of $2 billion per year. These estimates are based on what the profits would be if all of the bootlegged products were sold at full price. But at full price, the market for American software and video products would be far smaller, resulting in considerably less profits for American industries. Thus, the total loss to the United States of Chinese IPR piracy is but a small fraction of the total value of worldwide U.S. exports of these products. Moreover, even based on inflated price calculations, U.S. financial losses in 1996 from Chinese IPR piracy were approximately one half of the losses resulting from Japanese piracy.[47]

Given the limited stakes involved and the little likelihood of short-term resolution of the issue, U.S.-Chinese conflict over Chinese IPR piracy should be manageable. Indeed, limited successes should be possible. One of the most contentious issues has been Beijing's unwillingness to close large-scale factories mass producing pirated compact disks. Because these factories are easily identifiable, Washington has demanded that Beijing close them down. Following the 1995 U.S.-China agreement on PRC enforcement of Chinese IPR legislation, Beijing moved to close down these plants. In 1996 and 1997, Beijing closed 62 illegal CD and CD-ROM factories. In 1997 Beijing imposed stiff prison sentences on IPR violators. The business climate in China had become so unfriendly for illegal corporations that many had left China for Singapore, Taiwan, Macau, and Hong Kong. Although Washington is appreciative of Chinese efforts, Beijing's success has created a new problem—countless small Chinese businesses selling pirated software smuggled to China from Macau. Moreover, this problem may be more difficult for Beijing to manage than the prior problem of a small number of high-profile illegal factories. But, even here, the combination of PRC efforts and U.S. patience should allow for management of the problem.[48]

China will continue to pirate compact disks. Nonetheless, Chinese government progress in ending high-profile piracy and the minimal economic impact on U.S. industries of Chinese piracy suggests that U.S.-China economic cooperation can be insulated from ongoing conflict over Chinese IPR piracy.

U.S.-China Conflict over Human Rights

The United States and China have a fundamental conflict of interest over human rights. A broad sector of the American public is concerned with such Chinese practices as imprisonment of political dissidents and religious leaders, torture of Tibetan and Islamic independence activists, widespread use of the death penalty, sovereignty over Tibet, export of prison-labor products, and population planning. In the view of many Americans, the United States should not maintain cooperative relations with a regime that seriously violates the rights of its own citizens on a large scale. This broad-based concern has led to considerable controversy over the desirability of conducting normal trade with China, and each year the United States debates the wisdom of granting China MFN trade status.

It is not clear that the United States has sufficient leverage to alter Chinese human rights policies. China's harsh and unrelenting repression of dissidents, its prohibition on independent political activity, and its stifling of democracy challenges core American values regarding treatment of the individual, freedom of expression, and democracy. But it is also true that Chinese leaders value domestic stability and the political authority of the Chinese Communist Party far more than they value U.S.-China cooperation. No amount of American economic or political pressure will be able to coerce the Chinese leadership to give up its grip on power. U.S.-China conflict over Tibet reflects a similar dynamic. Although there is strong American support for the principle of self-determination and many Americans believe that the long and rich history of Tibetan culture makes Tibet a strong candidate for independence, the Chinese government considers Tibet an integral part of Chinese territory and no amount of U.S. pressure or persuasion will compel Chinese leaders to grant Tibet sovereign independence. U.S.-China conflicts of interest over human rights and Tibet are destined to bedevil relations for the long term.

Insofar as U.S. trade policy, such as threats to deny China MFN trade status, is not an effective instrument for achieving U.S. human rights interests, there is little reason for the United States to attempt to use it—"feel-good" diplomacy is counterproductive. Moreover, whereas short-term Chinese government policy toward independent political activity is deeply troubling, the long-term trend is encouraging. As the U.S. State Department acknowledged in 1998, the Chinese people are freer today than at any time since 1949 as government control over society continues to erode at a rapid pace. Moreover, individual access to global information sources has expanded and new social groups with economic resources have begun to play a role in community life.[49] This trend is the result of the opening of China to Western influence through trade and societal exchanges. Although porous borders, international trade, and economic modernization cannot guarantee political liberalization, over the long term they offer the greatest likelihood of success.

But such positive trends in China's human rights situation cannot eradicate U.S.-China conflict over Beijing's treatment of dissidents and its denial of political freedoms. It is, however, a manageable and containable conflict. Given the limited instruments available to the United States to alter Chinese behavior and America's stake in preventing human rights conflict from damaging the ability of the two sides to contend with other conflicts of interest, human rights should simmer but not explode. The United States can express opposition to and attempt to mobilize international condemnation of Chinese human rights violations in a wide range of international settings, including the U.N. Commission on Human Rights. For China's part, it can attack U.S. interference in its domestic affairs and try to block international organizations from focusing on Chinese abuses,[48] while tolerating outspoken American condemnation of its repressive policies. It can also retaliate with equally vocal attacks on what it believes to be violations of human rights in the United States.[51]

Finally, China can release jailed political dissidents to improve U.S.-China relations. The effect of Washington's human rights diplomacy is to hold cooperation with China hostage to the fate of Chinese dissidents. This encourages Chinese leaders to treat the dissidents as bargaining chips. When they believe that conditions are appropriate, they can release dissidents to realize their foreign policy objectives.[52] In November 1997, because Beijing was pleased with the outcome of the October U.S.-China summit and sought to promote subsequent cooperation, it released Wei Jingsheng from prison. Prior to the June 1998 summit in Beijing, China released Wang Dan and other dissidents from prison and agreed to sign the International Covenant on Civil and Political Rights. To the extent that Chinese leaders allow political dissidents to leave China, U.S.-China human rights conflict will be contained.

United States–Soviet conflict over human rights during the Cold War was similar to contemporary U.S.-China conflict over human rights. Although Soviet human rights violations were more abusive than contemporary Chinese violations, mutual superpower recriminations over human rights did not significantly impact U.S.-Soviet negotiations over other conflicts of interest, including the arms race, nor block summit meetings. Moreover, at times Moscow would release Soviet political dissidents to influence U.S. foreign policy. The United States and China should similarly be able to manage their human rights conflicts so that Washington can conduct human rights diplomacy and promote cooperation in other areas.

The Bilateral Dynamics of U.S.-China Negotiations

The United States and China have numerous conflicts of interests. Some are more amenable than others to a negotiated solution. But that they are manageable conflicts over nonvital interests does not preclude hard negotiations and tension. Despite each side's desire to avoid escalated conflict, each will nonetheless try to compel the other to make the compromises necessary to resolve the issues.

The course and character of these negotiations will inevitably reflect the nature of the conflict. But they will also reflect the disparity between the United States and China in the stake each side has in the relationship. Management of U.S.-China conflicts of interests will require compromise, but which side applies pressure and how much and which side compromises and by how much will necessarily reflect each side's interest in stable relations. In the post–Cold War world, both China and the United States have important interests in cooperation, but China's greater strategic stake in the relationship makes it far more vulnerable than the United States to the prospect of adversarial relations. This strategic asymmetry is a fundamental cause of the tension in U.S.-China relations because it combines with the post–Cold War ambiguity in U.S.-China relations to exacerbate the impact of domestic factors in policy-making.

The United States in Chinese Security Policy

In the post–Cold War era Chinese leaders remain concerned for the potential for heightened regional tension and great-power conflict. In these circumstances, they are intent on developing "comprehensive national strength," which includes the economic and technological as well as the military foundations of national power and international competition, and on forging stable bilateral relationships that can strategically position China in the emerging East Asian balance of power. The United States plays a critical role in determining whether China can realize both of these objectives.

It is difficult to overestimate the importance of the U.S. economy to China's economic modernization plans and its plans to catch up to its rivals and to compete in the twenty-first century balance of power. The U.S. consumer goods market has been a major contributor to Chinese modernization, and unimpeded access to the U.S. market has made many important contributions to the Chinese economy. The United States is China's third largest foreign investor. It provided 7 percent of direct foreign investment in China from 1979 to 1995. According to U.S. figures, total U.S. foreign direct investment in China in 1996 was $2.9 billion, an increase of 36 percent over 1995. Chinese statistics report that in 1996 the United States ranked third in foreign investment in China, providing over 8 percent of utilized direct foreign investment in China.[53] For much of the post-Mao era, the United States has also been China's largest market for manufactured goods, including textiles, toys, shoes, and inexpensive electronics. According to Chinese customs statistics, which undercount Chinese exports to the United States, in 1997 the United States was China's largest export market, purchasing over 18 percent of Chinese exports.[54] This has been a major stimulus to Chinese economic growth. The purchase by the United States of China's low-technology inexpensive consumer goods earns Beijing the hard currency it needs to import the high technology necessary to modernize its economy and upgrade its defense capabilities. Exports to America have also been a major source of employment and growth for the Chinese economy. In southern China, hundreds of thousands of Chinese workers produce goods for export to the United States. Loss of the U.S. market would not only cost these workers their jobs, it would also likely throw the southern economy into a recession. For all of these reasons, stable U.S.-China economic relations make a major and irreplaceable contribution to China's economic growth and future security.[55]

A crisis in U.S. trade relations would also have economic and political reverberations in China's economic relationships with all of the advanced industrial economies and with its economic partners in East Asia. It would place considerable pressure on policymakers in other countries to limit Chinese access to their own advanced technology and to limit China's access to soft loans and international financial assistance.

China has even more important political interests in maintaining stable U.S.-China relations. The Cold War may be over, but all of the East Asian countries are concerned about the possibility of a renewed instability and heightened tension among the great powers, and they are already making preparations. For China, the strategic imperative is to maintain an international environment in which it can focus its scarce resources on economic modernization. Among the worst possible scenarios for China would be heightened strategic conflict with the United States. America's overwhelming strategic power, its economic superiority, and its strategic influence in East Asia make China extremely vulnerable to conflict with the United States. Washington can challenge core Chinese interests, such as the status of Taiwan, and pose a severe challenge to the Chinese military, imposing prohibitively high costs on the Chinese economy and the national budget and fundamentally transforming China's strategic environment and derailing its modernization plans.

Recent trends in Washington's Japan policy underscores American ability to pose a strategic threat to Chinese security. Consolidation of the U.S.-Japan alliance in 1996–97 removed much of the uncertainty surrounding U.S. policy in East Asia and the future of the U.S.-Japan alliance. The alliance is apt to remain a permanent feature of East Asia for the foreseeable future, and China must now reconcile itself to long-term U.S.-Japan cooperation.[56] Moreover, by consolidating the U.S.-Japan alliance, Washington has enhanced its ability to further strengthen ties with Japan. Should the United States and Japan, the two most powerful countries in East Asia, target their combined resources on China, they would pose a menacing threat to Chinese security. Thus, it is incumbent on Chinese leaders to dissuade the United States from perceiving China as a threat not only because the United States is powerful but also because it can join forces with Japan.

China's political interest in U.S.-China cooperation also reflects its interest in developing cooperative relationships with its East Asian neighbors. It would be almost impossible for China to insulate U.S.-China conflict from its regional diplomacy. Should relations deteriorate, not only would Washington look for support from allies, but other East Asian countries, sensitive to changes in U.S. foreign policy and dependent on the United States for security and economic development, would feel pressure to participate in U.S.-China policy and to contribute to PRC diplomatic isolation. And should U.S.-China trade relations deteriorate in the context of strategic conflict, Chinese access to markets and technology in East Asia and throughout the world would be severely affected.

Finally, the United States can play a positive role in Chinese security policy. American distance from East Asia suggests to Chinese policymakers that despite recent trends in U.S. foreign policy the PRC's future rival may well be a resurgent Japan. While this concern may be colored by historical experience, it is a view shared to varying degrees in South Korea, Russia, the Philippines, and other East Asian countries. China must also focus on the possibility of a resurgent Russia. Russia's military, natural resources, and geographic and demographic size make it an imposing neighbor. For these reasons, although they rarely publicly mention it, Chinese leaders, along with the rest of East Asia, favor a continued U.S. military presence in the region. As long as the United States does not identify China as an immediate adversary and actively target its military and diplomatic resources on China, Chinese leaders will continue to perceive positive aspects in

America's strategic presence in East Asia and will have a strong interest in maintaining and consolidating U.S.-China cooperation.

In the aftermath of the Cold War, the United States poses a crucial challenge to Chinese leaders. Constructive management of U.S.-China relations offers China unmatched opportunities to modernize its economy and to build a benign international environment in which to prepare for an uncertain strategic future. On the other hand, the United States has unrivaled ability to destroy Chinese ambitions to modernize its economy and to achieve parity with its great-power neighbors. There is no greater foreign policy imperative for Chinese leaders than to manage and protect U.S.-China cooperation.

China in U.S. Security Policy

In contrast to China's stake in U.S.-China relations, the U.S. stake in the relationship is less vital to its economic and political interests. American benefits from trade with China are limited to well-defined sectors of the American economy. In 1996, the United States exported $2.3 billion of power-generating equipment and $1.4 billion of electrical equipment to China. In 1997, China agreed to purchase approximately $3 billion of Boeing aircraft. China is also a major importer of U.S. wheat and fertilizer. Businesses and workers in these and other industries benefit considerably from U.S.-China trade. On the import side, U.S. retailers of shoes, textiles, toys, and inexpensive electronics have profited from access to inexpensive Chinese products.[57] While gains to local communities, such as the farm states, the cities of Seattle and Kansas City, and high-technology centers, and to the consumer of inexpensive Chinese products create a significant U.S. interest in continued U.S.-China economic cooperation, trade with China represents a very small portion of overall U.S. trade. According to U.S. officials, China was only the United States's fourteenth largest export market in 1997, taking $12 billion of exports.[58] Disruption of U.S.-China trade would have a minimal impact on the overall size and growth of the U.S. economy.

There is also asymmetry in political relations. In the aftermath of the Cold War, U.S. foreign policy objectives have been limited to resolving regional conflicts, limiting proliferation of sensitive weaponry, promoting ideological and humanitarian objectives, and pursuing long-term interests in regional stability. China can play an important role in helping the United States achieve these goals. Chinese opposition to Khmer Rouge obstructionism was a central element in the Cambodian peace process during the late 1980s, and Beijing has been a stabilizing factor since the signing of the Cambodian peace agreement in October 1991. Chinese cooperation has been crucial in moderating North Korean policies, and its cooperation will remain important for continued reduction of tension on the Korean peninsula. Chinese assistance will also be necessary to moderate conflict in South Asia. Similarly, Chinese participation in nonproliferation regimes is important to U.S. security. Beijing's relative forbearance since 1988 regarding missile sales to Middle East countries and its expanding membership in nonproliferation regimes, including the Nuclear Non-Proliferation Treaty and the Comprehensive Test-Ban Treaty, are significant achievements for both U.S. interests and the post–Cold War global order. Continued Chinese cooperation will be necessary should the United States seek to strengthen nonproliferation regimes. Finally, stability in East Asia requires Chinese cooperation. In an emerging multipolar environment, Washington may well find China a useful partner in maintaining a regional balance of power or deterring regional conflict.

Nonetheless, the United States, in contrast to China, is not dependent on U.S.-China cooperation to realize its vital interests, including maintenance of its favorable position in the East Asian balance of power and territorial and economic security. This asymmetry also characterizes the likely costs to U.S. and Chinese interests of East Asian stability. Unlike China, the U.S. military and economic presence in East Asia is welcomed throughout the region—America has no major adversaries in East Asia. Most important, the United States and Japan are partners on a wide range of issues and can cooperate in the event of heightened U.S.-China conflict. In contrast, China considers Japan a potential formidable adversary.

U.S.-China cooperation is important to each country's pursuit of its respective interests. But the disparity in the Chinese and American stakes in the bilateral relationship affects their relative ability to allow peripheral factors to interfere with policy-making and to press for compromises over secondary issues in conflict. America's economic and political power compared to China's allows Washington to act with greater self-indulgence in foreign policy-making over such issues as human rights and trade issues and to risk heightened tension through the use of coercive measures, such as economic sanctions. Washington uses its strategic advantage to press for Chinese compromises, trying to move Beijing closer to American goals; Beijing seeks to establish limits beyond which it refuses to allow the United States to push.

But in the absence of an immediate security threat in the aftermath of the Cold War there are greater opportunities for domestic politics to interfere in policy-making. This is especially the case for the United States. Its status as the world's sole superpower encourages American policymakers and politicians to incorporate parochial political calculations into policy choices, contributing to the impulsiveness in U.S. foreign policy.[59] As Steve Teles and Robert Sutter argue in Chapters 2 and 3, respectively, U.S. policy toward China is buffeted by the pressures of domestic politics. Thus, despite the opportunities for Beijing and Washington to manage conflicts to their mutual advantage, it will be difficult for the two countries to reach compromise solutions to conflicts of interest.

The combination of U.S.-China conflicts of interest, American strategic advantage, and the impact of domestic politics in policy-making ensures that U.S.-China relations will be characterized by recurring tension and heightened conflict. But it precludes neither conflict management nor cooperation.

Managing U.S.-China Conflicts

The United States and China have few common interests and many conflicts of interest. But none of the conflictual issues in U.S.-China relations entails the vital strategic or economic interests of either country. Whereas during the early stage of the Cold War there were vital interests in immediate conflict that seemed to require Chinese and American antagonistic policies and during the latter stages of the Cold War there were common vital interests that required immediate U.S.-China cooperation, in the contemporary period there are no vital interests at stake in either U.S.-China conflict or cooperation.

U.S.-China conflicts of interest in East Asia primarily focus on potential trends rather than on current realities. Bilateral conflicts over weapons proliferation have yet to impact core security concerns of either China or the United States. Neither bilateral economic conflict nor cooperation have yet to affect national economic survival. U.S.-China conflicts over human rights are chronic but have primarily affected the tenor of the relationship and caused periodic setbacks rather than determined its fundamental direction.

This lack of clarity in U.S.-China relations provides the opportunity for parochial factors to influence policy-making in both countries. The absence of foreign policy imperatives creates expanded opportunities for opposition politicians to use foreign policy controversies to weaken incumbent leaders and for incumbents to use foreign policy to deal with domestic political problems. It also expands the susceptibility of politicians and policymakers to interest group pressures and to sectoral economic interests. This is especially the case for the United States, which can count on its global supremacy to minimize the cost of politically inspired policy impulses. The challenge of post–Cold War U.S.-China relations is to maximize cooperation and manage conflict in the absence of strategic imperatives and in the face of considerable domestic pressures. This challenge especially affects the United States. The significant asymmetry in U.S.-China relations suggests that U.S. policy-making will be even more susceptible to the influence of domestic factors than will be Chinese policy-making.

That U.S.-China cooperation does not encompass immediate vital interests and that the relationship is inundated with conflict and difficult to manage does not reduce its importance. The stakes in U.S.-China relations remain great, including the potential for costly conflict as well as the prospects for peace, economic prosperity, and regional stability. The greater difficulty in managing U.S.-China relations after the Cold War simply requires greater leadership and commitment on the part of U.S. and Chinese leaders.

Notes

1. Transcript of October 29, 1997, Jiang Zemin state dinner toast; *Zhongguo Xinwen She*, February 13, 1996, Foreign Broadcast Information Service, *Daily Report: China* (hereafter *FBIS/China*), February 14, 1996, pp. 2–3.

2. For a discussion of this process, see Robert S. Ross, *Negotiating Cooperation: U.S.-China Relations, 1969–1989* (Stanford, CA: Stanford University Press, 1995).

3. For a Chinese perspective, see the interview with Chinese Foreign Minister Qian Qichen in *Xinhua*, December 30, 1996, in *FBIS/China*, December 31, 1996; Tang Tianrui and Liu Jiang, "World Moves Toward Multipolarization," *Xinhua*, December 29, 1996, in *FBIS/China*, December 30, 1996; Song Yimin, "New Alignment of World Forces," *Renmin Ribao*, April 19, 1996, in *FBIS/China*, April 29, 1996, pp. 4–5. For Chinese military perspectives, see "Have a Clear Picture of General Trends of Relaxation, Be Prepared for New Challenges," *Jiefang Junbao*, January 8, 1996, pp. 27–32.

4. For a discussion of the U.S. Defense Department's appraisal of the "China Threat," see the department's 1997 *Quarterly Defense Report*.

5. *Trud*, January 4, 1996, in *FBIS/Central Asia*, January 5, 1996, p. 17; *ITAR-TASS*, June 28, 1997, in *FBIS/Central Asia*, July 1, 1997; *Xinhua*, July 2, 1997, in FBIS/China, July 3, 1997.

6. See the joint statement on the conclusion of the border demarcation in ITAR-TASS, November 10, 1997, in *FBIS/Central Eurasia*, November 12, 1997. Also see *Xinhua*, November 6, 1997, in *FBIS/China*, November 7, 1997. Russian sources report the demarcation agreement excludes the disputed islands in the Amur River. See *Interfax*, November 10, 1997, in *FBIS/Central Eurasia*, November 12, 1997.

7. For recent Chinese commentary on NATO expansion, see Yang Chengxu, "New Stage of Readjusting Relations," *Renmin Ribao*, May 28, 1997, in *FBIS/China*, June 9, 1997; Chen Zhi, Pan Yongming, and Yan Weimin, "Obstacles Facing the North Atlantic Treaty Organization's Eastward Expansion Remain," *Xinhua*, July 9, 1997, in *FBIS/China*, July 10, 1997; Yan Zheng, "Loud Thunder But Small Raindrops—NATO's Eastward Expansion Still Faces Numerous Difficulties," *Renmin Ribao*, May 28, 1996, in *FBIS/China*, June 26, 1996, pp. 1–3.

8. See the joint statement issued during President Yeltsin's April 1996 visit to China in *Xinhua*, April 25, 1996, *FBIS/China*, April 25, 1996, p. 14.

9. See the text of the November 10 joint declaration in ITAR-TASS, November 10, 1997, in *FBIS/Central Eurasia*, November 14, 1997, and the November 11 joint statement issued at the conclusion of the summit in ITAR-TASS, November 11, 1997, in *FBIS/Central Eurasia*, November 14, 1997. Also see the Chinese characterization of Chinese summitry with Russia and the United States in Lu Jin and Liu Yunfei, "From Beijing to Washington and from Moscow to Beijing: A Revelation of New-Type Relations Between Major Powers," *Xinhua*, November 9, 1997, in *FBIS/China*, November 12, 1997.

10. Perry's remark is in *Washington Post*, May 22, 1996. For sanguine U.S. reactions, see President Clinton's remarks in Reuters, April 25, 1997, and the remarks by Admiral Joseph Prueher, head of U.S. Pacific Command, in Reuters, May 20, 1997. On Soviet arms sales to China, see, for example, Yevgeniy Bazhanov, "Brothers in Arms—Brothers Forever: Should We Sell Military Equipment to China?" *Moscow Obshchaya Gazeta*, no. 31 (August 7–13, 1997), in *FBIS/Central Asia*, August 13, 1997; "Diplomatic Panorama," *Interfax*, June 27, 1997, in *FBIS/Central Asia*, June 30, 1997.

11. See the transcript of President Clinton's April 17, 1996, press conference in Tokyo; the transcript of Perry's April 13, 1996, remarks to the press en route to Tokyo.

12. See the authoritative statement by former U.S. Defense Department official Joseph S. Nye, Jr., "An Engaging China Policy," *Wall Street Journal*, March 13, 1997.

13. "Guidelines for U.S.-Japan Defense Cooperation," approved by the 17th United States–Japan Security Consultative Committee, November 27, 1978.

14. See Perry's April 13, 1996, discussion with reporters; Yoshiteru Oka, "Can 'Nodong' Be Intercepted and Destroyed?; Brain Racking Problem of TMD Study," *Sankei Shimbun*, June 29, 1997, in *FBIS/East Asia*, July 4, 1997.

15. Da Jun, "Where Will Japan Go?" *Xinhua*, December 7, 1995, in *FBIS/China*, December 7, 1995, pp. 4–5; Chen Lineng, "The Japanese Self-Defense Forces Are Marching Toward the 21st Century," *Guoji Zhanwang*, no. 2 (February 8, 1996), in *FBIS/China*, May 1, 1996, pp. 9–12; Lu Guozhong, "Japan's Position, Role and Future Trend in the New Situation," *Guoji Wenti Yanjiu*, no. 1 (January 13, 1997), in *FBIS/China*, May 7, 1997.

16. Zhang Guocheng, "Japan's Constitution Is Facing a Test," *Renmin Ribao*, April 23, 1996, in *FBIS/China*, April 29, 1996, pp. 3–4; Chen Zhijiang, "Japan-U.S. Joint Declaration on Security—A Dangerous Signal," *Guangming Ribao*, April 18, 1996, in *FBIS/China*, April 23, 1996, pp. 2–3. Also see Wei Yang, "Setbacks and Prospects for Sino-U.S. Relations, *Liaowang*, July 3, 1995, in *FBIS/China*, July 21, 1995, pp. 4–5; Sa Benwang, "Strategic Adjustment of U.S. Defense Policy—Comment and Analysis on U.S. 'National Defense Report' for New Fiscal Year," *Liaowang*, no. 14 (April 1, 1996), in *FBIS/China*, April 17, 1996, pp. 9–10.

17. "Commentary: A Dangerous Road," Beijing China Radio International, May 9, 1997, in *FBIS/China*, May 13, 1997; *Beijing Review*, no. 4 (January 27–February 2, 1997), pp. 7–10, in *FBIS/China*, January 31, 1997; Ni Feng, "Enhanced U.S.-Japanese Security Alliance: Cause for Concern," June 16–22, 1997, in *FBIS/China*, in *FBIS/China*, June 19, 1997.

18. On theater missile defense, see Liu Huaqing, "Evaluation and Analysis of China's Nuclear Arms Control Policy," *Xiandai Junshi*, November 11, 1995, in *FBIS/China*, December 22, 1995, pp. 6–11. On the Taiwan issue, see, for example, commentary, "Guard Against Japanese Official's Statement on Japan's Position," *Renmin Ribao* May 27, 1998, in *FBIS/China*, May 29, 1998. *Zhongguo Tongxun She*, May 1, 1998, in *FBIS/China*, May 6, 1998; *Zhongguo Tongxun She*, April 28, 1998, in *FBIS/China*, May 1, 1998; *Xinhua,* May 2, 1998, in *FBIS/China*, May 6, 1998; Kyodo April 28, 1998, in *FBIS/China*, April 30, 1998.

19. Reuters, March 12, 1996.

20. For a strategic analysis of Washington's Taiwan policy during the Cold War, see Xu Yimin and Wei Wenching, "The United States Must Correct Its Stance on Taiwan," *China Daily*, January 6, 1996, in *FBIS/China*, January 11, 1996, pp. 6–7. For a discussion of Taiwan's strategic significance to Chinese security, see Lu Junyuan, "Taiwan's Geostrategic Value Makes Unification Essential," *Taiwan Yanjiu*, no. 33 (March 20, 1996), in *FBIS/China*, September 4, 1996.

21. This was indeed the Chinese interpretation. See the discussion in the Chinese-controlled Hong Kong newspaper *Ta Kung Pao*, June 18, 1995, in *FBIS/China*, June 26, 1995, p. 7. For a discussion of the Pentagon statement, see *Far Eastern Economic Review*, August 3, 1995. For extended discussions of U.S. interest in East Asia and China's interests in the islands, see Douglas T. Stuart and William T. Tow, *A US Strategy for the Asia-Pacific*, *Adelphi Paper*, no. 299; Mark J. Valencia, *China and the South China Sea Disputes*, *Adelphi Paper*, no. 298.

22. See the rare and striking suggestion of PRC economic sanctions in the mainland-controlled *Ta Kung Pao* (Hong Kong), June 3, 1994, in *FBIS/China*, June 6, 1994, pp. 9–10. Also see the June 2, 1994, statement by the PRC Foreign Ministry spokesman in Agence France Presse, June 2, 1994, in *FBIS/China*, June 3, 1994, p. 1.

23. See Madeleine Albright's June 10, 1997, testimony before the Senate Finance Committee; Jeffrey Bader's April 23, 1997, testimony before the House International Relations Committee, Subcommittee on East Asian and Pacific Af-

fairs; and Winston Lord's October 11, 1995, testimony before the Senate Foreign Relations Committee, Asian and Pacific Affairs Subcommittee.

24. See, for example, Zhou Dewu, "Four-Party Talks Will Eventually Be Realized," *Renmin Ribao*, August 15, 1997, in *FBIS/China*, August 26, 1997; *Xinhua*, August 6, 1997, in *FBIS/China*, August 8, 1997.

25. *Xinhua*, July 30, 1996, in *FBIS/China*, July 31, 1996, p. 6; Shenyang Liaoning People's Radio Network, December 18, 1995, *FBIS/China*, December 18, 1995, p. 7; *Nihon Keizai Shimbun*, March 29, 1996, in *FBIS/China*, April 1, 1996, p. 15.

26. For Chinese and Malaysian discussions for their common position toward U.S.-led APEC proposals for trade liberalization, see Jiang Xiaoyan, "Dispute Over APEC Development Orientation, *Shijie Zhishi*, no. 21 (November 1, 1994), in *FBIS/China*, November 9, 1995; Chen Fengying, "Growing APEC Resists U.S. Domination," *Xiandai Guoji Guanxi*, no. 8 (August 20, 1996), in *FBIS/China*, October 17, 1996; Voice of Malaysia, November 15, 1994, in *FBIS/East Asia*, November 9, 1995; *The Star* (Malaysia), November 22, 1995, in *FBIS*, December 11, 1995.

27. See the discussion in Alastair Iain Johnston and Paul Evans,"China's Engagement with Multilateral Security Institutions," in Alastair Iain Johnston and Robert S. Ross, eds., *Engaging China: Managing the Rise of Major Power* (forthcoming).

28. For the U.S. position, see the October 2, 1995, State Department report; the October 24, 1995, White House press briefing by State Department and national security officials; *NYT*, October 2, 1995. On the "three-nos" and its variations, see, for example, U.S. Department of State Daily Press Briefing (Dpb 157), Friday, October 31, 1997; *Xinhua*, July 8, 1996, in *FBIS/China*, July 10, 1996; *Xinhua*, November 20, 1996, in *FBIS/China*, November 22, 1996. For Chinese policy, see, for example, Beijing's response to the transit visit to the United States by Taiwan foreign ministry head John Chang in AFP, June 17, 1997, in *FBIS/China*, June 18, 1997, and its response to Lee Teng-hui's September stopover in the United States in He Jixiong, "Lee Teng-hui's 'Transit Diplomacy' Can Hardly Succeed," *Zhongguo Tongxun She*, September 4, 1997, in *FBIS/China*, September 9, 1997.

29. *International Herald Tribune*, September 10, 1994.

30. See the discussion of Japan's nuclear weapons program in Liao Xinan and Sang Zhonglin, "A Potential Nuclear Power: Japan," *Bingqi Zhishi*, no. 6, 1995 (November 15), in *FBIS/China*, February 5, 1996, pp. 4–6. For a discussion of ongoing Japanese plans to stockpile plutonium, see *Far Eastern Economic Review*, March 3, 1994, p. 13.

31. Interview with U.S. State Department officials and Chinese military officials. Also see, for example, Qian Qichen's report on Under Secretary of State Lynn Davis's visit to China in *Xinhua*, November 5, 1996, in *FBIS/China*, November 7, 1996, and the statements by the spokesmen of the Chinese Foreign Ministry in Kyodo, November 5, 1996, in *FBIS/China*, November 21, 1996. See the report of the U.S. offer and China's response in the April 9, 1998, briefing by U.S. Acting Under Secretary for Arms Control and International Security Affairs John Holum.

32. For a discussion of Chinese motivations, see Karl W. Eikenberry, *Explaining and Influencing Chinese Arms Transfers*, McNair Paper, no. 36 (Washington, DC: Institute for National Strategic Studies, National Defense University, 1995).

33. *New York Times*, September 28, 1995; for Iranian recognition of this, see the Iranian press coverage of Foreign Minister Chen Qichen's statement in IRNA,

January 9, 1996, in *FBIS/China*, January 11, 1996, p. 3. Also see Winston Lord's confirmation of this in his October 24, 1995, press briefing. Regarding the 1997 agreement, see the October 29, 1997, background briefing by senior U.S. administration officials.

34. For a discussion of these developments, see the June 17, 1997, briefing by a "senior Department of Defense official." Perry's comments are reported in the *Far Eastern Economic Review*, September 11, 1997, p. 12.

35. Interview with U.S. State Department official; *Far Eastern Economic Review*, May 28, 1992. On the nuclear agreement with Iran, see the Chinese announcement in *New York Times*, September 11, 1992.

36. On recent Taiwan acquisitions, see Richard A. Bitzinger and Bates Gill, *Gearing Up for High-Tech Warfare?: Chinese and Taiwanese Defense Modernization and Implications for Military Confrontation Across the Taiwan Strait, 1995–2005* (Washington, DC: Center for Strategic and Budgetary Assessments, 1996); Reuters, May 23, 1996.

37. *Agence France-Presse*, June 9, 1998; Joint United States–People's Republic of China Statement on Missile Proliferation, October 4, 1994.

38. See the U.S. Department of State briefing on U.S.-China discussions on nonproliferation and nuclear-related exports, May 10, 1996. For the new export guidelines, see *Xinhua*, September 11, 1997, in *FBIS/China*, September 16, 1997. For a discussion of these regulations, see Ambassador Li Changhe's October 16, 1997, statement to the Zangger Committee. On the certification and export decision, see the October 29, 1997, White House background briefing conducted by senior administration officials; transcript of U.S. Acting Under Secretary for Arms Control and International Security Affairs John Holum's March 26, 1998, Beijing press conference.

39. See the June 3, 1998, remarks by President Clinton and Secretary of State Madeleine Albright and President Clinton's June 11, 1998, speech on U.S.-China relations.

40. U.S. Trade Representative, *1998 Foreign Trade Barriers Report*.

41. See Laura D'Andrea Tyson, "Trade Deficits Won't Ruin Us," *NYT*, November 24, 1997.

42. Nicholas R. Lardy, *China in the World Economy* (Washington, DC: Institute for International Economics, 1994).

43. See U.S. Trade Representative Charlene Barshefsky's June 10, 1997, testimony before the Finance Committee, United States Senate.

44. Robert S. Ross, "Enter the Dragon: China and the WTO," *Foreign Policy*, no. 104 (Fall 1996).

45. See, for example, Chinese Finance Minister Liu Zhongli's comments to U.S. Treasury Secretary Robert Rubin, in *Xinhua*, March 19, 1996, *FBIS/China*, March 18, 1996, pp. 2–3; Ren Zhong, "Forecast for China's Prospects for Joining the World Trade Organization," *Renmin Ribao*, February 6, 1996, in *FBIS/China*, February 6, 1996, pp. 54–55. On China's interest in an extended schedule for market opening, see Chen Weibin, "China's WTO Talks Have Entered a Crucial Stage," *Liaowang* no. 33 (August 18, 1997), in *FBIS/China*, August 29, 1997.

46. U.S. Trade Representative, "Intellectual Property Rights Enforcement in China: Fact Sheet," May 15, 1996.

47. See Berta Gomez, "Industry's 1996 Losses Estimated at $11,200 Million," United States Information Agency, May 7, 1997.

48. On the implementation agreement and the role of small business, see Office of the U.S. Trade Representative, "Fact Sheet: Chinese Implementation of the 1995 IPR Agreement," June 17, 1996; U.S. Trade Representative, *1998 Foreign Trade Barriers Report*; *NYT*, March 28, 1998. On the prison terms, see *NYT*, April 17, 1997. On the movement of production to elsewhere in Southeast Asia, see *Wall Street Journal*, August 22, 1997; *Wall Street Journal*, September 19, 1997. Also note that in 1997 the International Intellectual Property Alliance no longer targeted China as a priority for U.S. foreign policy. See Jeanne Holden, "Backgrounder on 'Special 301' Trade Law Review," United States Information Agency, February 25, 1997.

49. On the effect of sanctions, see Robert S. Ross, "China," in Richard Haass, ed., *Economic Sanctions and American Diplomacy* (Washington, D.C.: Brookings Institution, 1998). For the State Department's assessment of China's human rights situation, see United States Department of State, Bureau of Democracy, Human Rights, and Labor, "China Country Report on Human Rights Practices for 1997," January 30, 1998.

50. The United States will not always win such confrontations in international organizations. In 1996, China defeated U.S. efforts in the U.N. Commission on Human Rights, arousing considerable U.S. indignation. See Assistant Secretary of Human Rights John Shattuck's April 23, 1996, Geneva press conference on China.

51. China has not been reticent in its attacks on U.S. human rights violations. See, for example, Jin Jiang, "Such a 'Model of Human Rights'," *Renmin Ribao*, April 9, 1996, in *FBIS/China*, April 16. 1996, pp. 5–6.

52. For an extended discussion of this process, see Robert S. Ross, "Less Is Better: The Role of Sanctions in U.S. China Policy," in Richard Haass, *Economic Sanctions as an Instrument in American Foreign Policy* (Washington, DC: Brookings Institution, 1998).

53. See the testimony of Under Secretary of Commerce Stuart Eizenstadt to the House International Relations Committee, Subcommittee on Asian Affairs and the Subcommittee on International Economic Policy and Trade, May 16, 1996; U.S. Trade Representative, *1998 Foreign Trade Barriers Report*. For Chinese statistics for 1996, see Chinese State Statistical Bureau, *Zhongguo Tongji Nianjian* (Beijing: Zhongguo Tongji Chubanshe, 1997), pp. 606–607.

54. *China's Customs Statistics*, no. 100 (December 1997).

55. For a Chinese discussion of this situation, see Chen Baosen, "Quanmian Fazhan Zhong Mei Jingmao Guanxi Gonggu Zhong Mei Guanxi de Jingji Jichu" (Comprehensively develop China-U.S. economic and trade relations, consolidate the economic foundation of China-U.S. relations), *Shijie Jingji yu Zhengzhi* (*neibu*), no. 3, 1992.

56. Nye, Jr., "An Engaging China Policy."

57. U.S.-China Business Council; testimony of Under Secretary of Commerce Stuart Eizenstadt to the House International Relations Committee, Subcommittee on Asian Affairs and the Subcommittee on International Economic Policy and Trade, May 16, 1996; Office of the Press Secretary, The White House, "Fact Sheet: Accomplishments of U.S.-China Summit," October 29, 1997.

58. U.S. Trade Representative, *1998 Foreign Trade Barriers Report*.

59. For a forceful statement of the problem of interest groups in American foreign policy, see James Schlesinger, "Fragmentation and Hubris: A Shaky Basis for American Leadership," *The National Interest*, no. 49 (fall 1997).

2

Public Opinion and Interest Groups in the Making of U.S.-China Policy

Steven M. Teles

Realist theory generally assumes the primacy of diplomatic actors in the foreign policy process, although it is sometimes hard to distinguish wish from prediction, and also hard to determine how much this is based on regimes very different from the United States (i.e., those of a nondemocratic or parliamentary character, or with a high level of bureaucratic autonomy). In cases where the relations between nations are primarily strategic and military, this prediction has a certain force. However, the relations of the United States to China are particularly unsuited to this approach, since they are characterized only partially by strategic concerns, and much less so in the wake of the fall of the Soviet Union and the collapse of China's strategic role as a counterweight in the Cold War struggle.

The United States's relations with the People's Republic of China (PRC) are now increasingly dominated by "intermistic" issues: that is, issues that fall between international and domestic concerns.[1] Most favored nation (MFN) status, protection of intellectual property, human rights, forced sterilization and abortion, religious freedom, and the like are very different from the kinds of issues that predominate in a national interest/realpolitik relationship, and thus call into being a very different institutional and political set of actors and relationships.

The subject of this chapter is the role of two especially important influences on America's policy toward China: public opinion and interest groups. These two forces are not haphazardly joined. As we shall see, the character and level of public interest in our relations to China favor certain interests over others, and give interest groups differential access to influential institutions. I will begin with the subject of public opinion, since it is what sets the "frame," or context of policy, and then proceed to show how the new frame that public opinion has set for China policy has influenced the power and efficacy of interest groups.

Public Opinion on Foreign Policy

There is no more misused category of data compiled by modern social science than public opinion.[2] Newspapers and advocates trumpet answers to single questions given at one point in time, often on subjects where the public has little information, or even access to a conceptual screen. In the case of China, the situation is especially problematic, since the subject lacks many of the qualities that make the public's opinion in other areas coherent and substantive.

That said, there are some things we can say with certainty about the public's view of U.S.-China relations, and also about the role that public opinion (or, rather, policymakers' impression of public opinion) plays in the making of policy. I will start by giving a brief analysis of the public's larger views on foreign affairs, then examine their views on China, and then proceed to discuss how these views structure and bound the policy-making process that culminates in U.S.-China policy.

Americans are not, as a whole, isolationist, but it must be noted that they are more so than their leaders. While a substantial 65 percent of the public supports an active role for the U.S. in the world, an astounding 98 percent of leaders do.[3] This 1994 level is in the same general zone that it has been in since the early 1970s, when public support for an active role in foreign affairs dropped as a result of the Vietnam war.[4] The public and its leaders are split on other symbolically important issues in foreign affairs. A majority of leaders support U.S. soldiers serving under U.N. command, while the public is evenly split on this issue. Similarly, on the North American Free Trade Agreement (NAFTA), leaders supported the treaty at an 86 percent rate, while only 50 percent of the public did. These three polls all suggest enormous, near consensual support among leaders for internationalism, and the cosmopolitan values that underlie it, and substantial, if not majority-level, opposition to these values among the public.

Furthermore, the public is less likely to see foreign affairs as an autonomous sphere and more likely to see it as an extension of domestic policy. This is clear when one examines the areas of greatest distinction between the goals the public sees as "very important" and those leaders do. Of sixteen possible priorities, for only five are leaders more confident that they are "very important" than are the public: preventing the spread of nuclear weapons, securing adequate supplies of energy, defending our allies' security, maintaining superior military power worldwide, and helping to improve the standard of living of less developed nations. The first four are fundamentally interest-based goals, consistent with a realist framework of analysis. The last, while it gets somewhat more support from leaders, is at the bottom of both the public's and leaders' ranking of goals.

On the other hand, there are a substantial number of goals that the public is significantly more likely to see as very important priorities. Eighty-five percent of the public think "stopping the flow of illegal drugs into the U.S." is a very important priority (the goal that has the highest support of all sixteen possibilities), while only 57 percent of leaders view it as very important. The distinction is equally as sharp on the subject of protecting the jobs of American workers (83 percent to 50 percent), controlling and reducing illegal immigration (an astounding 73 percent to 28 percent), reducing our trade deficit with other countries (59 percent to 49 percent) and combating world hunger (56 percent to 41 percent).[5]

Taken as a whole, these responses suggest an aspect of public and elite opinion that is of particular relevance to the United States's relations with China. The public, both in absolute terms and when compared with their leaders, does not have a substantial conceptual screen for analyzing foreign policy goals that distinguishes them from domestic policy. This suggests that, in the absence of some very public conflict that mobilizes resources and elites' opinion-shaping role (such as the Cold War) to anchor the public's views and direct them toward strategic thinking, it is easy for American opinion on foreign affairs to devolve into a reification of domestic preferences. This will make it more likely that public pressure will push in the direction of making foreign policy a tool in the service of domestic policy problems, rather than as an instrument for the attainment of the U.S.'s interests in the world order.

For most of the post-WWII period, public opinion on foreign policy has been fundamentally stable, changing occasionally in response to shifts in the strategic situation (such as detente with Russia and the opening up of relations with China in the early 1970s, and in response to the more aggressive Soviet posture and reduction in U.S. defense effort in the late 1970s) or to changes in information or government policy.[6] While this trend is clear overall, it is much more certain where the larger structure of foreign policy is concerned, such as the nature of the role of the U.S. in the world. Where relations with specific countries and the content of policy toward those countries are concerned, opinion is typically less well-anchored.

For most of the post-WWII era, American public opinion was driven by the Cold War. Traditionalist conservatives who had previously been isolationists were drawn into supporting an activist foreign policy as a result of the impression that the Cold War was a global moral conflict, one partially fought on U.S. soil.[7] Many Western conservatives of a libertarian streak were swayed to support internationalism as a consequence of the enormous military construction and spending that was directed toward their states. Of greatest importance, the Cold War provided a context for intense and protracted mobilization of public opinion, one that could draw the public's attention to an area of policy they had traditionally ignored. With the collapse of the Cold War, that conceptual screen has now been removed. In the absence of a new, well-understood strategic doctrine connected to a high-profile conflict, it is unlikely that a nondomestic orientation to U.S. public opinion on foreign policy will emerge. This is the context in which we must judge and understand the way the public views our policies toward China.

Public Opinion Toward China

The American public's relationship with China has been a long and rocky one. In 1951, 60 percent of the public supported bombing China in the context of the Korean conflict.[8] In the mid-1950s, 92 percent of the public opposed the admission of China into the United Nations. On a temperature plot ranging from −500 degrees to +500 degrees, between the mid-1950s and the early-1970s, the American people never gave China more than a very frosty −200-degree rating.[9] Furthermore, in the 1950s, large majorities of the public actively supported U.S. aid for the nationalist Chinese, and the question of "who lost China?" helped spark much of the McCarthy-era search for domestic commu-

nists. From the mid-1960s through the mid-1970s, the PRC was actually more disliked than the Soviet Union.[10] It is not an overstatement to
observe that, up through the early 1970s, American public opinion
toward China was on a virtually war-level footing.[11]

That said, the reversal in public opinion toward China since the
reestablishment of bilateral relations has been startling. For much of
the 1970s, public impressions of the Soviet Union and the PRC tracked
each other closely, but then in the early 1980s, public warmth toward
China increased dramatically, becoming positive by the middle of the
decade. Even at the height of President Reagan's attempt to turn public
opinion against the Soviet Union by branding it an "evil empire,"
Reagan resisted making a similar appeal toward China. This elite signal surely played an important role in softening opinion toward China,
as did the end of the Cultural Revolution and the gradual opening up of
China's economy. By the end of the 1980s, public opinion toward
China had begun to "normalize."

One cannot underestimate the role that the Chinese regime's brutal
crackdown on student dissidents in Tiananmen Square had on U.S. public
opinion. In early 1989, according to Gallup, 72 percent of the American
public was either very favorable or mostly favorable toward China, while
only 13 percent were mostly or very unfavorable.[12] By the end of the
year, these levels of support had completely collapsed. By August, 31
percent were favorable, while a remarkable 58 percent were unfavorable.
A similar reversal was found in a series of other polls taken in this
period.[13] Hostility to China has moderated slightly since 1989, but as of
June 1997, those stating an unfavorable opinion of China was still at the
50 percent level, with those with an favorable impression at 33 percent,
levels characteristic of the post-Tiananmen period.[14]

This shift in impressions of the Chinese regime spills over into more
particular concerns. Fifty-seven percent of the American people now
view the development of China as a world power to be a "critical
threat" to the United States, up from 40 percent in 1990. An even
more dramatic jump in the impression of China as a critical threat was
registered among leaders: up to 46 percent in 1994 from only 16 percent in 1990. Along with its increased visibility, relations with China
are now seen as a vital interest of the United States: between 1990 and
1994, the public's impression of China as a vital interest jumped from
47 percent to 68 percent, and among leaders from 73 percent to 95
percent (which is, for leaders, approximately the same rating possessed

by Japan and Russia). More leaders and the public now support spying on China than on Russia.[15]

When the subject narrows to U.S. policy toward China, the public is sharply divided, and opinion has tended to sway fairly widely within a narrow time frame. For example, in December 1993, 65 percent of Americans said the United States should demand that China improve its human rights record if it wants to continue its current trade status with the United States, while only 29 percent thought that the United States should retain good trade relations regardless of our human rights disagreements. By June 1994, the gap had narrowed to 42 percent against linkage and 50 percent for, but support for linkage soared to 60 percent in 1995 and 67 percent in 1997.[16] When the specific question of MFN status is asked, even numbers of Americans support and oppose MFN renewal, although slightly stronger majorities support MFN when it is not specifically identified as such. American China experts, on the other hand, strongly oppose revoking MFN, with 75 percent opposing outright revocation and 16 percent supporting (on the narrower issue of conditional MFN, academic China experts are evenly split).[17]

For the American public, China now feeds into a number of concerns of a fundamentally nonstrategic character. In addition to the human rights issues that became salient after Tiananmen, China's emerging trade surplus with the United States, combined with the public's concerns about wages and foreign competition, have made it vulnerable in the same way that Japan was in the mid-1980s. Furthermore, the collapse of the Soviet Union has left a strategic-threat vacuum, one that politicians primarily concerned with human rights or trade can exploit by pointing to China as the United States's next major global adversary. Overall, public opinion has shifted dramatically and, given the objective situation in both trade and human rights, probably durably. Furthermore, given the collapse of the strategic conflict between the United States and Russia, the protection that policy elites had from the public has eroded. As discussed in the following section, this rising salience of public opinion has changed the structure in which interest group activity operates.

The Influence of Public Opinion

Public opinion is shaped by interest groups, but it also shapes the environment in which those groups operate. Especially for groups that lack tangible resources that they can bring to bear in the policy process, such as money, the perceived degree of public interest in an issue and an interest group's claim to speak for that public opinion are crucial. When public opinion is highly activated, groups without tangible resources are at an advantage. When deactivated, those groups have less of a claim to be heard.

The case of China is a textbook example of this division. One may say, very crudely of course, that there are three general clusters of interests on China policy, each with a different level and type of access to power, and all differentially impacted by public opinion. The first, those whose interest is primarily strategic or military, including such issues as nuclear and missile proliferation, prefer a low level of public concern, because the "natural" state of foreign policy power in our system is one of executive dominance, and within that state, dominance by the Departments of State and Defense.[18] That natural state is most likely to exist where public concern is muted. The second, those whose interest is primarily economics and trade, prefer a moderate level of public concern: specific enough to support an open trading regime, and to encourage involvement by nondiplomatic agencies (such as the Department of Commerce), but not so interested that they pay a great deal of attention to the specific situation in China. Those with an economic interest prefer White House dominance, so as to direct policy away from State and Defense and toward the more economically minded agencies. Finally, those with human rights concerns prefer a high level of public interest in China policy, so as to counteract the institutional interests within the executive branch in trade and strategic/military issues. As a result, they prefer the branch closest to public opinion, Congress.

As a background to the current interest group alignment, its relation to public opinion, and the interrelationship this has in its effect on China policy, it is useful to examine the effect that the Cold War had on the politics of foreign policy. First, by drawing all countries and issues into the rubric of the overall struggle for world supremacy between the United States and the Soviet Union, the Cold War made it easier to justify a realistic, end-oriented foreign policy. Human rights abuses or violations of trading arrangements could be accepted, if the violator was friendly in the Cold War struggle, making it easier to keep the nation's eye on global strategy. This also made it easier to dismiss the arguments of those interest groups with more narrow agendas.

Second, the Cold War permitted policymakers to do things that, in the absence of a quasi-war context, the public would not have accepted. These include high levels of secrecy, favorable trading relationships with friendly powers, covert military supply of sympathetic groups, and so on. Finally, the Cold War also limited somewhat the power of interest groups in foreign policy, by making the pressure that those groups could bring to bear appear unseemly. Pushing for your interest in, say, agricultural supports is one thing. Pursuing such a narrow agenda when it undermines diplomatic strategy in the context of war is quite another. This rough formalism made it easier for the foreign policy establishment to resist public pressure.

With the Cold War over, however, this overarching context has broken down. The most dramatic element to go with the Soviet Union was deference. The constitutional system emphasizes congressional and public deference to the executive on foreign policy issues, especially in the context of war. This deference is a necessary element in the creation and maintenance of geostrategy, since it permits centralized decision making in the executive. When power ceases to be highly centralized, and disperses throughout the government, geostrategy becomes more difficult, and policy devolves into a series of diverse, and often unconnected, "issues." This is where the political context is now for U.S. policy toward China.

The other element to erode with the end of the Cold War, and also with the economic liberalization of the PRC, is the ideological dimension to U.S. policy, which began with Nixon's opening up relations with China in the early 1970s. Warm relations with the PRC continued to be very unpopular among conservatives well into the 1980s, however. Much of this ideological stridency among mainstream conservatives is now gone. Within the two largest conservative think tanks, Heritage and AEI, a generally sympathetic policy on economic issues holds sway, and scholars at both groups support military-to-military relations with the PRC, a position still controversial in Congress. Until quite recently, hostility toward the PRC among mainstream conservatives manifested itself primarily in support for Taiwan in such areas as arms sales and an increased world stature for the Republic of China (ROC).

The 1992 and 1996 presidential campaigns of Patrick Buchanan showed that opposition to the Chinese government is still appealing to some conservative voters. In his campaign against George Bush in 1992 and in the 1996 primary, Buchanan used the China issue to appeal simultaneously to conservatives and those afraid of losing their jobs to foreign competition. In New Hampshire in January 1992, Buchanan memorably referred to Deng Xiaoping as a "chain smoking Communist dwarf."[19] Ever sensitive to a winning issue, Bill Clinton followed up Buchanan's attack by referring to the Chinese government as "the butchers of Beijing." For Clinton, this attack had a very specific political purpose: helping to attract former Democratic neoconservatives (such as Joshua Muravchik and Martin Peretz) into the Clinton fold. In 1996, Buchanan was somewhat less *ad hominem,* but equally emotional. Just a month before Bob Dole's decision to support MFN status for China, Buchanan held a press conference designed to push Dole in the opposite direction. He stated that, "I think the policy [of the Clinton administration] has degenerated into reflexive accommodation and appeasement of Communist China."[20] He went on to observe that, "I think we have to stop babying this regime. It is not some lovable wayward child that merely needs indulgence and affection.... [We have] to stop empowering a potential enemy of the United States of America ... and make China pay some price for her belligerence, hostility and arrogance."[21] Buchanan repeatedly referred to the PRC as "Communist China," an appellation seldom used outside of the hard right since the end of the Cold War. Buchanan, a shrewd judge of the political winds, surmised that for his more strident fellows in the conservative movement, such rhetorical exercises in the direction of China still had force and influence.

There is little question that the prominence of the China question in the 1992 election, and the way he used the issue in the campaign, made it initially very difficult for President Clinton to backtrack once in office. Jim Prystup, a former member of the Bush administration now at the Heritage Foundation observed that, "China wasn't the issue. It was turning Bush's foreign policy expertise against him by saying he's a symp, he's [a] wimp."[22] China had become a proxy issue for presidential strength in foreign policy, meaning that any retreat on a confrontational policy needed to be accompanied by bellicose rhetoric and strong action on more minor issues (such as intellectual property). While China is still a fairly minor issue in election campaigns, elections remain one of the key mechanisms by which public opinion influences the outcome of the policy process and by which various interests are strengthened or weakened.

The Relations Between Interest Groups

Before addressing the relative strength of those groups pushing for a more or less confrontational policy toward China, it is worthwhile to pause by examining the way the two sides interact, and to a limited degree cooperate, with each other. While political scientists spend an enormous amount of time studying the relations between interest groups in coalitions, and between interest groups and the political process, the relations between opposing interest groups is virtually uncharted waters. Were one to judge merely by surface appearances, the relations between business and human rights groups concerned with China would seem to be perfectly awful. With mind-numbing regularity, Washington goes through its "rite of spring" on MFN status for China, with business groups attacking the human rights community as extremists totally lacking in reason, and the human rights community accusing business of cozying up to a brutal Chinese dictatorship. The reality is somewhat different from the appearances. Over the last few years, relations between the human rights community and business have improved substantially, although not across the board.

One indication of the older pattern in human rights–business relations is a recent letter from Amnesty International to a number of the largest American businesses. This letter begins rather calmly, by observing that business relations with human rights–abusing nations are dangerous, as a result of political instability and the danger of violating U.S. law in the conduct of business. A final danger the letter points out is rather ominous, and in the eyes of businessmen, a threat:

> Finally, there are a number of non-governmental organizations capable of orchestrating well-organized boycott, sanction, or disinvestment movements against companies which they target for maintaining business relations in countries with patterns of gross and systematic human rights violations. How can responsible corporate leaders address such concerns and risks? Amnesty International, the world's oldest and largest independent human rights organization, is offering to enter into a dialogue with you.

Amnesty International suggests that it can provide information to companies entering into a dialogue and provide model corporate codes of conduct, and that they will not call for a boycott or request a withdrawal from nations in which that business is operating. However, they also state that they will not "'go public' with a criticism of your company's human rights practices or policies until we have attempted to discuss our concerns with you first." Many businesses, quite reasonably, took this last statement as a threat. They have also been frustrated with the moralistic tone of Amnesty's communications, which suggest that the group will "educate" businesses and "convince you that it is in your best interest as a business manager to respect the human rights of your employees and others in your domain of operations." One business representative told this author that, "There's two worlds here, and there is an interest [on Amnesty's part] in reaching out and establishing some sort of dialogue, but the way of viewing the world is so different. This letter just shines a spotlight on how different it is, to the point where a company would just say, there is nothing to talk about."

A more fully developed relationship exists between business groups, especially the U.S.-China Business Council, and Human Rights Watch (HRW)–Asia. This reality is, at first blush, counterintuitive. Amnesty takes no public position on MFN status for China, while Human Rights Watch openly calls for strict conditions. Amnesty is generally considered more "moderate" than Human Rights Watch, for reasons that have a great deal to do with the different stakeholders of the two organizations. (Amnesty is a world organization driven by its many national delegations, while HRW is more staff-driven.) Ironically, it may be that the conflictual relations over MFN have driven Human Rights Watch and the U.S.-China Business Council into conversation and a certain level of cooperation, while Amnesty's lack of involvement in MFN has caused it to be less comprehending of the needs and style of the business community.

Mike Jendrzejczyk, the Washington director of Human Rights Watch–Asia, states that the relationship began with the height of the MFN debates, during the Bush administration. After a number of public arguments, on congressional panels and in the press, leaders of the U.S.-China Business Council began to have more private meetings, at which they "found that even though on policy questions we might not come out the same way, some of our objectives, our working assumptions, and our concerns were actually very similar. So that began the process of rather sporadic and now fairly consistent dialogue on a whole range of things."[23] Rich Brecher, of the U.S.-China Business

Council, remembers the initial contacts somewhat differently. "They approached us at first with a somewhat patronizing attitude that they would like to 'educate' us regarding the true situation in China. Business representatives, many of which have extensive background living and working in China, resented their presumption."[24]

When HRW–Asia published a report on prison labor in China, a number of companies asked the group to brief them on how they could avoid becoming entangled in this practice. This began a process of more substantive contacts, often with the U.S.-China Business Council as moderator. Jendrzejczyk observes that,

> The range of issues has been very broad, ranging from the rule of law in Hong Kong, to the very controversial report on orphanages and how that was going to play out in the U.S. policy area. . . . I have been asked to give presentations to meetings of the U.S.-China Business Council on U.S. policy issues, the UN Human Rights Commission, and its deliberations on human rights concerns. Much of this has been in the area of better understanding of where each other is coming from.

These ongoing contacts, even where they do not have explicit policy content, do provide a forum for closing the gap between the world views of the two groups, permitting them to seek out areas of overlapping interests. Brecher observes that, "most of our contacts have been off the record. But as a result they have a deeper appreciation of some of the positive influences that accrue from our activity in China. . . . There is a civility and a level of respect that might surprise folks who aren't a part of this process."

At the same time, this has not diminished the ardor with which the human rights community pursues the MFN debate. Again, Jendrzejczyk observes that,

> There is a certain kind of confidence and trust level that has evolved over time that has allowed us to have a framework for this kind of dialogue despite our policy differences. And roughly it is analogous . . . with our relationship to the administration. . . . We've had a parallel relationship, or maybe a bifurcated relationship, that has allowed us to separate the policy issues where we clearly were in different camps altogether, from issues where it was in the administration or the State Department's interest to get information from us. . . . We are playing a dual role. . . . We have to be able to play both roles almost simultaneously.[25]

This dual role—strenuous conflict over certain issues like MFN, but more cordial relations on specific areas of mutual interest—may become the general pattern for business–human rights group interaction in the future. And if the MFN debate cools off, and human rights groups find that their ability to influence government policy is limited, these business contacts may provide their only lever to affect Chinese government behavior, or at the least economic conditions in China.

Recent overtures to the Council of Foreign Relations by Andrew Nathan, chairman of Human Rights Watch–Asia's Advisory Council, may signal the increasing popularity of this strategy. Nathan, himself a member of the Council of Foreign Relations, has proposed a project that would bring together business leaders, academics, and human rights activists to discuss cooperative strategies to influence foreign countries' human rights performance. This overture, according to Nathan, reflects the exhaustion of the MFN debate and the discomfort that some in the human rights community feel being at loggerheads with the business community.[26] It is unclear, as of September 1996, whether the "establishment" represented by the Council of Foreign Relations will reciprocate. Regardless, the initiative is a symbol that the politics of U.S.-China relations may be entering a new era, one characterized more by subpolitical efforts than by governmental action.

Winning the Rhetorical War

Political scientists tend to underestimate the importance of rhetoric in shaping political outcomes. A focus on the conflict of interests obscures the importance of arguments and ignores the importance of convincing both the public and members of Congress of the rectitude of one's position. This is especially true in the case of China. First, the issue of China is not one with deeply rooted ideological anchors, either for the public or members of Congress. As a result, the ability to frame the issue—to succeed in determining what the conflict is about—is extremely important. As we shall see, despite the long odds against the human rights groups, their ability to frame public debate partially compensates for their lack of other crucial political resources.

With the end of the Cold War, the ideological anchor that steadied the definition of U.S. interest in China was cut loose. As a result, there was a new opportunity for groups outside the strategic community to frame the issue of China, as either primarily a commercial one or a conflictual one based on differences over human rights. As Jim Prystup, former State Department official in the Bush administration said, "Everything became equal. So then the real issue is who has the loudest voice, who screams the loudest gets the attention of the White House."[27]

The primary activity of the human rights groups interested in China is the production of information, typically exposés of the abuses imposed by the Chinese regime. The relation between these revelations of Chinese government behavior and the groups' agenda on U.S. policy is very delicate. The reasons for this are simple. The human rights groups clearly have an interest in painting the Chinese regime as a systematic violator of human rights, and the steady, careful documentation of government behavior sets a foundation on top of which all other conversations must be made. At the same time, the human rights groups do not want to link their information and their policy positions too closely. If they do, they threaten to tarnish their reputation as speaking for the moral, idealistic point of view in the debate, and this reputation is their most potent weapon.

One example of this reticence is the situation that emerged in the aftermath of the revelation of abuses in the Chinese orphanage system. Even though the report of Human Rights Watch–Asia was released while the debate on relations with China were continuing, especially on MFN, HRW attempted to avoid linking the two directly. Mike Jendrzejczyk explains:

> We were not interested in linking this issue to MFN or other issues. Maybe there were opportunities, but if there were we deliberately did not take them, to try to further demonize China, or let this issue with all the emotional connotations behind it push us into taking more radical kind of policy positions. Just the opposite. We wanted to keep the focus on the issue. Yes, we wanted the abuses of Chinese orphans to be part of the larger debate in places like Geneva, but we were not interested in this issue [being] the cutting edge of U.S.-Sino relations.

The strategy of the human rights organizations is to steadily create an image of the Chinese regime that will make it difficult for the government to ignore the human rights issue. It is not any particular abuse, but the accumulation of abuses, that is critical to their policy agenda.

It should also be noted that the human rights groups often do not have to work very hard to put the issue on the agenda, for two reasons. The first is that the Chinese regime often does a good job of that themselves. Whether Amnesty or Human Rights Watch existed at all, the press would have still covered the Chinese government's ruthless crackdown in Tiananmen, and it would have affected public opinion in the way that was described earlier. A source in the International Campaign for Tibet observed that the single factor that affects their ability to shape opinion on the subject is not their own activities, but those of the Tibetans themselves, and the government's response: "The number one [factor] is when the Tibetans inside Tibet raise their voices. When you have 2,000 people on the streets getting shot. . . ."[28] public opinion is bound to become hostile toward the PRC. Right or wrong, the PRC considers suppression of dissension in Tibet to be essential to its national interest, and from time to time this will require the use of violence. The Chinese government will have to accept that a certain degree of hostility from those concerned with human rights is the price of their Tibetan policy, as is sustained attention on the issue by the U.S. government. This attention was institutionalized in 1997 with the establishment of a "Tibet watcher" to coordinate U.S. policy, an action that will give Tibet-focused interest groups a permanent channel into the U.S. government.

The second factor is the press, which both the human rights groups and the business community see as being biased toward the human rights position in general, and toward accentuating China's abuses in particular. T. Kumar at Amnesty International says that even though they do not place disproportionate resources on China, they get disproportionate interest from the media. "It so happens that whenever we do something on China the media is after us. China is big time. . . . When we do a report on Afghanistan, nobody is interested, because it is a forgotten country."[29] Since Tiananmen, the subject of Chinese human rights abuses has been a salient issue for the public, and this drives journalists to cover the issue, for editors to give it priority, and for human rights groups to be seen speaking up on it. Admittedly, there is something of an internally regenerating cycle to press coverage. The issue becomes salient as a result of an event, human rights groups get access to the media as a result, they can then get additional attention for their information, which increases public interest, which spurs more press coverage, and so on. Either way, disproportionate press attention to China is not the result of groups "picking on China," as her advocates in the United States accuse. China's abuses get coverage, even where they are less severe than in other countries, because the PRC is a globally significant state in a way that Nigeria or Burma is not.

The ability of the human rights groups to frame the issue of China is, therefore, a result of the real situation in the PRC, a sympathetic press, the rhetorical skills of the human rights advocates, and the effect of public opinion. Taken together, these force human rights concerns onto the agenda and make purely interest-based justifications for policy difficult if not impossible to make. In order to be successful, business groups now have to fight the human rights groups on their own rhetorical turf. As one very important business group representative said, "If you pitch dollars versus freedom, people generally in the end come down to freedom, as they should, I guess."[30]

Business has, therefore, been forced to come up with an argument that admits the importance of human rights concerns, and deplores Chinese behavior, but states that commercial links are the best way to change the human rights situation in China. One business representative involved with the China issue stated:

> If you go up to talk to a member of Congress and you say that we want you to support MFN, they go, oh but these are terrible people, they do terrible things, human rights, human rights, human rights. The point is not to defend China, it is not to deny that terrible things happen there, it is not to be an apologist for China, the point is to say that you are absolutely right about some of this stuff, but what are we going to do effectively to deal with this matter?[31]

The business groups' strategy, which has been quite shrewd, has been to take the sting out of the human rights groups' revelations by admitting everything that they accuse China of, but then shifting the debate to what can actually change the behavior of the regime. When the debate has been reframed in this way, it is very difficult for the human rights groups to win. Mike Jendrzejczyk observes that, "they [the business groups] were also very effectively aiming to reconfigure the argument in the debate two years ago to say that trade was itself a human rights policy, that trade and economic engagement would itself lead to policy reform and solve the human rights problem in some indefinite point in the future, and therefore were able to turn the argument around and succeeded to a great extent. . . ." Where congressmen were concerned both with human rights and with maintaining the economic relationship with China, the business groups' rhetorical strategy provided a way to vote for MFN with a clear conscience, especially for members who had walked a long way down the plank in criticizing the Chinese. Jendrzejczyk observes that, "They needed cover—ideological cover—to allow them to backtrack from their own linkage of trade and human rights that drove Clinton to issue his executive order. And that's what the business community gave them. They not only gave them a reason to do it, they gave them a rationale to justify their own change of heart."

Furthermore, the business community has successfully popularized the concept of "engagement" as the keystone of American policy in China. Engagement suggests that if China is integrated into the world economic and political system, it will be significantly more constrained than it is today. If China is economically integrated with the other economies of Asia, it is less likely to threaten them militarily, for this would inevitably damage China's own interests. As with human rights, the economic argument seeks not to dismiss military or strategic concerns, but to subsume them.

This current framing of the debate, although already taking on the appearance of stability, is perhaps more tenuous than it looks. For one, the influence of the strategic community, which is generally on the side of those pushing for an open trading relationship with China, is rather muted. The business organizations continue to depend upon the intellectual prestige of those who have standing on geostrategy, but there is a sense that they are less influential than they once were, as this business organization representative suggests.

> The latest gig now is to get a Scowcroft or an Eagleburger to make a big statement or do some huge op-ed and that's supposed to effect the process. It does in some ways. I'm just cynical because having done four of these efforts, it's like roll out the foreign policy kings and get them to say something again. There is some clout and they won't say something they don't believe in. Certainly there is some clout in having a Kissinger saying he believes in X or Y.[32]

For most members of Congress, strategic concerns have been at the bottom of their list of priorities where China is concerned, and as a result the influence of geostrategists has been muted. However, if the recognition of the "rise of China" (discussed in Chapter 3 by Robert Sutter) continues to increase, the clout of the strategists would rise as well. The more important the relationship is, the less likely members of Congress will be to approach the issue in an parochial or symbolic manner, and the more receptive they will be to intellectuals who can tell how China fits into the world system. But up until very recently, the arguments of the geostrategists have had a certain sameness to them, and this lack of something "new" to add to the debate is a disadvantage in a conflict that occurs every year.

In this sense, there are advantages to those whose arguments have not yet thoroughly evolved. This suggests that certain groups, for example, labor, environmental, and conservative religious organizations, may be able to frame the China issue more effectively in the years to come. Although it has muted somewhat, for years the U.S. relationship with Japan was dominated by the presence of an enormous bilateral trade deficit, a focus driven largely by the labor movement. While this has only begun to structure the debate over China so far, the substantial and increasing trade deficit with China is already affecting the debate, albeit in a more piecemeal fashion, in such areas as intellectual property rights.

Currently, business groups are able to make the economic issue play to their advantage by stressing the exports that the United States sends to China. The U.S.-China Business Council has been especially adept at this, breaking down within states U.S. exports to China by state and by industry group. This sort of targeted information is, by all accounts, very convincing to members of Congress, as is the promise that China will spend "over $750 billion in new infrastructure over the next decade."[33] There are opportunities, however, for the labor movement and other essentially protectionist organizations to reframe the debate in terms of lost jobs due to low-wage competition, as they did in the debate over NAFTA. Furthermore, the increasing strength of unions in the aftermath of the Teamster's strike may give the AFL-CIO more power on trade issues than it has had in the past. When China applies for admission to the WTO, this potential reframing may take on particular importance.

How Does Public Opinion Affect China Policy?

Public opinion, as suggested by the previous section, has a number of influences on the outcomes of our policy toward China, but it is important to take care in specifying what they are. First of all, generally hostile public opinion toward China gives strength and access to human rights groups that they would lack otherwise. When human rights abuses are in the news, the ability of human rights groups to get a hearing jumps substantially. A source in the International Campaign for Tibet observes that, in distinction to the situation ten years ago, "There has been an increased visibility of Tibet. We can get into congressmen's offices [now]. People are more receptive. They know it is a problem." Mike Jendrzejczyk observes that, while his organization has access to policymakers in Washington, the relation between that access and the ability to affect policy outcomes is largely determined by the perceived strength of public opinion. "There are people in the White House we can talk to or who come and ask us for our advice or to come in for meetings. But whether that can be equated with real influence in policymaking is to a large extent conditioned by how visible we are in the press, and to what extent Congress is echoing and picking up our concerns, our information or our policy proposals." T. Kumar of Amnesty generally agrees: "If it is a hot topic, we can really sway Congress. There is less pressure when there is no media event."

The question remains, however, that even where the human rights community can attract public opinion around an issue and push congressmen to listen and speak out, how much actual influence on policy are they able to have. In a few specific cases, one can definitely state that public opinion did bound the kinds of policy that were preferred by either the president or the diplomatic community. This is especially clear in the case of policy in the immediate aftermath of the Tiananmen Square massacre, and especially to Brent Scowcroft's ill-fated trip to China. Jim Prystup stated that

> the reaction to the Scowcroft business really made it very dangerous on a political level to have any links with China. Very clear. . . . It [public opinion] can act as a constraint. . . . Obviously after the second Scowcroft trip, Scowcroft could not go to Beijing for another three years. That was history. Look how many times Baker went to China. It became simply a management issue. There was very little that we could do, post-Tiananmen. There was no high-profile initiative, I don't know if there could have been in those circumstances.

Despite the administration's desire to have closer ties to China, and to tighten the links between the two countries, the kind of high-level political contacts that could permit this were impossible, given the public opinion context.

A similar pattern emerged in the aftermath of the revelation that Chinese donors had contributed large sums to the Clinton/Gore reelection campaign. In addition to their consequences domestically, the hearings into "donorgate" made it difficult for policymakers to make trips to China or be seen to be taking other than hard-line positions. Introducing the hearings, Sen. Fred Thompson (R-TN) stated that they would examine "allegations concerning a plan hatched during the last election cycle by the Chinese government and designed to pour illegal money into American political campaigns. The plan had a goal: to buy access and influence in furtherance of Chinese government interests."[34] Ultimately, this attempt to suggest a Chinese plan to manipulate American elections fizzled, as attention focused more on why the Clinton administration was asking for and accepting such contributions, rather than why they were being offered. Donorgate also failed to make a substantial impact on public distaste for the Chinese regime, largely because opposition to the PRC was already at a relatively high plateau (as discussed earlier). Regardless, the atmosphere created by donorgate was one where China's friends in the United States were forced to make their case in a much more restrained way, at the same time that its enemies were raising the stridency of their attacks.

Public opinion, in some cases, sets the limits in which policymakers can operate, putting certain options outside the bounds of consideration. This kind of public constraint on elites is typical of a number of policy areas.[35] More typically, however, public opinion requires that additional time and effort be expended that might be used in other areas. Prystup observed that, "It can act as something you have to deal with, it can absorb time, and by absorbing time it can take away from other issues elsewhere that you should be focusing on." He observed that this pattern was especially clear in the efforts of the administration to broker a settlement in Cambodia.

> We basically decided that the safest thing to do was to keep the Khmer Rouge in the negotiation. Public opinion was hostile to that, they didn't want them in. But so, we had to come up to the Hill and do a lot of explaining. We just asked the $64,000 question, if you don't want them in, are you willing to send in the 82nd Airborne in Phnom Penh to keep them out? The answer was no and we said, "Okay, that's the way we're going to go."

It would be a mistake to assume that this extra time and effort is necessarily deleterious to the outcomes of policy-making, however. Even Prystup admitted that this may have improved the conduct of foreign policy-making in the Bush administration.

> I think that the one thing we had good during the Bush years, having the Congress controlled by the Democrats made us think things through. So, when you came up with something you really had it walked through all the way and you could defend it. The thing that really hurt Clinton in the first few years is he had a Democratic Congress and they gave him a free ride. So a lot of loose and sloppy thinking went down as policy. I tend to think of it, having a strong opposition has a beneficial effect on policy.

In the Bush administration, hostile public opinion and congressional opposition limited the kinds of policy that the administration could pursue, but they also sharpened the thinking that went into policy-making. In this sense, public opinion is most likely to be effective where there is divided government, because Congress is more likely to challenge the president when he is of a different party and when public opinion runs against the president's policies.

Coalition-Building and Interest-Group Strategy

Another element affecting the relative strength of the pro-MFN and anti-MFN interest groups is their relative strategy and the durability of their policy coalition. In this area, business clearly is at an advantage.

First of all, the coalition that business develops for a debate such as China's MFN status is substantially the same as the coalition they develop for other issues, including trade but also regulatory and fiscal policy. The U.S. Chamber of Commerce and the National Association of Manufacturers, the Emergency Committee on American Trade, and the National Foreign Trade Council are used to working with each other and do not have to go through substantial investments of time and effort to build successful collaborative structures. Furthermore, the more specialized parts of their coalition, such as the U.S.-China Business Council, have a similar view of the world as their larger compatriots, and are thus easy to integrate into preexisting coalitions. Furthermore, there is remarkably little dissension within the U.S. business community concerning MFN for China. Even those companies, such as Microsoft and AST, that have specific trade conflicts with China support the overall business community's position on MFN.

On the other side, the situation is much messier. The anti-MFN coalition is a motley assortment of a number of groups, each of which has a particular reason for opposing MFN, driven by a different worldview and often sharply varying ideologies. The human rights community, although united in its concern with China's human rights behavior, is not as united in the vehemence with which it pursues opposition to unconditional MFN. Some human rights groups, such as Amnesty International, take no official position on MFN whatsoever, while many of the others support conditional MFN for leverage purposes, even though they privately will admit to wanting to preserve the trade relationship that MFN makes possible. Even within the community of activists interested in Tibet, for example, there are differences as to policy preferences. My Tibetan source told me that, "There is some tension between some of the more radical groups who want revocation, and groups in Washington who are more of the philosophy that we should achieve something, don't want to take something on principle and lose.... In some ways it can help our position, if they are calling for revocation, it makes it easy for those of us in the middle." Clearly, this dissension cuts two ways. It does make it easier for the mainstream human rights groups to pose as moderates, but it also somewhat weakens the consistency of their message.

The labor movement is interested in MFN for an entirely different set of reasons. The AFL-CIO is in favor of revocation of China's MFN status, and its motivations, depending upon the source, are some amalgam of legitimate human rights concerns concerning forced labor in China and trade protectionism. While the human rights groups take a fundamentally agnostic position (or even supportive) toward U.S. trade with China, the labor movement is opposed, for a set of reasons not substantially different from those at issue in the NAFTA debate, in particular its interest in avoiding additional foreign competition. Unlike the human rights groups, which have the potential for relatively wide-ranging cooperation with business on non-MFN–related issues, this potential for cooperation is not present with labor unions, which are on the other side of business on most other issues with an economic motivation. This is clearly shown by the labor movement's choice of issues, in particular their focus on prison labor in China. This issue, while certainly legitimate on human rights grounds, is tailor-made for keeping certain goods out of U.S. markets, and out of competition with U.S. workers.

Right-wing ideological organizations have a different set of motivations for interest in China. While the more mainstream think tanks, such as AEI and Heritage, are generally supportive of a non-confrontational relationship with China, those closer to the fringes still retain much of the old Cold War fervor. The group with the most clout in Washington that opposes unconditional MFN is the Family Research Council (FRC), which is, along with the Christian Coalition, the most important Washington presence of the Christian Right. Other important parts of the conservative anti-MFN coalition include Freedom House (the conservative human rights organization), the Eagle Forum, and Concerned Women for America. The motivation of all these groups is similar, focusing primarily on China's one-child policy, forced abortion and sterilization, oppression of Christian groups, and, to some degree, concern about China as a potential strategic threat.

Starting in 1996, this conservative-labor coalition on China policy began to spread, drawing in more mainstream groups and, of genuine significance, major opinion magazines. FRC and the AFL-CIO have worked closely with each other on the issue, both behind the scenes and in more high-profile ventures. But the most meaningful change has been in the high-brow media. Just between March and July of 1997, the *New Republic* published four cover stories on China, all severely critical of the engagement/economic strategy of the Clinton administration, and has maintained a uniformly critical stance on its editorial page. On February 4, 1997, the *Weekly Standard* published an entire issue devoted to pushing a hard line on China policy. William Kristol, the *Standard*'s editor, has made China the cornerstone of a new conservative foreign policy, one that can distinguish it from the economistic consensus that has driven policy in the Clinton administration. *New York Times* columnists William Safire and A.M. Rosenthal have repeatedly pummeled the Chinese government and U.S. policy toward it in the most important newspaper in the world. As Jacob Heilbrunn has argued, this hard-line coalition of conservatives, unions, pundits, and intellectuals concerned with human rights strongly resembles the array of forces that existed during the Cold War.[36] Just as it is difficult (although by no means impossible) to stray from the pro-life position if you are a national Republican, a focus by Christian conservatives on a lower-priority issue (and one with less downside electorally) like China could make it very hard for Republicans to support a policy of engagement. At the least, the interest of Christian conservatives in the China issue has put the treatment of Christians in China on the agenda of the U.S. foreign policy bureaucracy.[37] What is more, support for a hard line from a mainline center-left magazine like the *New Republic* may give moderate Democrats more self-confidence in challenging the prevailing China strategy.

Obviously, there is little reason for any of these groups to work together on issues other than MFN. While labor unions applaud conservatives' opposition to open trading borders, they despise their support of right-to-work and other antiunion laws. While conservative groups agree with the human rights community about China's cavalier approach to fundamental freedoms, the political backgrounds and overall view of the world of activists on either side are radically different. Because there are few ongoing links between the parts of the anti-MFN coalition, and because of the varying policy preferences and overall agendas of the groups, fusing the parts of the coalition into a whole is a very difficult process. This means that changes in the political environment, such as the balance of partisan power in Congress and the presidency, can cripple what is already a very tenuous coalition. It also means that the opponents of unconditional MFN cannot take advantage of preexisting mobilization, as the business community can. However, time and the increasing prominence of the issue may make it easier for these strange bedfellows to maintain their uneasy coalition.

Finally, the business community has the advantage of a very sophisticated political strategy, one that builds upon their ongoing activities. The business community, organized under the umbrella of the U.S. Business Coalition for Trade with China, brings together all of the business organizations supportive of China MFN on a weekly basis to "talk about what people are hearing is happening on China, and you talk about who is setting up a Heritage Foundation briefing, who is setting up a staff briefing or something like that."[38] But the coordinating function goes beyond the informational. "The way it works is that we get together on message, and position papers and stuff like that, and we have a letter that says we support MFN and this is why, and we have certain talking point pages." This ability to coordinate and simplify the business community's message gives them a substantial advantage over the anti-MFN groups, which do not have the same level of coordination.

Furthermore, the pro-MFN side has a powerful grass-roots and Washington-based organization, which is especially useful in identifying swing votes and targeting attention. The first part of the strategy is centered in Washington, and it focuses on locating congressional members' preferences.

> The target list comes from the Hill. . . . We found members who we knew were going to be there . . . like [Representative Lee] Hamilton, [former Representative Robert] Matsui . . . and you get their staff together and you see what they can do. You divide up the country by region or whatever else makes sense. . . . Then you draw up a target list. . . . Once you split up the target list between businesses, between members of Congress who also whip their colleagues, you come back and report in.

This sophisticated and coordinated organization permits the business community to sharply target their resources, which are greater than those of the anti-MFN groups to start with.

Finally, the largest advantage that the business community has is its presence in members' districts, a presence that political scientists generally consider to be a powerful factor in congressmen's decisions.[39] But "grass-roots" rarely emerge spontaneously. Diane Sullivan, the National Association of Manufacturers' primary staff member on China MFN, is instructive in this regard.

> We have twelve field offices. The first thing I did when I came in was I called all of them and said, hi, you don't know me but we have this [China MFN] coming down the pike, let's get to work on this. . . . We set up congressional dialogues out there in the district. I sent them a two-pager on what we're saying in Washington, and asking them to augment it with stories that they have of locally how they are affected. I let them know procedurally what is going on in Washington . . . then organize follow-up from the field. . . . We try to get the field to tell us when they talk to members so that we in Washington will know where we might have soft spots so that we can fill in gaps. I think it adds a lot. . . . Members of Congress react to the people who elect them.[40]

This unity and coordination, which links the District with Washington-based business groups, who are themselves tightly coordinated, gives business a substantial advantage and makes their lobbying much more efficient. These are advantages that the anti-MFN side, because of their smaller resources, more varied constituency, and more ambivalent policy preference, cannot match.

While the business community has been essentially invincible on the issue of MFN status (although they have not been successful in making MFN permanent, and thus avoiding an annual debate), individual business concerns have not succeeded across the board. One important example is U.S. opposition to the Three Gorges Dam on the Yangtze River. This dam, perhaps the largest such project in world history, was a major priority for U.S. environmental groups, including the Sierra Club, the Environmental Defense Fund, the International Rivers Network, Friends of the Earth, Defenders of Wildlife, and the World Wildlife Federation. While the environmental community was overwhelmingly opposed to U.S. support for the dam, support for U.S. financial participation in the project within the business community was narrower. While engineering and construction machinery companies, especially Caterpillar, were very supportive of the project, and had special access to the agencies within the U.S. government that would fund or support the dam, they were routed by the environmentalists. The Treasury Department opposed World Bank aid for the Three Gorges project, which led the bank to drop its support for the project. Perhaps even more surprising, environmentalists successfully pressured the Export-Import Bank to withhold financial assistance to China for the project (in the form of loans to purchase U.S. goods and services associated with the project). The difference between Three Gorges and MFN is simple: in the latter case, business support was strong across the board, and there was an intellectually respectable case that a policy of engagement would improve human rights, while in the former business support was concentrated among a few firms in a few sectors, and there did not exist a compelling case that U.S. support would help improve the environment. Where the issue is narrower than MFN, therefore, opponents of Chinese policies in the United States may be more likely to get their way.

Conclusion: The Future of U.S.-China Policy

American policy will, in all likelihood, continue to be rather schizophrenic toward China in the near future, at least so long as the PRC persists in its current military, economic, and domestic human rights behavior. The persistence of the public's distaste with the Chinese regime, encouraged and concentrated by the activism of the human rights community, will make "normal" relations very difficult and will create incentives for American officials to maintain a hard rhetorical line on China. In fact, the maintenance of such a rhetorical position is the main victory that the critics of China have won in the years since Tiananmen. Since voters judge more with their ears than with their eyes or their hands, this rhetorical victory will probably compensate for continuing open relations on a substantive level.

At the same time that they face difficulty on the rhetorical level, the business community will probably continue to be successful in the areas that are of the greatest importance to them. This may be even more true if China is admitted to the WTO, a change that could effectively transfer much of the U.S. and China's economic conflict to the level of global organizations. Even so, the experience of NAFTA is instructive. Despite the overwhelming support of the economics profession, which is very powerful on issues like trade, NAFTA passed only narrowly. There is a substantial plurality of the public and members of Congress ready to be convinced of the dangers of foreign trade. If economic conditions for working Americans decline over the next few years, organizations pushing for trade restrictions, such as the labor opponents of China MFN, will be much stronger than they are today. Moreover, counterproductive Chinese behavior can rekindle American opposition to trade with China. A substantial use of force to suppress dissent in Hong Kong would be one such trigger. It appears that Chinese officials are cognizant of this fact and are likely to eat away at the liberties of Hong Kong's people, if they choose to do so, in small bites, so as not to draw foreign attention.

On the other side, the American friends of the Chinese government have only recently embarked upon a large-scale attempt to influence the American public's impressions of China. This effort has been led primarily by the Boeing Corporation, which sees a fast-growing market for its planes in China.[41] In addition, groups such as the National Committee on U.S.-China Relations, have attempted to undercut the arguments of human rights groups, on such issues as the status of Tibet. Sustained efforts in this area, combined with restrained behavior by the Chinese government, especially avoiding high-profile human rights abuses or military tensions, could gradually knock down public opposition to the Chinese regime and limit the pressures on the U.S. government toward symbolic or rhetorical conflict. In addition, as Robert Sutter notes in Chapter 3, the 1996 Taiwan Strait crisis has encouraged members of Congress to adopt a more cautious attitude toward China in recognition of Chinese power and its ability to harm important U.S. strategic interests. This, too, should contribute to greater stability in U.S.-China trade relations.

Finally a note on the dog that has not bitten in the China debate so far: experts. Much of the importance of any policy elite is determined by their degree of consensus.[42] An elite consensus represents to policymakers the "right thing to do." On issues such as tax reform in 1986[43] or deregulation in the 1970s[44], policymakers were faced by a phalanx of economists all arguing the same thing, a consensus that made opposition to their preferred policies difficult. On China, however, there is not such an overwhelming consensus. While most China experts agree that it is in the U.S. interest to integrate the PRC into an international, rule-based economic and political system, which will pressure the regime toward the rule of law and conformance with international standards, there is not yet consensus-level agreement that a primarily economic, conflict-averse relationship is the way to get there. Until there is, policy will lack the larger strategic and international framework that could discipline both the public's and policymakers' opinion. Without such a discipline, of the kind that only experts can provide, and presidential leadership can cement, policy toward China is likely to sway with the relative power of interest groups, shifts in public opinion, and the salience of various domestic public policy issues.

Notes

1. For a discussion of intermistic issues, see Bayless Manning, "The Congress, The Executive, and Intermistic Affairs: Three Proposals," *Foreign Affairs,* January 1977, pp. 306–324.

2. See Steven Teles, *Whose Welfare? Elite Conflict and AFDC* (Lawrence: University Press of Kansas, 1996), pp. 41–43.

3. John Reilly, ed., *American Public Opinion and U.S. Foreign Policy 1995* (Chicago: Chicago Council on Foreign Relations, 1995), p. 6.

4. Robert Shapiro and Benjamin Page, "Foreign Policy and the Rational Public," *Journal of Conflict Resolution,* v. 32, no. 2, June 1988, p. 221.

5. All goals questions are from John Reilly, ed., *American Public Opinion.*

6. Shapiro and Page, "Foreign Policy and the Rational Public," passim.

7. See, in particular, Whittaker Chambers, *Witness* (New York: Random House, 1952).

8. Shapiro and Page, "Foreign Policy and the Rational Public," p. 236.

9. Bruce Russett, "Doves, Hawks, and Public Opinion," *Political Science Quarterly,* v. 105, no. 4, 1990–1991.

10. Ibid.

11. For an overview of American public opinion on China, and its effect on U.S. policy prior to the 1980s, see Leonard Kusnitz, *Public Opinion and Foreign Policy: America's China Policy, 1949–1979* (Westport, CT: Greenwood Press, 1984).

12. Wynne Pomeroy and Marianne Ide, "The Polls: China and Human Rights," *Public Opinion Quarterly,* v. 59, p. 137.

13. Ibid.

14. Source: Roper. Question: "What is your overall opinion of China—very favorable, mostly favorable, mostly unfavorable, or very unfavorable?" Results for May 1996 were 39 percent in the favorable range/51 percent unfavorable; in June 1995, 41 percent/53 percent.

15. John Reilly, *American Public Opinion,* p. 24.

16. Pomeroy and Ide, pp. 142–143. For 1995 and 1997 data: Source: Roper. Question: "Which one of the following statements comes closer to your point of view on our relationship with China? Statement A: We should maintain good trade relations with China despite disagreements we might have with its human rights policies. Statement B: We should demand that China improve its human rights policies if China wants to continue to enjoy its current trade status with the United States." Dates: August 1997 and December 1995.

17. Tao Wu and Yang Zhong, "Political Science and U.S. Policy Toward China," *PS,* December 1993, p. 799.

18. Aaron Wildavsky, "The Two Presidencies," *Trans-Action,* December 1966. For a view of the president's power in foreign affairs, which makes a claim to greater natural congressional involvement, see Louis Fisher, *Presidential War Power* (Lawrence: University Press of Kansas, 1995).

19. "Buchanan Criticizes China," *Gannett News Service,* January 13, 1992.

20. April 16, 1996, news conference by presidential candidate Patrick Buchanan, transcript from *Federal Documents Service.*

21. Ibid.

22. Interview conducted May 15, 1996.

23. Interview conducted May 17, 1996.

24. Interview conducted May 16, 1996.

25. Interview conducted May 17, 1996.

26. Interview with Andrew Nathan, September 5, 1996.

27. Interview conducted May 15, 1996.

28. Interview conducted May 14, 1996.

29. Interview conducted May 15, 1996.

30. Interview conducted May 16, 1996.

31. Ibid.

32. Ibid.

33. Source: "Indiana Trade Statistics with China," produced by U.S.-China Business Council as lobbying material.

34. Senator Fred Thompson, Senate Governmental Affairs Committee Hearing on Campaign Finance, July 9, 1997.

35. See, for example, Wilson Carey McWilliams, "The Two-Tiered Polity," in Martin Levin and Marc Landy, eds., *The New Politics of Public Policy* (Baltimore: Johns Hopkins University Press, 1995).

36. Jacob Heilbrunn, "Christian Rights," *New Republic,* July 7, 1997, pp. 19–24.

37. One example of this is the State Department's stinging rebuke of China in its 1997 report on the treatment of Christians worldwide. See Steven Erlanger, "U.S. Assails China Over Suppression of Religious Life," *New York Times,* July 22, 1997.

38. May 16, 1996, interview in Washington with business community representative.

39. See, in particular, Richard Fenno, *Homestyle* (Ann Arbor: University of Michigan, 1989).

40. Interview conducted May 16, 1996.

41. David Sanger, "Analysis: Boeing, a Giant in Jets and Foreign Policy," *New York Times,* December 17, 1996.

42. See, in particular, Levin and Landy eds., *The New Politics of Public Policy* .

43. See Jeffrey Birnbaum and Alan Murray, *Showdown at Gucci Gulch* (New York: Random House, 1987).

44. See Martha Derthick and Paul Quirk, *The Politics of Deregulation* (Washington: Brookings Institution, 1985).

3

Domestic Politics and the U.S.-China-Taiwan Triangle

The 1995–96 Taiwan Strait Conflict and Its Aftermath

Robert G. Sutter

The Clinton administration and the Congress have been unable to reach a consensus on important issues in U.S.-Chinese relations. For much of the first two years of the administration, policymakers wrestled with the issue of whether or not to place conditions on the annual U.S. presidential waiver granting most favored nation (MFN) tariff treatment to Chinese imports. The administration's decision in May 1994 to "delink" U.S. MFN tariff treatment and Beijing's authoritarian human rights practices temporarily eased the debate in the United States over China policy. By the end of 1994 the previous wide-ranging differences within the administration were narrowed as President Clinton and his advisers pursued "engagement" with Beijing, especially in commercial and defense relations. Prominent examples of engagement were the visits to Beijing by Commerce Secretary Ron Brown in September 1994 and Defense Secretary William Perry in October 1994.

But just as the administration appeared to be settling on its China policy, the 1994 congressional elections brought forth the Republican-led 104th Congress. Republican congressional leaders proved to be more

The views expressed in this chapter are the author's and are not necessarily those of the Congressional Research Service.

inclined than their predecessors to question the administration's emphasis on "engagement" and to press for more assertive policies on such sensitive issues as Taiwan, Tibet, arms proliferation, and human rights.

The Clinton administration's decision to change its previous stance and "delink" MFN and human rights concerns reflected competing political pressures. Particularly influential was the growing perception among U.S. business circles and their supporters within the government of the opportunities the Chinese economy held for U.S. business. They argued that by conditioning or withdrawing MFN, the administration would invite Chinese retaliation that would undercut U.S. economic interests in this "Big Emerging Market"—as the Department of Commerce refers to significant international markets. Closer economic relations were also said to promote a long-term interest in greater Chinese interdependence with the world economy and in economic, social, and, ultimately, political change in China. On the other hand, they argued that cutting off MFN would have prompted a hardening of Chinese official policy on human rights questions—in effect producing the opposite result as desired by the administration.[1]

Behind the business interests lobbying for the decision to delink was the People's Republic of China (PRC) as well as the governments of Hong Kong and, more discreetly, Taiwan, that would have been adversely affected by a U.S. decision to condition or withdraw MFN. PRC authorities made no bones about their firm stance during Secretary of State Warren Christopher's visit to China in April 1994. They apparently believed that a tough stance would add to the pressure on the administration to end linkage between MFN and Chinese human rights practices.

Mustered against these forces was an array of Americans advocating a tougher U.S. approach toward Chinese human rights violations. Although some in the Clinton administration were sympathetic to their views, they found themselves defeated in the face of the arguments and power of those pushing for the decision to delink.

The experience over MFN and China policy was a graphic illustration that the Clinton administration had not established a firm China policy and that it would reconsider policy in the face of strong pressure. Policy advocates were quick to recognize that if the administration's policy was not to their liking, there was a chance that the policy could be changed given enough persuasive arguments and political pressure. Following delinkage, the president's reputation for vacillation contributed to a crisis when pressure on the administration compelled it to switch positions on a sensitive aspect of U.S. policy toward Taiwan—it permitted President Lee Teng-hui from Taiwan to travel to Cornell University.

The pressure for change had been growing for some time. Indeed, Taiwan's supporters in the 103rd Congress had forced the administration to sign a law requiring that the Taiwan president be granted a visa to visit the United States.[2] The administration had side-stepped this challenge, but growing pressure from an increasingly assertive Taiwan and an increasingly assertive China, along with contending pressures in the United States, set the stage for a policy change of considerable significance. In effect, the background to the decision was defined by emerging challenges to the U.S.-PRC-Taiwan triangular relationship that had existed up to that time, reinforced by domestic determinants in each capital.

Challenges to the status quo have come from a variety of directions.[3] Several years of remarkable Chinese economic growth have been followed by predictions of continued development well into the next century. This gives PRC leaders a growing sense of confidence in their ability to survive the trauma of the Tiananmen incident and the collapse of international communism to become an increasingly influential player on the world stage. It also has allowed for an increase in China's military capabilities and reluctance on the part of Chinese leaders to defer to U.S. pressures. Second, Taiwan has also been more assertive. Fed by impressive economic growth and rapidly changing social conditions, Taiwan has moved quickly to democratize its political system. This has led to debate of such long-repressed issues as the identity of the people on Taiwan and the role of Taiwan in world affairs. Democratization has led Taiwan to seek greater stature in international organizations and to move away from rigorous adherence to a one-China policy, challenging China's stance regarding sovereignty and reunification with Taiwan. Third, U.S. uncertainty has destabilized U.S.-China-Taiwan relations. The end of the Cold War, generational change in the U.S. leadership, and a more pluralistic foreign policy-making process have produced confusion throughout the world about the American role in world affairs. Washington seems to lack a clear sense of priorities.

The politics of foreign policy in the United States have contributed to U.S. policy vacillation. The Republican-controlled Congress has vied with the Democratic president for leadership on important policy issues. On the issue of President Lee's visit, President Clinton became isolated from almost all members of his own party, as well. This situation complicated administration efforts to reach a consensus response to Lee's request for a visa before reaching a decision. Moreover, broader questions of U.S. policy toward Taiwan and China became embroiled in the 1996 congressional and presidential election campaigns.

Domestic politics in China and Taiwan have also influenced relations among the three actors. Chinese leaders have been embroiled in a succession struggle. In such circumstances, it is politically expedient to support policies expressing suspicion or even hostility to challenges to Beijing's nationalistic goals. It has been widely reported that the prevailing view among Chinese senior leaders is that the United States is hostile to China and that Taiwan is moving slowly but surely to a more autonomous and independent posture. Lee Teng-hui's visit to the United States was seen as the capstone of these sinister U.S. and Taiwan efforts. As a result, Beijing has reacted with frustration and hostility to defend itself from U.S. pressure and to halt Taiwan's drive toward autonomy.

Taiwan has not been dissuaded by Beijing's actions. Pressed by a widespread domestic demand that policymakers seek greater stature for Taiwan in world politics, the ruling Nationalist Party and the main opposition party have been active in seeking opportunities to enhance Taiwan's international role. They have focused their efforts on the United States, especially on the Congress. Visits by senior leaders from Taiwan to Congress in the first half of 1995 were among the most numerous of any country. In many cases, these leaders have sought support for Taiwan's growing role in world affairs and to use congressional support to enhance their position in Taiwan domestic politics. The atmosphere in Taiwan remained politically charged as politicians prepared themselves for the elections of a new legislature at the end of 1995 and for the presidential election in early 1996.

Post–Cold War Debate in U.S. Foreign Policy

The absence of a clear direction in U.S. policy toward China has broader roots than the vagaries of U.S.-China policy. Perhaps a more experienced president, with a clearer vision of China policy and a greater election mandate than the 43 percent of the popular vote gained by Bill Clinton would be more decisive in formulating China policy. Such a president could set a course of action and stick to it—thereby avoiding the spectacle of repeated tugs-of-war among competing interests. On the other hand, since the end of the Cold War Americans have been deeply divided over foreign policy, and the contending policy perspectives cannot easily be bridged to develop coherent policy toward China or other important areas.[4]

Because the primacy of security issues and opposition to Soviet expansion no longer drive U.S. foreign policy, economic competitiveness, democracy, and human rights have greater prominence in policy-making, and various pressure groups and other representative institutions have enhanced influence in policy-making. This fluidity and competition among priorities has more often than not been the norm in American foreign policy. Presidents Woodrow Wilson and Franklin Roosevelt both set forth comprehensive concepts of a well-integrated U.S. foreign policy, but neither framework lasted long. The requirements of the Cold War were much more effective in establishing rigor and order in U.S. foreign policy priorities, but that era is over.

There is consensus that foreign policy should not be expensive. The fate of the international affairs budget in the U.S. Congress indicates that Americans want foreign policy both to cost less and to give more benefit. Unfortunately, Americans do not agree on how to accomplish this. There appear to be at least three distinct tendencies or schools of thought regarding post–Cold War U.S. foreign policy. An understanding of what these schools stand for underscores how difficult it is to gauge the direction of U.S. policy toward China.

One prominent school stresses the relative decline in U.S. power and its implication for U.S. ability to protect its interests. It calls for the United States to work harder to preserve its important interests while adjusting to its limited resources and reduced influence. Advocates of this position expect continued international instability and limited U.S. ability to respond. They observe that there is no international framework to shape policy and that U.S. policy must use a complex mix of international, regional, and bilateral efforts to achieve policy goals and that security, economic, and cultural-political issues will compete for priority in policy-making. They argue that in this uncertain environment, pressing domestic problems will divert U.S. attention from international affairs and restrict the financial resources available for foreign policy. They also believe that policy-making will remain difficult because the executive branch may well remain in control of one political party and the Congress in control of another party.

This school argues that these circumstances require the United States to work closely with traditional allies and associates. They argue that it is inconsistent with U.S. goals not to preserve long-standing good relations with Japan and with friends and allies in Asia whose security policies and political-cultural orientations complement U.S. interests. They acknowledge that opinion surveys indicate that the American public and some U.S. leaders see Japan as an economic "threat," but they stress that few opinion polls reflect support for a confrontational foreign policy. They argue for caution in policy toward other regional powers—Russia, China, and India. All three are preoccupied with internal political-development crises and do not appear to want regional instability. All seek closer economic and political relations with the West and with the advancing economies of the region. Washington would be well advised, they say, to work closely with these governments wherever there are common interests. In considering U.S. assets available to influence regional trends, they call on the United States to go slowly in reducing its regional military presence. The economic savings of cutbacks would be small; the political costs could be high insofar as most countries in Asia encourage the United States to remain active in the region to offset the growing power of Japan and/or China.

A second major school of thought argues for significant cutbacks in U.S. international involvement and a renewed focus on solving such domestic problems as crime, drug use, lagging economic competitiveness and educational standards, homelessness, poverty, and decaying cities and transportation infrastructure. Variations of this view are seen in the writings of William Hyland, Patrick Buchanan, and other well-known commentators, and in the political rhetoric of Ross Perot. Often called an "American First" or "Neoisolationist" school, these advocates argue that the United States has become overextended in world affairs and has been taken advantage of in the current world security–economic system. They call for sweeping cuts in spending for international activities, favoring a complete U.S. pullback from foreign bases and major cuts in foreign assistance and foreign technical/information programs. They are skeptical of the utility of international financial institutions and the United Nations and of international efforts to promote free trade through the World Trade Organization (WTO). They advocate termination of international economic talks that help to perpetuate a liberal world trading system. Some favor trade measures that are seen as protectionist by U.S. trading partners.

The third position argues that U.S. policy needs to promote more actively U.S. interests in international political, military, and economic affairs and to use U.S. influence to pressure countries that do not conform to their view of an appropriate world order. Advocates of this position want the United States to lead strongly in world affairs and to avoid compromises and accommodations.

This school of thought has always been present in American politics. But for several reasons it is stronger today than at any time since the 1960s. During the Reagan administration, after a prolonged period of introspection and doubt following the Vietnam War, oil shocks, and the Iran hostage crisis, the American public became much more optimistic about the future of the United States. This trend coincided with the Cold War victory for the U.S.-backed system of collective security and for U.S. political and economic values. The outcome of the 1991 Gulf War inspired confidence in U.S. military doctrine, equipment, and performance and in America's international leadership ability.

These opinion leaders acknowledge that America faces serious economic difficulties, but they are optimistic that the United States can successfully compete in a competitive world economy. They also insist that the United States is better positioned than any other country to exert leadership in the realm of ideas and values, political concepts, lifestyle, and popular culture. They are encouraged by the perception of a global power vacuum that allows the United States to exert influence. They are not deterred by the seeming decline in U.S. economic resources. They argue that Russia, China, and India will remain preoccupied with domestic problems. They acknowledge that Japan and Germany are economically powerful but also that they are uncertain how to use their new power and that they lack American cultural influence.

In recent years, advocates of this third tendency have been most vocal in pressing for strong policy in support of democracy and human rights. They have argued for a more active U.S. foreign policy, leading some target countries to view U.S. policy as illegitimate interference in another country's internal affairs. They have reinforced U.S. opposition to economic or trading policies seen as inequitable or predatory and have pressed for strong policy against proliferation of weapons of mass destruction. Members of this school also press for sanctions against countries that practice coercive birth control, seriously pollute the environment, harbor terrorists, and promote the drug trade. They have pushed the United States to be more assertive in promoting humanitarian relief and in recognizing the legitimacy of people's right to self-determination.

Three Approaches in U.S.-China Policy[5]

In recent years the third group—advocates of active U.S. leadership—has been most forceful in advocating policy opposing Chinese human rights violations, weapons proliferation, and trade practices. They have pressed Beijing to meet U.S.-backed international norms and called for retaliatory economic sanctions. By contrast, the more cautious and accommodating first group believes that the advocates of strong U.S. assertion of its values and interests are unrealistic about U.S. power and unwilling to make needed compromises with the Chinese government to protect U.S. interests in promoting regional stability.

There remains little indication as to which approach will ultimately determine China policy. Some in the Clinton administration and in Congress advocate the moderate, less confrontational posture of "engagement" with China. Some are concerned with perceived weaknesses in China and urge a moderate policy for fear that to do otherwise could promote divisions in and a possible breakup of China with potentially adverse consequences for U.S. interests in Asian stability and prosperity. Others are more impressed with China's growing economic and national strength and the opportunities this provides for the United States. They promote U.S. engagement with China as the most appropriate way to guide the newly emerging power into channels of international activity compatible with American interests.

Underlying this moderate approach is a belief that trends in China are moving inexorably in the "right" direction, that China is increasingly interdependent economically with its neighbors and the advanced industrial economies, and that it is increasingly unlikely to destabilize these relationships. Economic growth is seen as promoting a materially better-off, more educated, and cosmopolitan populace that will, over time, press for greater political pluralism and democratic institutions. U.S. policy should seek to work closely with China to encourage these long-term trends.

A second, tougher approach is that of some U.S. advocates inside and outside the U.S. government who have doubts about the interdependence argument. These policymakers and opinion leaders stress that PRC officials still view the world as a state-centered competitive environment where interdependence counts for little and compromises Chinese power. China's leaders are seen as determined to use any means to increase China's wealth and power. At present, Beijing is merely biding its time, conforming to many international norms to build its economic strength. But once it succeeds with economic modernization, the argument goes, Beijing will not sacrifice nationalistic and territorial ambitions for economic stability. This group encourages U.S. leaders to be firm with China. Rather than try to persuade Beijing of the advantages of cooperation, the United States is advised to rely on military power as a counterweight to rising Chinese power, to remain firm in dealing with economic and security conflicts, and to work closely with traditional allies and friends along China's periphery to deal with Chinese assertiveness.

A third approach is favored by some U.S. officials and other leaders who believe that China's political system needs to change before the United States can establish a constructive relationship with Beijing. China's communist leaders are seen as inherently incapable of participating in cooperative relationships. U.S. policy should seek to change China from within while maintaining a vigilant posture to deal with disruptive Chinese foreign policy. It should not abet the development of an authoritarian superpower more advanced economically than the former Soviet Union.

Close observation suggests that these differences, though real, have been a matter of degree. For instance, although the Clinton administration is closely identified with "engagement," there is plenty of evidence that many administration officials are inclined to support the second, tougher approach noted earlier. In Congress, a lot of publicity goes to Republican foreign policy leaders like Senator Jesse Helms (R-NC) and Congressman Ben Gilman (R-NY), who are closely identified with the third approach, calling for change in China's political system before pursuing U.S.-China cooperation. But such viewpoints are a distinct minority among congressional members. Far more common are members favoring the second approach; and perhaps as many or more favor the moderate policy of "engagement."

Given the continued wide range of opinion over appropriate U.S.

policy toward China, it is likely that U.S. policy will continue the pattern of trying to accommodate elements of all three approaches. On some issues, like linking MFN treatment with China's human rights policies, the White House believes that U.S. interests are best served by acknowledging PRC interests. But on intellectual property rights protection and proliferation of missile technology, the U.S. government has threatened sanctions to compel Beijing to conform to U.S.-backed norms. Meanwhile, although many U.S. officials would see as counterproductive any declaration that the United States aims to change China's political system, there is widespread agreement that greater "engagement" will encourage such change.

Whether the synthesis of these three tendencies is done smoothly or is accompanied by the strident policy debates accompanying recent policy depends partly on leadership. The Clinton administration's vacillation has been widely criticized as reflecting a lack of leadership.[6] Critics argue that the president has devoted insufficient attention to U.S. interests in U.S.-China relations, in contrast to his attention to events in Japan, Korea, and the Balkans. As a result, China policy has been seen more as a liability than a success for the president. The administration's sensitivity in dealing with China is backed by strongly negative U.S. media treatment of China and by strong levels of disapproval of the Chinese government by public opinion.

At the same time, the administration is seen as devoting insufficient effort to develop positive and negative incentives to support its China policy. In particular, it is seen as reluctant to take the initiative against political pressure. When Taiwan lobbied Congress to press the administration to change U.S. policy toward Taiwan, provoking a crisis in U.S.-China relations, the administration did not act to curb future Taiwan efforts. When Beijing resorted to the use of force in the Taiwan Strait, the administration did very little for seven months, only taking action when seemingly compelled to by domestic pressure.

Given the Clinton administration's passive and reactive China policy, it is not surprising that not only Beijing and Taipei but also domestic interest groups are putting pressure on the administration to set policy. Thus, the White House encounters pressure from all sides. Especially active in U.S. politics are groups involved in human rights (including the influential movements favoring "right to life" and religious freedom), weapons proliferation, and trade policies. Backed by negative media coverage of PRC policies, these groups drive U.S.

policy to be critical of China. Moreover, these groups enjoy good access to the Congress. The different institutional imperatives of Congress and the president and the end of the Cold War have given Congress and the interest groups that work through Congress more influence in the making of U.S. foreign policy. Simultaneously, divided government and the partisanship of election politics have set Congress and the president on separate tracks on China policy. Thus, the debate over China policy is seemingly reduced to Congress arguing for a tougher policy and the administration arguing for a more moderate one.

The Taiwan Crisis of 1995–96 and U.S. Domestic Politics

The Taiwan crisis of 1995–96 had deep roots in the respective policy aspirations and domestic politics of Taiwan, China, and the United States. Throughout most of the crisis, the United States was generally reactive in the face of competing pressures coming from Taiwan and the PRC. This Taiwan-PRC competition occurred in the context of the U.S. domestic debate over U.S. policy toward Taiwan-PRC-United States triangular relations.

During the previous two decades, the U.S.-PRC-Taiwan triangular relationship, while often presenting problems for U.S. policy, basically met U.S. interests. The United States was able to develop relations with the PRC while sustaining ties with Taiwan—all within an atmosphere promoting broad U.S. security and economic interests in Asian and world affairs. So the question naturally arises, where did the recent crisis come from?[7] It was clearly not sought by the United States. Rather, the catalyst for change was a changing Taiwan. As Taiwan has become economically advanced, better educated, more cosmopolitan, and politically democratic, its people have demanded that their leaders adopt a policy to end Taiwan's status as an international pariah. Taiwan leaders who run against this tide do not do well in elections.

In response to changing domestic circumstances, Taiwan's leaders are prepared to use its influence as one of the world's largest trading nations and holder of one of the world's largest reserves of foreign currency to achieve greater international recognition and respect. In a word, Taiwan is prepared to put its money where its mouth is. The calculus seems to be that by using financial resources to attract international attention Taiwan will be able to develop economic and political relationships with important countries. One consequence will be ever broader political influence and respect for the people of Taiwan and their democratically elected leaders.

Taiwan's growing assertiveness ran up against PRC assertiveness. After the 1989 Tiananmen incident and the collapse of communism in the Soviet bloc, Chinese leaders were beleaguered and fairly isolated in world politics. But through effective economic policies and adroit diplomacy, Beijing reversed its situation. China's remarkable economic growth has attracted widespread international attention. All major powers, with the possible exception of the United States, have acknowledged the legitimacy of China's leaders and have developed close ties to capitalize on economic and other opportunities.

This diplomatic success has elicited greater China assertiveness. Beijing has actively pressed its claim to disputed territories in the South China Sea. It drove a hard bargain with world powers striving to achieve a comprehensive nuclear test ban. And it is prepared to go head-to-head with the United States in threatening sanctions and countersanctions over economic disputes ranging from MFN tariff treatment, market access, and intellectual property rights.

In addition, just as Taiwan's assertiveness has been pushed by domestic pressures and politics, it appears that domestic influences have contributed to PRC assertiveness. Chinese leaders have fostered an atmosphere of nationalism in China. This nationalism portrays China, rightly, as having been victimized by international pressures in the past. It implies that China now has the moral high ground in reasserting its claim to disputed territories and world leadership that were taken from China during the age of imperialism. As a result, it may be difficult for Chinese leaders to propose policy suggesting that Beijing should compromise its claims to Taiwan or disputed territories and its terms for membership in the WTO. Moreover, the leadership succession in the PRC, with the passing of Deng Xiaoping, seems to reinforce PRC's assertiveness. During the transition, it is difficult for leaders to promote policy that suggests compromise of China's moral right to its nationalistic aspirations. Conciliatory policies could be used against them in the ongoing struggle for power.

The United States has long been an important arena for Taiwan and the PRC to compete for influence. For some time in the late 1980s and early 1990s, the competition was not as acute as it is today. Although PRC leaders were concerned over democratization in Taiwan and the attendant rise of proindependent politicians, they were also encouraged by how democratization in Taiwan was forcing Taipei leaders to open economic and other contacts with the mainland. In short, Beijing endeavored to use growing cross-Strait economic, social, and cultural contacts to build ties with Taiwan that would offset the perceived negative trend caused by Taiwan's growing assertiveness for international recognition. Meanwhile, U.S. policymakers had made clear to both the PRC and Taiwan the broad outlines of U.S.-China policy. Both Taiwan and Beijing had come to terms with this consensus in U.S.-China policy in the late 1980s.

The context of policy-making changed after the Tiananmen incident and the end of the Cold War. Nonetheless, the Bush administration was able to protect the broad guidelines of policy toward the PRC and Taiwan, despite heavy pressure from the media, Congress, and interest groups. But the Clinton administration was not as strongly fixed in its direction on China policy. It entered office on a platform decidedly critical of China and soon changed Bush administration policy by linking China's MFN trade status to its human rights practices, only to end linkage in the face of heavy pressure from the PRC, U.S. businesses with an interest in China, and opinion leaders.[8] The lesson for both Taiwan and the PRC in their newly assertive approaches seemed clear: the Clinton administration did not possess a strongly fixed policy and pressures could be applied in the hope of prompting policy change favoring one side or the other.

The Lee Teng-Hui Visit and Chinese Views of the United States

The Clinton administration's decision to bow to congressional pressure to allow Taiwan's President Lee Teng-hui to visit Cornell University in June 1995 prompted an extraordinary reaction by the PRC. Beijing issued strong protests, suspended or canceled important bilateral dialogues, suspended important dialogues with Taiwan, and conducted provocative military exercises near Taiwan. It warned that a Taiwan move toward *de jure* independence would lead to a PRC invasion of Taiwan and a protracted cold war with the United States.[9]

U.S. efforts to reassure Beijing of its cooperative intentions and Beijing's reassessment of the costs of its hard-line policy led to a temporary thaw in relations. The October 24, 1995, meeting in New York between Bill Clinton and China's President Jiang Zemin proceeded smoothly despite wrangling over the protocol level and the site of the meeting.[10] U.S. and Chinese officials portrayed the session at New York's Lincoln Center as the most positive of the three sessions.[11] The New York meeting was accompanied by other signs that both governments were interested in improved relations. China agreed to the appointment of U.S. Ambassador-designate James Sasser; the return of China's ambassador to the United States after his abrupt withdrawal in June; and the U.S. dispatch of Assistant Secretary of Defense Joseph Nye to Beijing to resume high-level defense discussions suspended in mid-1995.

Nonetheless, the decision to allow Lee Teng-hui to visit the United States not only resulted in the suspension of diplomatic and other official ties, but perhaps of more importance it also resulted in a strongly negative view of U.S. policy intentions on the part of Chinese officials, intellectuals, and policy analysts.[12] This reinforced prior PRC suspicions that the United States had decided to "contain" China. For some time, this view of U.S. policy was prevalent among Chinese government officials and military officers.[13] It holds that the United States is opposed to the rise of China and has adopted corresponding policies, including improved relations with Taiwan, to "hold back" China's power. Despite the lively debate in the United States over many issues in U.S.-China relations, Chinese leaders have maintained that U.S. policymakers act as though China's growing power threatened the United States and that the United States must weaken China through security, economic, and political measures.

Many Chinese officials and intellectuals trace the alleged U.S. desire to weaken and hold down China to the reevaluation of U.S. policy following the 1989 Tiananmen massacre and the concurrent collapse of the Soviet empire. They claim that U.S. leaders took a number of economic, military, and political measures against China that were designed to help bring down Beijing's communist system. U.S. leaders expected that in a mere few years the Chinese regime would be swept away by the forces of history that had just removed their ideological comrades in Europe. But instead the PRC economy grew at a remarkable rate, leading to greater military power, expansion of China's foreign relations, and greater self-confidence and assertiveness by Chinese leaders both at home and in world affairs.

In response, the Chinese claimed, the U.S. stepped up its effort to curb the growth of China's power. In addition to Lee Teng-hui's visit to Cornell University, U.S. foreign policy legislation in 1995 and 1996 (e.g., H.R. 1561, S. 908) regarding Taiwan, Hong Kong, and Tibet were seen as measures designed to keep the PRC preoccupied with protecting its sovereignty and territorial integrity and to reduce its ability to exert influence elsewhere. In 1994 and 1995 the United States pressed Beijing to observe intellectual property rights, open its markets to outside goods and services, and meet strict conditions to gain entry into the WTO. Many Chinese leaders saw these steps as designed to keep the PRC economically weak. The United States also maintained restrictions on exports to China of military-related equipment and technologies and warned Russia about the dangers of such sales to China, further encouraging views that Washington aimed to keep China from becoming stronger.

The Clinton administration's Asia policy also aroused PRC concern. Chinese leaders viewed the administration's February 1995 statement about the security environment in East Asia[14] as critical of China's assertiveness and growing military power. At the same time, the administration gave greater emphasis to Japan as the cornerstone of U.S. policy, which suggested greater effort to "contain" China.[15] Then, following Chinese military actions in the South China Sea that had alarmed its neighbors in Southeast Asia, the administration stated a stronger position about U.S. interests in the South China Sea and Congress considered legislation (H.R. 1561, S. Res. 97) taking aim at China's policy. Some in Congress advocated that the United States move ahead with diplomatic relations with Vietnam as a way to counter PRC expansion.[16]

U.S. analysts differed on the importance of such a conspiratorial Chinese view for U.S.-China relations. On one side were those who judged that Chinese government leaders were deliberately and cynically manipulating Chinese opinion mainly for other motives. Thus, Chinese criticism of the United States was seen as part of a broader effort by PRC leaders to use nationalistic themes, which enjoy widespread support in China, to fill the ideological void caused by the collapse of world communism and to help shore up the sagging prestige of PRC leaders in the wake of the Tiananmen massacre. By associating PRC policies with Chinese nationalism, Beijing portrayed criticism of those policies by the United States as affronts to the Chinese people. This could have the beneficial effect of alleviating pressure on the leadership to deal with substantive problems in Chinese society. Another perceived ulterior motive is to put the United States on the defensive. U.S. officials anxious to restore meaningful dialogue with China would be expected to "prove" their intentions with gestures showing that China's conspiratorial view of U.S. policy was incorrect. Chinese leaders were said to have used similar techniques against Japan in the 1970s and 1980s—using strident campaigns against Japan's alleged "militarism" to compel Japan to agree to several billions of dollars of grants or low-interest loans for China. Once the money was promised, the charges against Japanese "militarism" subsided.[17]

A very different view comes from U.S. analysts who see the Chinese leaders' conspiratorial view of U.S. policy as misguided but genuine. They believe it has reflected the mix of U.S. pressures on China, the suspicious view of the outside world of many Chinese leaders, and the pressures of domestic Chinese politics during a period of leadership succession. The combination was thought to incline PRC leaders to adhere to more narrow, somewhat chauvinistic views of foreign powers, especially those like the United States with an ability to threaten Chinese interests. They argue that this Chinese perception has now reached the point that PRC leaders are convinced that the United States is "out to get them" and that they would almost certainly interpret future U.S. policy along those lines.

Based on extensive contacts with Chinese officials and experts, these analysts argue that U.S. policy has encouraged PRC apprehension. The Clinton administration's reversal on the Lee Teng-hui visit was said to have undermined those in the Chinese leadership arguing for a more moderate approach toward the United States. Because many Chinese leaders, including Foreign Ministry officials and U.S. specialists, had predicted that the administration would keep its commitment and not allow Lee to visit, they were discredited when the United States reversed policy and the advocates of a more suspicious view of U.S. intentions experienced enhanced influence. The U.S. policy reversal also prompted PRC specialists in the U.S. to "play it safe" and accommodate the hard line, even though they may not have agreed with it. Finally, Lee's determination to visit the United States and fears that he was seeking independence for Taiwan undermined Jiang Zemin's efforts in January 1995 to encourage a dialogue with Taiwan's leaders on the basis of a flexible-sounding PRC eight-point proposal. In the view of some PRC specialists, Jiang's "flexible" approach on Taiwan was now seen as naive.[18]

Evolution of Beijing's Approach to the United States, June–October 1995

Despite Clinton administration reassurances that the United States was not attempting to contain China's development, Chinese officials remained unmoved. In June and July 1995 Beijing indicated that only "concrete" action by the U.S. government—at minimum a pledge by the Clinton administration that it would not give a visa to other senior Taiwan leaders—would allow U.S.-China relations to go forward. To underline the point, Beijing called home its ambassador, refused the U.S. offer to send Under Secretary of State Tarnoff to China for talks, and rebuffed reported U.S. queries about a possible U.S.-China summit. Beijing also escalated political and military pressure on Taiwan in general and Lee Teng-hui in particular.[19]

On August 1, 1995, Secretary of State Christopher and Chinese Foreign Minister Qian Qichen met in Brunei.[20] Christopher confirmed that the United States would not promise to prohibit senior Taiwan visitors from traveling in a private capacity to the United States. But some Chinese officials did point to U.S. reassurances, including a letter from President Clinton to Chinese leaders reaffirming past U.S. policy on Taiwan. Soon after the meeting in Brunei, China altered its view of U.S. policy. PRC officials acknowledged that Washington was not working to contain China, but affirmed that leaders in Beijing continued to believe this.[21] Senior leaders endorsed interaction with Congress. Foreign Minister Qian stated on August 18 that "China is willing to increase contacts and exchanges with the U.S. Congress and welcomes more U.S. congressmen to visit China."[22] Beijing also reversed policy by agreeing to a visit by Under Secretary Tarnoff and by discussing plans for a U.S.-China summit. For the first time it expressed willingness to accept former Senator James Sasser as ambassador to China[23] and it returned its ambassador to Washington following his withdrawal in June. China also improved the overall atmosphere in U.S.-China relations by releasing detained human rights activist Harry Wu after his conviction in August, easing the way for Hillary Clinton to attend the International Women's Conference in Beijing in September.

China's moderate approach to the United States stood in marked contrast to Beijing's continued harsh pressure against Lee Teng-hui. In effect, Chinese officials and media now acknowledged that Lee's visit reflected more the strong desire of Lee and others in Taiwan to assume a greater role in international affairs than it did a U.S. conspiracy to use the "Taiwan card" to check the growth of Chinese power and influence.

A sharply worded New China News Agency commentary of August 22 provided the most authoritative justification of Beijing's moderation toward the United States.[24] The commentary criticized "hegemonists" in the U.S. media and elsewhere who had brought Sino-U.S. relations to their "lowest ebb" in sixteen years.[25] But it differentiated between so-called "hegemonists" and "quite a few sensible people" in the United States who oppose the containment strategy advocated by the "hegemonists." The commentary clearly implied that the Clinton administration was among the "sensible people" and that the "hegemonists" were increasingly "unpopular" in the United States. The commentary did not link Congress with one side or the other in the American debate.

Chinese officials privately offered a different rationale for China's shift and provided a somewhat more optimistic outlook for relations. One official, after spending many weeks in consultations in Beijing, reported that in August 1995 at the seaside resort of Beidaihe senior Chinese leaders concluded that the United States may be conspiring to contain China, but that China needed a workable U.S.-China relationship. While determined to resist alleged efforts to "contain" China, Chinese leaders recognized the need for pragmatic policy. The official added that Chinese leaders recognized that "China needs the United States more than the United States needs China."[26] Another Chinese official in August 1995 explained that since the United States refused to provide Beijing with the concrete action it sought on Taiwan, there would remain a coolness and distance in the U.S.-PRC relationship for some time to come. Nonetheless, Beijing would move forward in areas of Sino-American relations where it saw advantages for China.[27] The official was cautiously optimistic about the outlook for Under Secretary of State Tarnoff's visit to China and for a summit meeting between President Clinton and President Jiang. Subsequent reports by Chinese officials and observations by U.S. officials and experts pointed to Chinese President Jiang Zemin's enhanced authority as key to the policy shift.[28] Some Chinese officials asserted that at important leadership meetings Jiang defended a moderate U.S. policy and achieved a consensus, despite skepticism and criticism from Chinese leaders urging a harder line.

Americans knowledgeable of the negotiations leading to the Clinton-Jiang meeting in New York noted that China's changed posture was not merely a retreat toward a realistic posture in line with Chinese interests but also reflected Beijing's assessment that its militant policies had achieved several objectives. It had intimidated Taiwan, at least temporarily, from taking further assertive actions to lobby Congress for greater international recognition and prompted second thoughts by some pro-Taiwan advocates in the U.S. Congress on the wisdom of supporting Taiwan's agenda. It heightened sensitivity in the Clinton administration regarding PRC policy toward Taiwan, eliciting official U.S. assurances that any future visits by Taiwan leaders would be only under exceptional circumstances.[29] It also caused some pro-independence advocates in Taiwan to reassess their claim that Chinese warnings against independence were mere bluffs and to adopt a more skeptical view of the likelihood that the United States would intervene militarily to support Taiwan should China attack.

Lessons Learned—PRC

Chinese officials and specialists consulted in the latter part of 1995 gleaned several lessons from the crisis over Taiwan. Many in China recognized that Beijing overplayed its hand in pressing the United States for "concrete" pledges against Taiwan official visits and in pressing the Taiwan people to abandon Lee Teng-hui in favor of a leader more committed to reunification. Beijing also appeared to recognize that charges of U.S. "containment" and that shunning dialogue until the United States proved otherwise merely strengthened the hands of U.S. officials suspicious of China and weakened the arguments of administration officials and members of Congress who argued for a moderate approach to China.

China's interest in a working relationship with the United States encouraged it to develop common ground in U.S.-China relations and to play down bilateral differences. Beijing tried to use Jiang's October 24, 1995, meeting with Clinton in New York for this purpose. After the meeting, Chinese officials privately made known China's interest in a "smooth" relationship with the Clinton administration. Some Chinese officials averred that whereas in mid-1995 Beijing appeared prepared to await the results of the 1996 presidential election, it now judged that working constructively with the current administration was in China's best interest. In particular, they said that Beijing now understood that domestic pressure from a wide array of critics of China in the Congress and the media as well as the politics of China policy in the 1996 presidential campaign could destabilize relations. It thus decided to try to develop closer relations with the Clinton administration.

China was also determined to do a better job of influencing U.S. politics. Jiang Zemin told U.S. reporters in mid-October that lobbying Congress would be an important priority in the year ahead. China's U.S. specialists said that the PRC would put more effort into winning support from other U.S. sectors, notably the media and business.[30] They also acknowledged that Beijing's strident invective against Lee Teng-hui had strengthened support for Lee on Taiwan. Ultimately, China would need to adjust its hard line to open a dialogue with Taiwan.

On the other hand, many Chinese understood the delicate condition of U.S.-China relations. Some Chinese leaders remained suspicious of U.S. intentions toward China. Other leaders who were more flexible and moderate toward the United States had little confidence that the United States would develop policy on sensitive issues like Taiwan that would avoid a future crisis. In their view, the United States lacked a clear sense of priorities toward China in particular and foreign policy in general. As a result, Washington dealt with issues on a case-by-case basis, making it difficult to predict U.S. policy. The Clinton administration's reversal on the Lee Teng-hui visit was said to represent just such a phenomenon. Chinese specialists feared that without a sense of order and priorities in U.S. policy toward China, similar policy reversals could occur with possibly very negative results for U.S.-China relations.

Lessons Learned—The U.S. Congress

Clinton administration officials and many in Congress acknowledged that Beijing's harsh response to the Lee Teng-hui visit took them by surprise and that the United States needed to exercise greater care in dealing with Taiwan-related issues. Because the Lee visit reflected congressional pressure on the administration, the effect of the PRC actions on congressional attitudes has been most important in determining U.S. policy.

Some congressional officials acknowledged that in the aftermath of the PRC's 1995 military maneuvers Congress had "pulled back" on Taiwan-related issues. In part, this reflected greater discretion by Taiwan, which adopted a lower profile on Capitol Hill in the second half of 1995 than it did in the first half. It also reflected the wish of many members of Congress to avoid difficulties in the U.S.-PRC-Taiwan triangular relationship. Thus, H. Res. 63 expressing support for Taiwan's representation in the United Nations was delayed because some members of Congress believed that raising and passing the resolution would undermine U.S. interests in relations with China and Taiwan. Such resolutions passed in the past.

On the other hand, some members of Congress not normally associated with a hard-line policy became more rigid after Beijing's mid-1995 provocations. They suspected that Beijing used military force not only to intimidate Taiwan but also to intimidate the United States to weaken ties with Taiwan, that it was testing the resolve of an administration seen by some as less than resolute in foreign policy. This bipartisan group wanted the United States to stand firmly on Taiwan and related issues and urged the president not to "reward" PRC "temper tantrums." They also believed that the United States was within its rights under agreements with the PRC to allow Lee Teng-hui to visit Cornell University in a private capacity. Some members asserted that the administration did not respond strongly enough to the PRC military exercises in the Taiwan Strait.

Renewed Crisis—March 1996

The thaw in U.S.-China relations in late 1995 was only temporary. Despite the avowed interest of some Chinese officials to maintain smooth U.S.-China relations during the election year, renewed PRC military pressure on Taiwan and rigid PRC economic policies prompted a sharply negative reaction in the United States. Press reports in late January 1996 that Chinese officials were accompanying intimidation tactics toward Taiwan with threats to attack U.S. cities in the event U.S. forces intervened in the Taiwan Strait affected media and congressional attitudes.[31]

China's provocative use of force in the Taiwan Strait in March 1996, timed to coincide with Taiwan's first presidential election, headed the list of U.S. grievances against Chinese leaders. Other major issues included the estimated $2 billion in annual losses suffered by U.S. firms as a result of China's violations of U.S. intellectual property rights, despite past Chinese agreement to halt such violations; China's reported continued cooperation with Pakistan's effort to build a nuclear weapons capability; reports of China's sale of surface-to-surface missiles and related technology to such troubled areas as Iran and Pakistan; and Beijing's hard-line stance toward any signs of political dissent.[32]

Against the backdrop of a deluge of media criticism and congressional and interest group pressures on the Clinton administration's comprehensive engagement policy, the White House toughened its stance. During the PRC military exercises near Taiwan in March 1996, the United States deployed two U.S. carrier battle groups to the area, postponed the visit of China's defense minister to the United States, and suspended approval of Export-Import Bank financing for new projects in China, pending a review of options to deal with reported Chinese export of nuclear technologies. But the administration also tried to sustain long-term engagement through dialogue between U.S. and PRC senior leaders. President Clinton reportedly gave newly appointed U.S. Ambassador James Sasser a letter for China's leaders requesting such a dialogue. China responded by sending to Washington in March 1996 Liu Huaqiu, the State Council's senior foreign policy expert, for discussions with White House and congressional leaders.[33]

Congress was not assuaged by the administration's actions, and it sought additional measures to reinforce the U.S. posture. The House and Senate passed separate nonbinding resolutions expressing support for Taiwan in the face of PRC intimidation. Many members were adamant that the administration adopt a stronger response to reported Chinese nuclear and missile proliferation and to violations of the intellectual property rights of U.S. businesses. The House and Senate also passed the 1996–97 State Department authorization bill (HR 1561) that contained over one dozen provisions targeted directly or indirectly at strengthening U.S. policy on Taiwan, Tibet, human rights, and Chinese membership in the World Trade Organization.[34]

Postcrisis U.S.-China Relations, 1996–97

Following Lee Teng-hui's election, with a strong showing gathering 54 percent of the vote in a field of four candidates, both Taipei and Beijing took steps to ease bilateral tensions. However, the U.S. show of naval power in the face of PRC military exercises brought the situation in the Strait and in U.S.-PRC relations to a new and important juncture. In particular, several months after Washington and Beijing had managed to ease their earlier tension over Taiwan, the United States was now once again of central and immediate importance in PRC policy toward Taiwan.

There were many critical factors in China and the United States that needed to be considered to assess U.S.-China relations and U.S. policy in the aftermath of the crisis.[35] On the U.S. side, the Clinton administration used a series of high-level meetings with Chinese leaders both in the United States and in Beijing to sustain its engagement policy. The administration hoped that the U.S. show of force in the Taiwan area would deter Beijing while cooling U.S. domestic pressure to take a tougher line toward the PRC. Some in the administration wanted to continue engagement because they believed it was in the U.S. interest. Others wanted smooth relations with China so that the issue did not rise prominently in the 1996 presidential campaign. They worried that Republican presidential candidate Senator Bob Dole could do to President Clinton what candidate Clinton did to President Bush over China in 1992—use the China issue to weaken the incumbent. Still others in the administration really did not believe in the policy of engagement. Press reports suggested that the State Department's Human Rights Office opposed engagement.

Many in the media and the Congress, backed by a wide variety of anti-PRC interest groups, sensed weakness in the administration's policy. They also judged that China's leadership sensed the administration's weakness and pressed the United States hard, especially on Taiwan. Therefore, these Americans pressed hard in the opposite direction, trying to make sure that the administration did not accommodate Chinese pressure and its violations of U.S.-backed international norms.

In China, senior PRC leaders still said that they wanted a stable relationship with the Clinton administration because they feared the consequences of politicization of China policy. But this calculus seemed to have changed in early 1996. Underlying the change was a basic belief held by the senior Chinese leaders that the United States was fundamentally determined to "contain" China and that its Taiwan policy was part of this effort. This view was said to be widespread among senior PRC leaders. It added to Beijing's equally alarmist view about Lee Teng-hui and Taiwan. The PRC concluded that Lee was trying to lead the people of Taiwan toward independence. It refused to consider the fact that Lee had not advocated *de jure* independence and that his views favoring continued separation and greater international recognition of Taiwan reflected widely held views on the island.

Based on these views, PRC leaders in 1996 developed an assertive military effort to intimidate Taiwan, the United States, and the rest of Asia. Any concern about a relationship with the Clinton administration was put aside so Chinese officials could show how determined they were to deal with the Taiwan issue and any U.S. or other outside interference. This hard-line stance played well in the Chinese domestic politics of leadership transition. It also may have reflected an underlying calculus of some Chinese leaders that by pushing Taiwan and the United States hard, they might be able to achieve through intimidation what they could not get from more conventional means.

Taiwan was temporarily cowed by PRC pressure. It avoided egregious efforts to gain international recognition for the rest of 1996, but over the longer term it appeared determined to seek international "space." This not only reflected a strong desire on the part of the Taiwan electorate that their leaders do more to gain Taiwan greater respect and recognition in world politics, it also reflected the private calculus of Taiwan leaders of their strong need for the international political support that comes from recognition. They believed that the PRC would become stronger economically and politically than Taiwan and that Taiwan would become more dependent on the PRC economy. To safeguard Taiwan in the face of these trends, Taiwan needed broader and deeper political contacts to reinforce its strong economic contacts with much of the world, especially with the United States and key developed countries.

China's neighbors in Asia wanted stability to be restored. At first, they were very critical of Taiwan for precipitating PRC anger over Lee's visit to the United States in 1995. But some were equally concerned with Beijing's militant behavior and the need to deter PRC aggression while avoiding protracted confrontation. Japan was probably the most concerned with the PRC aggressiveness and welcomed U.S. efforts to solidify the U.S.-Japan security relationship during the summit meeting with President Clinton in April 1996.

In short, the outlook for U.S.-PRC-Taiwan relations remained subject to many variables. In the United States, many in Congress, the media, and anti-PRC interest groups had an active agenda that aimed to influence the presidential campaign and postcampaign policies. Pressure on the White House was building to take steps to support Taiwan with more arms transfers; to reinforce the U.S. defense posture in East Asia; to build a missile defense system against China; to sanction China over trade, proliferation, and other issues; and to slow the flow of multilateral lending and advanced technology to China. Such actions were sure to antagonize PRC leaders, who might have responded with strong rhetoric and maybe some retaliatory actions of their own.

It was not inconceivable that military tensions in the Taiwan Strait would reoccur. Nonetheless, there emerged in the United States, especially in the wake of the U.S.-Chinese military face-off in the Taiwan area in 1995–96, tentative signs of policy convergence among executive branch officials, some members of Congress, and opinion leaders, and of the emergence of a more coherent China policy. For a time in 1996 and 1997 there was less debate in the United States pushed by single-issue advocates demanding that their interest be the top priority of U.S. policy toward China. There was more awareness of China's rise as a great power, of the multifaceted challenges this poses for U.S. interests, and of the need for the United States to establish carefully crafted and effective policies and contingency plans to deal with those challenges. Evidence of the more serious, sober, and careful U.S. approach to China was seen in:

- President Clinton's more careful use of negative and positive incentives in dealing with China in 1996. The show of force in the Taiwan Strait and the president's tough stance on intellectual property rights provided a good atmosphere for the administration's renewal of MFN treatment and its accommodation with Beijing over the sale of nuclear-related technology to Pakistan.
- Senator Dole's speech on Asia on May 9, 1996, which avoided a wide difference with the direction of administration policy.
- Secretary Christopher's first major address on China, on May 17, 1996, which laid out a balanced U.S. approach to the rise of China's power and influences.
- President Clinton's postcrisis willingness to take the initiative in discussing issues in U.S.-China relations, despite the sensitivity of election-year politics.

- The administration's decision to send National Security Adviser Anthony Lake to China, paving the way for a U.S.-China summit meeting.
- Low-key efforts by U.S. critics to cut off MFN tariff treatment for Chinese imports during the annual debate over granting MFN for China in 1996.
- Growing evidence that congressional leaders were willing to give voice to the idea that "punishment" of China through withdrawal of MFN needed to be replaced by more carefully crafted and serious efforts to "deal" with the "rise of China."

Perhaps the main reason the United States appeared to be developing a more coherent China policy in 1996 and early 1997 was growing awareness of China's strategic importance. Although rising Chinese power poses opportunities as well as challenges, opinion leaders and officials increasingly focused on the challenges. China was seen as a strategic power undergoing rapid economic growth and social change and as ruled by authoritarian leaders. China had made great strides in conforming to many international norms, but rising Chinese power and nationalistic assertiveness posed serious problems for U.S. interests in regional stability, curbing proliferation of nuclear and missile technologies, the stability of the international economic system, and international management of such issues as human rights and environmental protection.

Experience suggested that the United States would be unable to reach any "grand bargain" resolving the challenges posed by Chinese power. Rather, U.S. leaders would need to devote continuous high-level policy attention, issue by issue, case by case, both to deter Chinese assertiveness and to encourage Chinese accommodation of U.S. interests. In so doing, the United States would not rely solely on policies designed to moderate Chinese assertiveness through accommodation and greater integration in world affairs.

Although many were hopeful that positive changes could come from China's economic modernization and social change, fundamental political change remained a distant prospect. As a result, U.S. policymakers were striving to establish clearly defined negative and positive incentives that would prompt PRC behavior more compatible with U.S. interests. At the same time, a U.S. policy of containment against China was seen as both premature and unworkable. An effective U.S. strategy was considered in the context of a broader strategy for Asia—one requiring a strong U.S. military, economic, and political presence, as well as cooperation from important allies and friends in the region. Policy recommendations focused on establishing clear priorities that took account of U.S. interests along with Chinese concerns and those of interested third parties. To formulate these priorities and to ensure that they were met required consistent high-level attention, including regular U.S.-PRC summit meetings. That such meetings gave prestige to PRC leaders seen as illegitimate by many Americans posed perhaps the most serious, immediate dilemma for sustained U.S. efforts to deal with the rise of China.[36]

Chinese specialists and other observers in the United States and Asia were optimistic in late 1996 that there would be substantial progress in U.S.-China relations in 1997. They were surprised by the vehemence of the U.S. debate that impeded progress during that year. In early 1997, they saw President Clinton, Vice President Gore, and senior administration officials strongly committed to a policy of "engagement" with Chinese counterparts. This seemed likely to provide the impetus for U.S.-Chinese agreements on China's entry into the World Trade Organization (WTO), possible U.S. consideration of granting permanent MFN for China, and other issues during the high-level U.S.-Chinese exchanges planned during 1997 and 1998. The Clinton administration was seen as backed strongly by many U.S. businesses with interests in China's advancing economy, U.S. strategists who judged that U.S. policy needed to deal constructively with China's rising power and influence in Asian and world affairs, and others. Specialists and others acknowledged that the U.S. media appeared to remain critical of the Chinese government, U.S. public opinion continued to have a negative view of the Chinese government, and a number of U.S. groups critical of Chinese government policies and practices on issues ranging from human rights, trade, and proliferation of weapons remained active.

The Clinton administration's public commitment to the engagement policy weakened in mid-1997, particularly as a result of the campaign contribution controversy that was highlighted by the U.S. media since late 1996. Most damaging were charges in the U.S. media that the Chinese government was involved in funneling campaign contributions to U.S. candidates with the intention of winning their support for favorable U.S. trade or other treatment of China.[37] As a result, President Clinton, Vice President Gore, and other administration leaders were seen to have adopted a lower public posture in defense of the engagement policy with China. At the same time, U.S. critics of the engagement policy were seen to use the controversy to launch a varied attack on China's policies and practices and on the Clinton administration's approach to China issues.

Specialists saw "partisan" elements in both the U.S. Democratic and Republican parties allegedly using the debate over China policy for partisan reasons. Thus, they charged that some of the U.S. criticism of Vice President Gore over China policy reflected a design by some elements within the Democratic party to use China issues to weaken Mr. Gore's standing in the party and his chances to serve as the Party's presidential candidate in 2000. Some Republican politicians were thought to hold to a similar reasoning in their criticism of Mr. Gore's China policy. Meanwhile, some Republican activists, who adhere strongly to the socially conservative agenda of the religious right, were said to be using China issues against some leaders in the Republican party who were seen as not suitably conservative on social and other issues important to these activists. Many suspected that these partisan charges would continue well after the 1997 debate on MFN treatment for China and might become a fixture of U.S. domestic politics for the next few years.

It is important to note that the Taiwan issue did not figure prominently in the renewed U.S. China policy debate of 1997. Pro-Taiwan advocates were still on the defensive in the face of charges that they had recklessly endangered Taiwan's security and prosperity, as well as U.S. and regional security interests, in their headlong push to seek Lee Teng-hui's visit to Cornell. The Taiwan government also adopted a low-key lobbying approach in Washington in the wake of the donor controversy of late 1996–97. Many of the early press reports had linked Taiwan government and private interests with allegedly illegal or inappropriate donations to U.S. politicians. Taipei presumably calculated that a low-key posture would allow those allegations to fade while U.S. investigators focused on alleged illicit actions by the PRC and others.

Sino-U.S. Summits—Alternative Outlooks

Specialists in the United States, China, and elsewhere have differed over the outlook for U.S.-China relations over the next year.[38] Some optimists have judged that the Clinton administration's policy of "engagement" with Chinese leaders would result in productive Sino-American summit meetings in Washington in October 1997 and in Beijing in 1998. In this view, the two governments would use these and other opportunities to consolidate common ground on economic, environmental, regional security (e.g., Korean peninsula), and other issues, while making progress on various human rights, trade, weapons proliferation, and other questions that divide them.

Chinese President Jiang Zemin is fresh from his success at the Chinese Communist Party's 15th Congress in September 1997; he is anticipated to be more willing and able than in the past to reach compromises on issues important to the United States. U.S. President Bill Clinton is said to be focused on the long-term importance for the United States, and also for his presidency, of managing effectively China's emergence in world affairs. Thus, the president is thought by some specialists to be ready to make compromises and gestures aimed at promoting forward movement in relations with China, and thereby facilitating China's integration into constructive international relations.

On the other hand, there are specialists who have argued that progress in Sino-American relations will be limited over the next year, and possibly longer, because of constraints and trends in both China and the United States. In this view, Chinese leaders headed by President Jiang Zemin have little of the will and/or power needed to reach significant compromises with the United States on the various human rights, trade, weapons proliferation, and other issues that divide the two governments. Clinton administration leaders also are viewed as constrained, as their engagement policy faces a continuing barrage of opposition from important U.S. leaders in the Congress, the media, and elsewhere in U.S. public affairs.

Lessons of the Recent Past

Past patterns of behavior are not always good indicators of future behavior. Nonetheless, a careful review of developments in U.S.-China relations since the Tiananmen incident of 1989[39] appear to support the arguments of those who are more pessimistic than optimistic about future progress in U.S.-China relations over the next year.

1. Although Chinese officials hold different views of the U.S. government's China policy, senior Chinese leaders remain deeply sus-

picious of U.S. policy. At times, at least some Chinese leaders suspect that the United States is intent on "containing" China and "holding back" its rise in international power and influence. A more common view among Chinese leaders is that the United States is determined to maintain its status as the world's only superpower and a dominant strategic power in East Asia, and to maintain strong ties with Taiwan and support the island against military pressure from the Chinese mainland.

They also are more uniform in suspicion of a long-term U.S. effort—publicly articulated by President Clinton in his first second-term press conference,[40] and by President Bush before him—to seek a changed Chinese politicai system along lines compatible with U.S. interests.[41] But in recent years, Beijing's broad internal and international policies have enjoyed support among various segments of the Chinese leadership, often as a result of protracted Chinese leadership negotiations.[42] As a result, Beijing is not inclined to change policy to accommodate the United States.

2. In the 1990s, Beijing's confidence in its own economic power and its increased standing in world affairs has grown. At the same time, Chinese leaders have become increasingly aware of, and able to use to their own advantage, the sharp divisions in the United States over policy toward China, in order to avoid undesired changes in China's policies and practices. For example, some U.S. business groups and some groups representing interests important to the United States in Hong Kong and other parts of Asia have seen their concerns as best served by aggressively countering the arguments of U.S. critics of China's policies and practices. The result has been particularly important in allowing Beijing to offset pressures from the United States pushing for changes in the Chinese government's policies and practices over human rights, proliferation, trade, and other sensitive issues.

3. Admittedly, Beijing has made several adjustments in policy and practice in recent years in ways that favor U.S. interests and facilitate forward movement in Sino-U.S. relations. But it has generally done so when the costs of not changing have outweighed the costs of change. Thus, when Chinese leaders feared China might lose U.S. most favored nation (MFN) tariff treatment in 1990 and 1991, they made several last-minute but important concessions on sensitive human rights, proliferation, and other issues in order to buttress U.S. support for continued MFN. Later, when U.S. and world opinion pressed China

on the issue of the Comprehensive Nuclear Test Ban, China changed
its stance in order to avoid isolation and possible sanction.[43] China also
agreed several times to accommodate the United States on market
access, intellectual property rights, and other trade issues, when it was
clear that the alternative was loss of several billions of dollars of trade.
When China realized that suspending ambassadorial ties with the
United States after Taiwan President Lee Teng-hui's visit to the United
States in June 1995 was hurting Chinese interests without much likelihood of concessions from the United States, Beijing returned its ambassador and resumed normal relations.

4. On the U.S. side of the equation, China's inertia and resistance to
change in policy areas of concern to the United States add to the reasons
why U.S. officials, critical of Chinese policies and practices, are likely
to continue to press hard for strong U.S. efforts to promote changes in
China. Strong support from U.S. media, interest groups, and others who
adamantly disapprove of China's behavior appears likely to continue.
As noted earlier, such strong criticism and pressure constrain efforts by
the Clinton administration and others to promote forward movement in
U.S. relations with China. Ironically, Chinese government inertia also
gives assurance that those U.S. critics likely will face few immediate
negative consequences from China for their attacks on China.

It is logical that U.S. officials, especially in the Congress, and others
concerned with human rights, weapons proliferation, trade, and other disputes with China will see China's continued recalcitrance or slowness to
change as reason for a tougher U.S. policy. At the same time, it is also
logical that since China follows current policies for its own reasons,
deeply rooted in protracted Chinese leadership deliberations over how
they protect and enhance China's interests, Beijing is not likely to disrupt
them for the sake of "punishing" China's critics in the United States.
Indeed, China continues to be solicitous of numerous congressional members who are sharply critical of China, urging them to carry out visits to
China for meetings with high-level Chinese leaders.

Meanwhile, the Clinton administration thus far has given little sign
that it is prepared to take concrete action against congressional and
other critics of its policy of engagement toward China. Some U.S.
specialists criticize the Clinton administration for not doing enough
both to rally U.S. supporters to its engagement policy and to sanction
those Americans who attack and criticize the policy. At minimum, they
believe the president should be more direct in publicly confronting the

critics of his China policy, thereby warning the critics that they face public censure and possibly other retaliation within the power of the executive branch.

Trends in Chinese and U.S. decision making since the Tiananmen incident add to evidence that U.S. and Chinese leaders will have difficulty making major progress in their high-level meetings through 1998. The trends depict Chinese leaders as deeply suspicious of changes advocated by the United States, more confident of their power and influence in world affairs and of their ability to use sharp divisions in the United States to China's advantage, and determined to adhere to long-standing Chinese policy approaches reached after often protracted efforts to achieve consensus among diverse Chinese leaders. The trends also show that the many official and other U.S. critics of China's policies and practices have ample incentives and few immediate disincentives for continuing their harsh attacks against Chinese government behavior and the Clinton administration's engagement policy.

U.S. and Chinese leaders could choose to depart from recent patterns in order to achieve a significant breakthrough in Sino-American relations over the next year. Thus, as noted earlier, some specialists are optimistic that the senior U.S. and Chinese leaders will see their interests well served by "successful" summit meetings marked by major improvements in U.S.-China relations. On balance, however, the pattern of decision making on both sides in recent years reflects important constraints on Chinese and U.S. leaders in seeking greater flexibility, compromise, and forward movement in U.S.-China relations.

Longer-Term Challenges[44]

For the reasons just noted, the Taiwan issue has not been a leading element in the U.S. debate over China policy in the period leading up to the U.S.-PRC summits of 1997 and 1998. In large measure this reflects the calculus of the Taiwan government and pro-Taiwan interests in the United States that their concerns remain best served by a low-key posture over the next year. Beyond that, the course of U.S. policy over the Taiwan issue depends in great part on the policies of the PRC and Taiwan. PRC-Taiwan competition for international support will continue and perhaps intensify. Leaders in Taipei and Beijing have strong political and strategic reasons to maintain assertive policies. For Taiwan, the search for international space seeks to secure Taiwan's separate status at a time of growing PRC economic and military power. For their part, PRC leaders are said to recognize that China needs to control Taiwan's diplomatic posture if it expects to play a great-power role in Asian and world affairs. A China preoccupied with an unfriendly or uncooperative Taiwan along its seaward periphery will be constrained in Asian and world politics. Taiwan under the influence of another great power can undermine PRC security.

As in the past, the main international arena for this competition will be Washington. Greater coherence in U.S. policy may ultimately allow U.S. leaders to deal more effectively with the tug-of-war for influence that has characterized U.S. policy on the U.S.-Taiwan-PRC triangular relationship in recent years. The president may be able to define a clear policy reflecting broadly accepted U.S. interests and stick to it. He may also be more willing to employ positive and negative incentives on interest groups, lobbyists, and others that might otherwise be prompted to push hard for change in the president's policy. But, if recent practice is any guide, U.S. policy could also be a muddled drift, moving in one direction or another depending on the shifting relative strength of international and domestic forces pushing it along.

White House policymakers and other U.S. leaders argue that China is an important country, that U.S.-China relations are at a delicate stage, and that U.S. policy should strive to put relations back on track. In so doing, U.S. policy will foster tendencies in China toward economic, social, and political change advantageous to the United States and foster greater Chinese interdependence in world affairs. These leaders point out that Taiwan officials sometimes privately aver that Taiwan is dependent on the United States, so that the United States does not have to assuage feelings in Taiwan with actions sure to antagonize the PRC. They argue that the United States should maintain the status quo in its relations with Taiwan and build relations with the PRC.

Opposed to this view are many members of Congress, the media, and various interest groups who emphasize Taiwan's positive features. Close U.S.-Taiwan relations provide trade and investment opportunities for U.S. businesses and campaign contributions and votes of blocs of Taiwanese-Americans for American politicians. Taiwan's competitive economic system and its recent democratization have attracted American ideological and moral support. In contrast, members of this group tend to doubt that there will be any significant PRC movement toward political pluralism or international interdependence. They also emphasize the asymmetry of power between the United States and China. China will press the United States on Taiwan or other questions only when it senses U.S. weakness. If the United States is strong and demonstrates negative consequences for Beijing if it adopts confrontational policies, PRC leaders will pull back to protect Chinese interest in stable relations with the United States.

Which side will win in this debate in U.S. policy?[45] Since Richard Nixon's opening of diplomatic relations with the PRC, the PRC has won the big decisions. This was evident in the U.S. policy choices in Nixon's initial visit to China, U.S. inability to maintain Taiwan's seat at the United Nations, the U.S. decision to normalize diplomatic relations with Beijing, and the U.S. decision to sign the 1982 communique limiting U.S. arms sales to Taiwan. And yet, for the most part, these developments were heavily influenced by an overriding strategic rationale that drove U.S. policy toward the PRC and against the Soviet Union.

Even during the Cold War, when the PRC was winning the big U.S. decisions, Taiwan made important gains. Since 1978, when the U.S. broke relations with Taiwan to establish relations with the PRC, Americans have increased the breadth and scope of relations with Taiwan. The Taiwan Relations Act expressed U.S. support for Taiwan security. Washington protected Taiwan's membership in the Asian Development Bank and has supported its membership in the WTO. It aided Taiwan's development of a new jet fighter, and in 1992 sold it 150 F-16 fighters. In 1994 it upgraded the protocol level of diplomatic exchanges, and in 1995 it issued a visa for Lee Teng-hui to visit Cornell University.

The end of the Cold War eliminated the strategic rationale for the pro-PRC decisions in U.S. policy in the 1970s and 1980s. As noted earlier, a new strategic rationale has emerged. Policymakers recognize that China is a growing power and possesses the strategic importance of a great power. But Chinese power does not guarantee that U.S. policy will tilt toward China. China's importance, strength, and assertiveness may also strengthen U.S. resolve to support Taiwan against Beijing's threat.

This inventory of U.S. domestic forces on the Taiwan issue reveals that whatever administration exists in Washington, it is going to feel strong pressure from members of the media, Congress, and interest groups who feel that Washington should do more to help Taiwan. If Taiwan maintains its close and cooperative relationship with the United States and avoids provocative actions that unnecessarily exacerbate cross-Strait relations, U.S. policy will likely tilt toward Taiwan.

If Taipei, Beijing, and Washington pursue pragmatic and moderate policies, this may encourage domestic convergence on policy toward China and Taiwan and allow policymakers to reinforce tendencies toward policy coherence, perhaps leading to policies that provide an appropriate balance between Taipei and Beijing. Moderation and pragmatism by one party can reinforce trends toward moderation and pragmatism by the other, leading to a pattern of realistic but mutually beneficial contacts and reduced tensions. U.S., PRC, and Taiwan actions would then focus on the common ground all three share in avoiding war and promoting regional development, goals shared by other East Asian nations and powers with an interest in the region.

Notes

1. For background, see David Michael Lampton, "America's China Policy in the Age of the Finance Minister: Clinton Ends Linkage," *China Quarterly*, pp. 597–621. For analysis on the interaction of U.S. business groups and human rights groups during the debate over MFN, see the article by Steve Teles in this volume.

2. Reviewed in CRS Issue Brief 94006, *Taiwan: Recent Developments and U.S. Policy Choices* (updated monthly).

3. For a discussion of the background and determinants, see *China Policy: Managing U.S.-PRC-Taiwan Relations After President Lee's Visit to the U.S.*, CRS Report 95-727S, 5 pp.

4. See discussion in, among others, Robert Sutter, *Shaping China's Future In World Affairs* (Boulder, CO: Westview Press, 1996), pp. 69–85.

5. These are reviewed, notably in Sutter, *China's Future In World Affairs*, pp. 15–18.

6. Speech by Robert Dole on Asian Affairs, May 9, 1996.

7. For background to the crisis, see among others, Robert Sutter, *Taiwan: Recent Developments and U.S. Policy Choices*, CRS Issue Brief 94006 (updated regularly).

8. For background, see Kerry Dumbaugh, *China-U.S. Relations*, CRS Issue Brief 94002, (updated regularly).

9. For background, see CRS Report 95-727S, and CRS Report 95-750S.

10. For background, see *China-U.S. Relations*, CRS Issue Brief 94002.

11. *New York Times*, October 25, 1995.

12. For details on China's breaking off contact with the United States and other reaction to the Taiwan president's visit, see Robert Sutter, *China Policy: Managing U.S.-PRC-Taiwan Relations After President Lee's Visit to the U.S.*, CRS Report 95-727S, June 19, 1995, 5 pp.

13. This finding is based on interviews and in-depth consultations with sixty Chinese specialists during two visits to China in 1994, consultations with thirty Chinese specialists who visited the United States in late 1995, and consultations with twenty-five U.S. specialists who traveled to Beijing in recent years for consultations on U.S.-China relations. For background, see CRS General Distribution Memorandum *Sino-U.S. Relations: Status and Outlook—Views from Beijing*, August 15, 1994.

14. U.S. Department of Defense, *United States Security Strategy for the East Asia-Pacific Region*, Washington, February 1995, 32 pp.

15. *Washington Post*, February 19, 1995.

16. These latter events are reviewed in CRS Issue Brief 94002.

17. See among others, Allen Whiting, "Sino-Japanese Relations," *World Policy Journal*, v. 8, Winter 1990–91, pp. 107–134.

18. For background on PRC-Taiwan relations, see *Taiwan-Mainland China Relations*, CRS Report 95-968S, September 8, 1995, 14 pp.

19. For background, see CRS Issue Brief 94002, *China-U.S. Relations*, and CRS Issue Brief 94006, *Taiwan*.

20. *Los Angeles Times*, August 2, 1995.

21. Consultations, Washington, D.C., and/or New York, August 23, 25, and 28, 1995.

22. New China News Agency, August 18, 1995.

23. Radio Beijing, August 2, 1995.

24. New China News Agency, August 22, 1995.

25. U.S. media reaction to the Chinese commentary focused on the harsh anti-U.S. rhetoric in the piece. See, for example, "China Bitterly Attacks Critics in U.S.," *Washington Post*, August 24, 1995.

26. Consultations, Washington, D.C., August 29, 1995.

27. Consultations, New York, August 8, 1995.

28. Consultations, Washington, D.C., October 17, 1995.

29. Interviews, Washington, D.C., November 9, 13, 1995.

30. *U.S. News & World Report*, October 23, 1995, p. 72.

31. *New York Times*, January 24, 1996.

32. For background, see *China-U.S. Relations*, CRS Issue Brief 94002.

33. Reviewed in *China, Congress and Sanctions*, CRS Report 96-348F, April 17, 1996, pp. 1–2.

34. Ibid.

35. These are reviewed in CRS general distribution memorandum for Congress, March 18, 1996.

36. See notably, discussion in *China's Rising Power: Alternative U.S. National Security Strategies—Findings of a Seminar*. Congressional Research Service Report 96-518 F, June 6, 1996, 16 pp.

37. For background, see, among others, *Congressional Quarterly Weekly Report*, April 26, 1997, pp. 967–972.

38. These judgments are based on consultations with over 100 specialists in China, Japan, South Korea, England, and the United States since May 1997. For background on some of those consultations, see CRS General Distribution Memoranda for Congressional China Watchers dated June 10 and July 8, 1997. For background on recent U.S.-China relations, see *China-U.S. Relations* by Kerry Dumbaugh, CRS Issue Brief 94002.

39. Those interested in more detail on this period can consult, among others, *China. Interest Groups and Recent U.S. Policy—An Introduction* by Robert Sutter, CRS Report 97-48 F, pp. 1–62; and David M. Lampton, "America's China Policy in the Age of the Finance Minister," *The China Quarterly,* 1994, pp. 597–621.

40. See coverage in *New York Times,* January 30, 1997, p. 20.

41. For recent background on such Chinese suspicions, see Congressional China Watchers Memorandum of July 8, 1997.

42. For background on Chinese decision making, see, among others, *China After Deng Xiaoping,* CRS Issue Brief 93114.

43. For background on Chinese weapons proliferation policies and practices, see *Chinese Proliferation of Weapons of Mass Destruction* by Shirley Kan, CRS Report 96-767F.

44. This is based on a panel discussion held at the Heritage Foundation, March 5, 1996.

45. This section is based on a panel discussion held at the Heritage Foundation, March 5, 1996.

4

U.S.-China Economic Relations

Marcus Noland

The United States is the world's largest economy. China will soon be the second largest economy if it is not already (Table 4.1), and, according to one Chinese scholar, it will surpass the United States to become the world's largest economy by 2030.[1] Relations between these two countries are crucial to the future development of the world economy. Unfortunately, economic relations between the two countries are troubled. China is large, rapidly growing, and still in the process of devising and implementing fundamental economic reforms. Despite its size and importance to the global economy, it is still not a member of the World Trade Organization (WTO), the primary multilateral institution for managing the world trade system. As a consequence, trade disputes between China and the United States are resolved almost exclusively in public, acrimonious, bilateral negotiations.

This pattern exposes both the strengths and the weaknesses of the U.S. position. By pressing China bilaterally and using the leverage of access to its large and lucrative market, the United States can largely set the agenda without concern for third-party interests. At the same time, U.S. trade policy-making is a complainant-driven system prone to capture by special interests. Consequently the United States can set the agenda, but the agenda may reflect the very particularistic demands of narrow groups and detract from the achievement of broader aims.

Paper prepared for the conference on Domestic Factors in U.S.-China Relations, Peking University, June 24–25, 1996. Copyright © 1998 by the Institute for International Economics. All rights reserved.

Table 4.1

World Income Shares

	1993	2003		
		Low	Medium	High
North America	26.3	22.8	24.0	25.5
United States	21.9	18.2	19.2	20.6
Canada	2.1	1.9	2.0	2.0
Mexico	2.3	2.7	2.8	2.9
Asia-Pacific	26.1	28.1	31.0	33.6
Japan	8.8	7.6	8.1	8.8
China	8.8	10.8	13.0	15.5
Rest of Asia-Pacific	8.5	8.4	9.9	10.8
Korea	1.5	1.4	1.9	2.1
Taiwan	1.0	1.0	1.2	1.3
Hong Kong	0.6	0.5	0.7	0.8
Singapore	0.3	0.4	0.4	0.5
Malaysia	0.4	0.5	0.6	0.7
Thailand	0.8	0.9	1.2	1.4
Philippines	0.4	0.4	0.5	0.5
Indonesia	0.9	1.0	1.3	1.4
Australia	2.2	1.9	2.0	2.1
New Zealand	0.3	0.3	0.3	0.3
Western Europe	22.5	18.3	19.1	19.9
Latin America	6.0	5.6	5.9	6.1
Rest of the world	19.1	19.2	20.0	21.9

Source: Marcus Noland, "Implications of Asian Growth," Asia Pacific Economic Cooperation Working Paper Series Number 94–5, Washington, DC: Institute for International Economics.

Notes: Shares are calculated from purchasing power–adjusted national income figures. See footnote 4 for explanation of derivation of "high" and "low" shares; they do not sum to 100.0.

This chapter reviews U.S.-China economic relations and reaches a number of major conclusions:

- China's large bilateral surplus acts as a political lightning rod in the United States and contributes to trade tensions, regardless of the economic merits of these political concerns.

- The impact of the rapid growth of bilateral trade on the U.S. economy is positive, though probably not particularly large: imports from China have largely displaced imports from third countries, not domestic production, and exports have been higher than expected as well.
- In the recent dispute over intellectual property rights (IPR) the industry loss claims appear greatly exaggerated.
- Self-inflicted export disincentives probably do more to discourage U.S. exports than Chinese policies do.

Based on this analysis, these are the recommendations for U.S. policy:

- The United States needs to get its own house in order, reducing its budget deficit (so as to reduce the trade deficit), and reform both disincentives to export and the way in which the trade policy agenda is set.
- The annual debate over most favored nation (MFN) status is counterproductive and the Jackson-Vanik amendment should be repealed.
- In light of the apparent consolidation of power by Jiang Zemin at the 15th Party Congress, the United States should renew its efforts to resolve issues such as WTO accession that have been left to drift.

Overview of China's Economy

Since the inception of economic reforms in 1979, China's economic performance has been nothing short of spectacular. Between 1979 and 1995, China's real growth rate has averaged more than 9.5 percent annually (Figure 4.1). Yet difficulties in the development of effective tools of macroeconomic management have led to a stop-start pattern of growth and problems with inflation. The time path of Chinese economic growth is subject to considerable uncertainty.[2]

The level of output in China is likewise subject to considerable uncertainty, and various attempts to measure the purchasing power adjusted level of gross domestic production (GDP) have generated a wide range of estimates (Lardy 1994, Table 1.3).[3] Indeed, the estimate of Chinese GDP per capita reported in the most widely cited source,

110

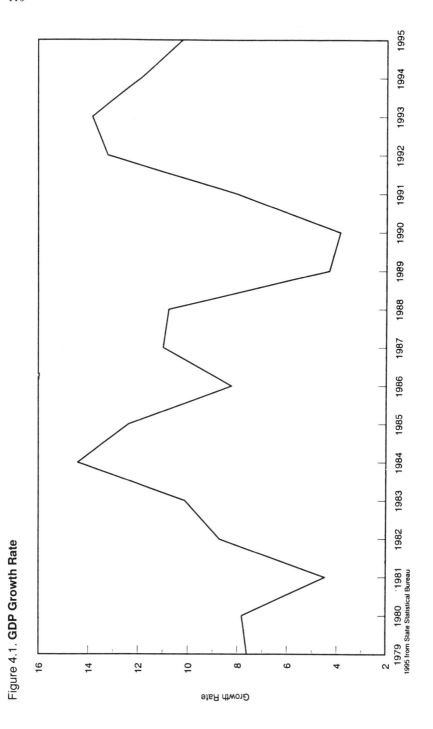

Figure 4.1. GDP Growth Rate

the Penn World Tables, changed by 40 percent in successive versions of the tables. Thus any attempt to put the size of the Chinese economy into international perspective is subject to enormous uncertainty. With this caveat, an estimate of the Chinese share of world output derived from purchasing power–adjusted data reported by the United States Central Intelligence Agency is reported in Table 4.1.[4]

As can be seen in the first column of Table 4.1, China accounted for just under 9 percent of world output in 1993, making it the world's third largest economy following the United States and Japan. The remaining columns show China's share ten years hence under various scenarios.[5] The Chinese growth rate is subject to the greatest uncertainty due to questions about the character of Chinese economic policy in the post-Deng era. The bottom line is that even under the slow growth scenario, China clearly emerges as the world's second largest economy in the next decade. This conclusion is further reinforced if the figures for Hong Kong's share of output are added to China's.

China's participation in international trade also has grown rapidly during the period of reform, and its share of world trade has risen from 0.6 percent in 1977 to 4.9 percent in 1994, making it the world's eighth largest trading nation (Figure 4.2). Chinese economic reforms not only spurred an enormous growth in trade, but the reforms have transformed the commodity composition as well, aligning China's pattern of trade more closely with its true pattern of comparative advantage (Table 4.2). Between 1980 and 1994, the share of exports accounted for by the light manufactures of Standard International Trade Classification (SITC) 8 rose from 16 percent to 47 percent. Similarly, imports of capital equipment (SITC 7) rose from 25 percent to 42 percent during this period.

In addition to its rapid emergence in goods markets, China has also become a major player in international capital markets. China is now the leading developing country destination for foreign direct investment. The stock of inward foreign direct investment (FDI) now exceeds $100 billion, though some of this is due to "roundtripping" as Chinese investment is routed through Hong Kong to take advantage of the more favorable treatment of foreign investors. Firms with foreign equity participation accounted for two thirds of the increase in Chinese exports in 1992 and 1993.

With regard to portfolio investment, external debt does not appear to be a problem: World Bank figures estimate annual repayments on the order of $12–14 billion, well within China's service capacity, though

Figure 4.2. **Merchandise Trade**

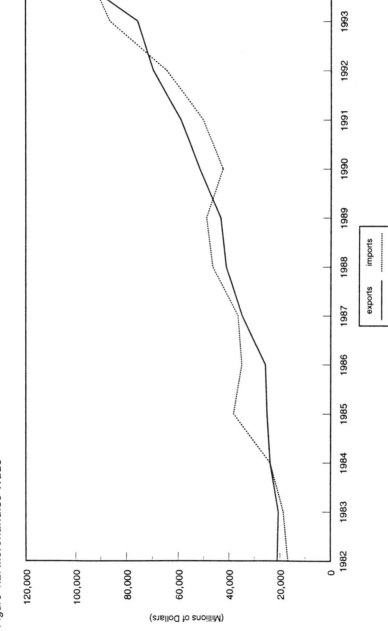

Source: IMF "International Financial Statistics"

Table 4.2

Changes in Chinese Export and Import Shares

	Exports		Imports	
	1980	1994	1980	1994
Food and live animals	0.15	0.07	0.15	0.02
Beverages and tobacco	0.00	0.01	0.00	0.01
Crude materials, inedible, except fuels	0.09	0.03	0.18	0.06
Mineral fuels, lubricants and related materials	0.21	0.03	0.01	0.03
Animal and vegetable oils, fats and waxes	0.00	0.00	0.01	0.00
Chemicals and related products	0.06	0.04	0.10	0.11
Manufactured goods (classified by primary material)	0.20	0.16	0.25	0.27
Machinery and transport equipment	0.03	0.19	0.25	0.42
Miscelleneous manufactured articles (includes textile and apparel)	0.16	0.47	0.03	0.06
Others	0.09	0.00	0.01	0.02
Total, 1.00	1.00	1.00	1.00	1.00

Source: Statistics Canada, *World Trade Database 1980–1994.*

some private analysts claim the burden is higher. Much of Chinese finance is intermediated through Hong Kong, however, and a crisis of confidence surrounding the transfer of sovereignty or Chinese policy and administration in its aftermath could greatly complicate the situation for China and the region as a whole.

China is a major recipient of multilateral and bilateral official lending. The United States has recently questioned whether China should continue to receive concessional finance through the International Development Agency (IDA), the World Bank's soft loan window. IDA funds have accounted for about a quarter of China's $22 billion in World Bank loans since 1980, and China has been receiving approximately $1 billion annually from IDA for the last several years. Other countries (most notably Japan), while decrying U.S. arrears in its payments to IDA, have tended toward the U.S. position. The Chinese share of IDA funds is expected to decline, and China may well be graduated from the program when the current IDA replenishment is exhausted.[6]

Environmental issues are likely to play an increasingly prominent role in China's economic relations. Already the U.S. Exim Bank has refused to grant export finance to participate in the Three Gorges Dam project because of environmental concerns. China is also predicted to emerge as a major source of hydrocarbon emissions in the twenty-first century due to its rapid growth and reliance on dirty coal for energy. If there were to be an international tax on hydrocarbon emissions, it would presumably fall heavily on China. It is not difficult to imagine China insisting on enhanced multilateral and bilateral concessional financing or increased access to developed country markets as quid pro quos for adherence to a strict antiemissions regime.

Two fundamental points must be kept in mind when analyzing U.S.-China economic relations. First, China is an incompletely reformed centrally planned economy.[7] Second, China is huge. It is no longer a marginal player in the world economy. It is increasingly central to the world economy, and interaction with the Chinese economy is potentially highly beneficial and highly disruptive to its partners. It is for these reasons that it is entirely appropriate, indeed prudent, for China's partners to keep a close watch on Chinese economic policy.

U.S.-China Economic Relations

The rapid integration of China into the global economy has posed particular problems for high-income countries, including the United

States. China has a rapidly growing aggregate bilateral trade surplus with the United States, and in June 1996 the U.S. deficit with China exceeded the deficit with Japan for the first time. This trend is apparent even according to Chinese data, and even when the miscounting of reexports through Hong Kong is taken into account (Table 4.3). Nor can this growing Chinese surplus be explained away as a function of the relocation of production from Hong Kong and Taiwan to China as was conceivable a few years ago (Table 4.4), though Naughton (1997) notes that some of the unknown amount may be due to Japanese and Korean factories relocating in China.[8] Differences in political values, the growing bilateral imbalance, and the concentration of imports in light manufactures all act as political lightning rods in the United States.

As shown in Table 4.5, at the one-digit SITC level U.S. exports to China in 1994 were concentrated in the machinery and transportation group ($5.1 billion), followed by chemicals ($1.5 billion), and mining products ($1.2 billion). In terms of more narrowly defined three-digit SITC categories, exports were the greatest in aircraft ($1.9 billion), fertilizers ($944 million), cotton textile fibers ($648 million), and telecommunications equipment ($563 million).

U.S. imports from China were overwhelmingly concentrated in the broad miscellaneous manufactures category (SITC 8, which includes footwear and apparel as well as a variety of other light manufactures— $24.2 billion), followed by machinery and transportation equipment ($9.0 billion), and manufactured goods classified chiefly by material ($3.3 billion), which includes textiles, wood products, pottery, and so on. Chinese exports to the U.S. exceeded $1 billion in ten more narrowly defined three-digit SITC categories: toys, games, and sporting goods ($5.5 billion), footwear ($5.3 billion), women's and girls' coats ($2.0 billion), articles of apparel not elsewhere classified ($1.7 billion), telecommunications equipment ($1.6 billion), luggage ($1.6 billion), radios ($1.4 billion), headgear ($1.2 billion), plastic products not classified elsewhere ($1.2 billion), and the three-digit SITC miscellaneous manufactures category that includes things like umbrellas, baskets, and brooms ($1.1 billion). These imports are almost wholly labor-intensive manufactures, and economic theory suggests that this exerts downward pressure on the wages of import-competing domestic low-skilled labor, if production in such activities is actually carried out domestically.[9] It is for this reason that the role of international trade—especially with China—has come into scrutiny in domestic discussion over the growing income inequality.

Table 4.3

U.S.-China Bilateral Trade Balances ($billions)

	U.S. data	Chinese data	Adjusted U.S. data	Adjusted Chinese data
1989	−6.2	3.5	−4.9	−3.7
1990	−10.4	1.4	−9.1	−7.8
1991	−12.7	1.8	−11.0	−9.9
1992	−18.3	0.3	−15.9	−15.4
1993	−22.8	−6.3	−19.5	−24.9
1994	−29.5	−7.5	−25.8	−29.1
1995	−33.8	−8.6	−28.9	−31.2

Source: K. C. Fung and Lawrence J. Lau, "The China–U.S. Bilateral Trade Balance: How Big Is It Really?" Department of Economics, Stanford University, Stanford, California. April 1996.

Note: The adjustments correct for the mistreatment of Hong Kong's entrepot trade services in the accounts of both China and the United States.

Table 4.4

Bilateral U.S.-Chinese Economic Area Trade Balances ($ billions)

	Chinese Economic Area	PRC	Hong Kong	Taiwan
1987	−25.9	−2.8	−5.9	−17.2
1988	−20.6	−3.5	−4.6	−12.6
1989	−22.6	−6.2	−3.4	−13.0
1990	−24.4	−10.4	−2.8	−11.2
1991	−23.7	−12.7	−1.1	−9.8
1992	−28.4	−18.3	−0.7	−9.3
1993	−31.4	−22.8	0.3	−8.9
1994	−37.4	−29.5	1.7	−9.6
1995	−39.6	−33.8	3.9	−9.7

Source: Department of Commerce.
Note: Customs valuation.

Table 4.6 lists the U.S. industrial sectors of greatest dependence on China in 1994, the most recent year for which comparable production and trade data were available, using a different data set based on a different (Standard Industrial Classification) scheme. With respect to exports, as shown in the top panel, the industrial sector with the greatest dependence on exports to China was agricultural pesticides, which exported 40 percent of domestic production there. It was followed in

Table 4.5

Commodity Composition of Trade

SITC Code	Industry Sector	U.S. exports to China	U.S. imports from China	Trade balance
0	Food and live animals chiefly for food	276,845	528,433	-251,588
1	Beverages and tobacco	6,401	12,331	-5,930
2	Crude materials, inedibles, except fuels	1,152,257	251,414	900,843
*263	Cotton textile fibers	648,128		
3	Mineral fuels, lubricants, and related materials	61,146	362,691	-301,545
4	Animals and vegetable oils, fats and waxes	134,812	3,279	131,533
5	Chemicals and related products, N.E.S.	1,507,859	722,823	785,036
*562	Fertilizers (except crude)	944,121		
6	Manufactured goods classified chiefly by materials	407,734	3,344,552	-2,936,818
7	Machinery and transport equipment	5,118,675	9,056,750	-3,938,075
*792	Aircraft and associated equipment; spacecraft vehicles and parts	1,910,641		
*764	Telecommunications equipment	563,437	1,641,813	-1,077,376
*762	Radiobroadcast receivers		1,367,653	
8	Miscellaneous manufactured articles	508,463	24,175,559	-23,667,096
*894	Baby carriages, toys, games, and sporting goods		5,536,493	
*851	Footwear		5,259,130	
*842	Women/girls' coats, capes, etc.; textile fabric, nonknit		2,037,599	
*845	Articles of apparel of textile fabrics N.E.S.		1,660,921	
*831	Trunks, suitcases, vanity cases, briefcases		1,560,660	
*848	Headgear		1,225,162	
*893	Plastics		1,217,666	
*899	Miscellaneous manufactured		1,096,224	
9	Commodities and trans. not classified elsewhere	112,569	323,312	-210,743
TOTAL		9,286,761	38,781,144	-29,494,383

Source: U. S. Foreign Trade Highlights, 1994, p.7
Note: SITC stands for Standard International Trade Classification. Large three-digit SITC entries broken out as memoranda items.

Table 4.6

Sectors of Greatest Import and Export Dependence

SIC code	Name	Exports as share of production
2879	Agricultural pesticides and other agr chemicals, NSPF	0.40
2874	Phosphatic fertilizers	0.33
3449	Structural metal parts, NSPF	0.16
3548	Welding apparatus, and parts, NSPF	0.14
2824	Manmade fibers, noncellulosic	0.11
3261	Vitreous plumbing fixtures	0.10
3535	Conveyors and conveying equipment and parts	0.08
3728	Aircraft equipment, NSPF	0.08
2076	Veg oils & byprod exc corn, cottonseed & soy beans	0.08
3542	Machine tools, metal-forming, and parts, NSPF	0.08
3543	Molders' patterns for the manufacturing of castings	0.08
3792	Travel trailers and campers, and parts, NSPF	0.07
3553	Woodworking mach, parts & attachments	0.07
3533	Oil and gas field equipment, and parts, NSPF	0.07
2075	Soybean oil and byproducts	0.07
3536	Hoists, ovrhd trvlng cranes & monorls pts att NSPF	0.06
2812	Alkalies and chlorine	0.06
3671	Electron tubes	0.05
3564	Fans & blowers ex hshld; dust collection, etc.	0.05
3568	Mech power transmission equip NSPF & pts, NSPF	0.05
3571	Electronic computers	0.05

(continued)

turn by phosphatic fertilizers (33 percent), structural metal parts (16 percent), welding apparatus (14 percent), noncellulosic man-made fibers (12 percent), and vitreous plumbing fixtures (10 percent). The sectors listed in the upper panel of Table 4.6 might be described as mostly chemicals and capital goods.

The import figures in the bottom panel of Table 4.6 are both larger, and in a sense, more systematic. Sectors in which imports from China account for more than half of domestic consumption include dolls (75 percent), rubber and plastic footwear (66 percent), narrowly defined miscellaneous manufactures (which includes a laundry list of items such as cigarette lighters, umbrellas, and wigs—55 percent), leather wearing apparel (53 percent), and leather gloves (51 percent), all of which are simple light manufactures.

These figures refer to merchandise trade. The Department of Commerce estimates that the United States exported $2.5 billion in services

Table 4.6 *(continued)*

SIC code	Name	Imports as share of consumption
3942	Dolls and stuffed toy animals	0.75
3021	Rubber and plastics footwear	0.66
3999	Manufactured articles, NSPF	0.55
2386	Leather wearing apparel, NSPF	0.53
3151	Leather gloves and mittens	0.50
3171	Women's handbags and purses	0.47
3142	House slippers	0.47
3944	Games, toys, and children's vehicles, except dolls	0.45
3272	Concrete products, NSPF	0.42
3634	Electro-mech hshld appl NSPF electro-thermic, etc.	0.40
2391	Curtains and draperies	0.40
3172	Personal goods, of leather, ex handbags & purses	0.38
3648	Lighting equipment, NSPF (including commercial)	0.37
2675	Die-cut paper and paperboard; cards and cardboard	0.36
3149	Footwear, NSPF	0.36
2591	Venetian blinds & pts, ir/stl or aluminum, etc.	0.35
2392	House furnishings, NSPF	0.35
2394	Tarpaulins, tents, awngs, sails, & oth mde-up cnv gds	0.34
3161	Luggage	0.34
3143	Men's footwear, NSPF; work footwear, NSPF	0.30

Source: Department of Commerce.
Note: The abbreviation NSPF stands for Not Specifically Provided For.
Note: The abbreviation SIC stands for Standard Industrial Code.

to China in 1995, while importing $1.6 billion, for a positive balance on services trade of $937 million.

The stock of U.S. investment in China in 1995 was $2.0 billion (USTR, 1997). The Department of Commerce's 1993 survey of foreign direct investment provides a considerable amount of detail on this investment. According to the survey, in 1993 U.S. firms had eighty-eight Chinese affiliates (sixty-five of which were majority owned), with nearly $4 billion in assets that generated almost $3 billion in sales on which the affiliates earned $120 million.[10] These affiliates paid over $250 million in compensation to more than 37,000 employees. Most of this activity was in the petroleum, wholesale trade, machinery, and chemicals sectors.

Unfortunately, most of the data on intrafirm trade and the destination of sales is not reported to avoid disclosure of data for individual firms. As a consequence it is impossible to tell how much of affiliate output is exported back to the United States, or conversely what share of U.S. exports to China are from parents to Chinese affiliates. What the data that is reported indicates is that for majority-owned affiliates, 20 percent of output is sold to related parties, which is slightly lower than the average for U.S. majority-owned affiliates worldwide (25 percent). In other words, intrafirm trade is probably somewhat less important in the case of U.S. trade with China than with other countries. Production by majority-owned affiliates is exported to third countries at a noticeably lower rate (16 percent) than the worldwide average (23 percent). The overall picture that emerges is for a pattern of investment that is probably a bit more geared to serving the needs of the host market, China, than is the case with other U.S. direct investments around the world. A corollary is that intrafirm trade is probably not a big contributor to the bilateral trade imbalance.

U.S. Policy Toward China

The outside world has limited abilities to affect the development of the Chinese economy—the outcomes of the major economic policy issues that China faces will largely be determined internally. To give but one example: If the political leadership in China began to fear that centrifugal forces were pulling the country apart, there might well be a retrenchment of economic reform, and the Chinese government would become less responsive to the interests of foreigners and to fulfilling international obligations. In such circumstances there would probably not be a whole lot that foreigners could do to reverse such a tendency. Similarly, without domestic constituencies for change, there is little foreigners can do to expedite the process of reform.

Contrary to recent calls to "contain" China, the overarching goals of U.S. *economic* policy toward China are to promote political and economic liberalization within China (which the Clinton administration explicitly views as linked), integrate China into global institutions, and pursue U.S. commercial interests (which the administration largely identifies as exporters' interests). The U.S. also has strategic and political goals (which may at times conflict with economic interests) though there appears to be a lack of consensus in the domestic foreign policy establishment about prioritizing among these possibly conflicting goals as well as the effectiveness of alternative strategies and tactics to achieve them in the post–Cold War world. Policy is also influenced by the demands of a variety of domestic special interests (import competing sectors, exporters, human rights activists, etc.) with their own particular agendas. As a consequence, U.S. policy toward China is probably best regarded as a manifestation of competing interests in which no single goal predominates, and special interest groups may hold sway on particular issues. This sometimes gives the impression of an inconsistent policy, but to a certain extent this is probably inherent in the structure of the U.S. political system and the lack of domestic consensus over goals, strategies, and tactics in the post–Cold War world.

In the economic sphere, relations with China are played out in bilateral, regional, and global forums, and involve both trade and financial issues. There are obviously interrelationships between these different modalities, but for expository reasons, it is probably simplest to consider them separately in turn.

Bilateral Issues in U.S.-China Relations

The U.S. government interacts with China bilaterally in two basic ways. The first is proactively through U.S. policies to encourage economic reform in China, and China's responsible integration into the international economy. The administration regards technical assistance as the primary channel through which it can influence economic reform in China (and by extension encourage political liberalization). Among the avenues of technical assistance that have recently been created (or revitalized) has been the U.S.-China Joint Economic Committee led by the Treasury Department, with working groups on financial reform and the foreign exchange system. The Securities and Exchange Commission has a group that works on securities regulation, and the Treasury and the Federal Reserve Board have a group to provide assistance on banking regulation and the implementation of monetary policy. Private nongovernmental organizations (such as the American Bar Association) also engage in institution building. The primary channel of economic cooperation is private business trade and investment, though.

Similarly, bilateral intergovernmental relations are dominated by a second track of reactive trade conflict, largely a function of China's rapid growth, partially reformed economic system, and the complainant-driven U.S. trade policy-making system.[11] Noland (1996) presents evidence that indicates that bilateral trade conflict is most closely associated with the magnitude of bilateral imbalances and the extent of intraindustry trade.[12] Presumably, bilateral imbalances, whether caused by "natural" trading patterns, trade impediments, or macroeconomic disequilibrium, attract the attention of politicians and policymakers, giving rise to trade conflict either to resolve real issues or to provide political cover that the ostensively responsible politicians are "doing something." Intraindustry trade may be associated with less trade conflict, because trade in similar products is thought to usually involve less economic dislocation and a smaller impact on factor returns (including wages) than interindustry trade. As noted earlier, the impact of interindustry trade—especially with China—on the income distribution has become a particularly controversial issue in the United States. Moreover, Noland (1997) presents evidence that U.S. negotiators have been singularly ineffective in resolving trade disputes with China, in a sense of ending the recurrence of disputes on similar issues from year to year. In light of China's large and rapidly growing bilateral surplus with the United States and the relative predominance of interindustry trade over intraindustry trade in bilateral exchange, the "fundamentals" are in place for highly contentious relations.

Indeed, the potential for Sino-American economic conflict is likely to worsen. Table 4.7 reports the shares of U.S. trade accounted for by different trade partners, and projections of how these shares might change obtained by plugging the Table 4.1 figures, estimates of per capita income, measures of distance, and other factors into a gravity model of bilateral trade.[13] As indicated in Table 4.7, China's share of U.S. trade is likely to grow significantly, and China may become the United States's fifth largest trade partner after Canada, Mexico, Japan, and the European Union. Size counts in terms of political attention, and China's rapid growth is likely to translate into increased scrutiny of its trade practices by the U.S. government (Noland 1996, 1997).

Most Favored Nation Trade Status

Under the Jackson-Vanik amendment to the Trade Act of 1974, most favored nation (MFN) status can be extended to nonmarket economies only if the president grants a waiver certifying that the country does not impede emigration. (The law was originally passed to encourage

Table 4.7

U. S. Trade Shares

	1993	2003		
		Low	Medium	High
North America	28.3	27.5	30.3	31.5
Canada	20.5	16.5	18.2	19.2
Mexico	7.8	10.8	12.1	12.5
Asia-Pacific	35.2	34.7	37.6	41.1
Japan	14.7	12.2	13.2	15.0
China	3.8	4.2	5.3	6.7
Rest of Asia Pacific	16.6	16.4	19.1	21.6
Korea	3.0	2.5	3.4	4.1
Taiwan	3.9	3.7	4.5	5.3
Hong Kong	1.9	1.6	2.1	2.6
Singapore	2.3	2.3	2.6	3.0
Malaysia	1.6	1.8	2.1	2.4
Thailand	1.2	1.2	1.5	1.9
Philippines	0.8	0.8	0.9	1.0
Indonesia	0.8	0.8	1.0	1.1
Australia	1.1	0.9	1.0	1.1
New Zealand	0.2	0.2	0.2	0.2
Western Europe	22.2	17.4	18.5	20.2
Latin America	6.8	5.9	6.3	7.0
Rest of the world	7.5	6.9	7.3	8.1

Source: Marcus Noland, "Implications of Asian Economic Growth," *Asia Pacific Economic Cooperation Working Paper Series* Number 94–5, Washington, D.C.: Institute for International Economics.

Note: See footnote 5 for explanation of derivation of "high" and "low" share estimates. The "high" and "low" shares do not sum to 100.0.

the Soviet Union to permit the emigration of Soviet Jews.) China first gained MFN status in the U.S. market in 1980, and its annual renewal under Jackson-Vanik was routine until the Tiananmen Square incident of 1989.[14] Since then the annual renewal has been a point of contention with a bipartisan congressional coalition of anticommunists, human rights proponents, and protectionists attempting to use the threat of nonrenewal as leverage to encourage human rights, discourage nuclear proliferation, promote open markets, and reduce the bilateral trade imbalance. President Clinton exacerbated this tendency, first by criticizing President Bush during the 1992 campaign, and then in 1993 by tying renewal of MFN explicitly to immediate improvements in human rights in China. The executive order signed by President Clinton in 1993 to extend MFN until 1994, included a laundry list of human rights objectives as conditions for future renewal.

Relations between the two countries continued to be rocky in 1994: the Chinese government cracked down on dissidents following a visit by Assistant Secretary of State for Human Rights John Shattuck, and Secretary of State Warren Christopher was snubbed during his spring 1994 trip to China. Despite this, economists and business leaders successfully argued that revoking China's MFN and the ensuing retaliation would only hurt American exports while doing little or nothing for human rights. The Chinese, for their part, made a number of superficial concessions on human rights while cultivating the support of U.S. business. Despite an outcry from many congressmen, human rights activists, and the press, the administration decided to announce that China had met the minimum requirements necessary for renewal.[15] It also declared that in the future it would delink MFN and nontrade issues. The administration adopted the new line that encouraging China's economic liberalization and integration into the world economy would be the best way to pursue U.S. foreign policy objectives of democratization, development, and economic reforms in China (Economic Report of the President, 1996). Although the renewal of MFN in 1994 was correct substantively, the apparent climb down from the earlier statements of explicit conditionality made the president appear unsteady.

Relations subsequently worsened. Soon after the 1994 MFN renewal, the United States designated China as a priority foreign country under the Special 301 intellectual property rights protection provision. In May 1995, the U.S. Congress voted overwhelmingly to support the admittance into the United States of Taiwan's President Lee Teng-hui to receive an honorary degree at his alma mater, Cornell University.[16] The vote to admit Lee was a reflection of both fundamental American values and the fact that while the U.S. public regards China as important, this is not translated into warm feelings.[17]

Over the next year relations between the two countries plunged to their lowest level in recent memory. Several reports were released criticizing China's human rights policy; the American public was particularly outraged when China imprisoned (but later released) human rights activist Harry Wu, a U.S. citizen. China also conducted large-scale military exercises off the coast of Taiwan in an effort to influence behavior before the island's first democratic elections in which Lee Teng-hui scored a resounding victory. Evidence was uncovered that Chinese firms had sold Pakistan magnetic rings that could be used to enrich nuclear fuel, which could then be used in the production of nuclear weapons, and were involved in smuggling illegal weaponry into the United States. And just as the intellectual property rights (IPR) dispute was reemerging as a hot political issue, it was time to renew China's MFN status for another year.

MFN renewal in 1995 passed with little fanfare, but as tension on the trade, human rights, IPR, and proliferation fronts increased, the debate over renewal in 1996 became yet another occasion for addressing American concerns. The president announced that he would certify China's MFN status for another year, and the administration strenuously resisted congressional efforts to link the 1996 MFN debate with human rights, the IPR issue, and proliferation concerns. The United States Trade Representative (USTR) made it clear that it would handle the IPR issue independently of the MFN renewal. And while failed Republican presidential candidate Pat Buchanan railed against the Chinese, Republican presidential nominee-apparent Senator Bob Dole closed ranks with the president, reaffirming his support for renewal of China's MFN status.[18] Similarly others have long argued that China's MFN status should only be dependent on substantive progress in meeting criteria of trade liberalization, transparency, and other preconditions in China's effort to join the WTO. Indeed, the Taiwan crisis, while reinforcing China's image as an illiberal bully, appeared to temper attitudes in both the administration and Congress. South Carolina Senator Ernest Hollings, a long-time opponent of China's MFN status, announced that he would switch his vote and support MFN extension on the grounds that the yearly Washington debate serves only to increase tension and harm U.S.-China relations without accomplishing anything positive.[19] Alaska Senator Frank Murkowski, a long-time "friend" of Taiwan's, took a similar position. What is truly striking about the trade politics in the United States is how MFN policy has been driven by exporters and investors, not import-competing interests, and in the end the administration prevailed.[20]

The 1997 Rite of Spring was distinguished by mobilization of fundamentalist Christian political groups in opposition to MFN renewal.[21] Other issues invoked in the annual brouhaha included the governance of Hong Kong, and allegations (never substantiated) that the Democratic party received campaign contributions from the Chinese government. When it came to a vote, MFN renewal passed again (though by a smaller majority and with reduced votes from both parties). Right-wing Republican congressmen produced a package of legislative initiatives including a voluntary set of corporate conduct principles (modeled after the Sullivan Principles for doing business in apartheid-era South Africa), increased funding for Radio Free Asia, the National Endowment for Democracy, a State Department registry of Chinese political prisoners, the publication of a list of firms operating in the United States with links to the Chinese military, and visa denial for Chinese government officials implicated in human rights abuses. The legislative future of this package is highly uncertain.

Despite the almost comical aspects of the annual renewal debate, in reality the economic stakes alone are potentially quite large—according to the World Bank (1994). Loss of MFN treatment by the United States would cost China between $7 billion and $15.2 billion in lost export earnings, while costing U.S. consumers up to $14 billion a year in higher prices.

Import-Competing Sectors

Nevertheless, even if the issue of MFN did not exist, the United States and China would continue to have trade disputes. Historically, the focal point of trade tensions has been protectionist demands by U.S. light manufacturers. To cite one example, China's share of the U.S. bicycle market increased from 14.6 percent in 1993 to 23.7 percent in 1994, and in April 1995 three American manufacturers filed an anti-dumping suit against China.[22] The most important action has come in textiles and apparel, however, where the historic inability of the U.S. government to resist protectionist demands, import surges from China, and Chinese evasion of legal textile and apparel trade restrictions have combined to make this a major point of contention.

China circumvents its bilateral textile and apparel quotas, mainly by transshipping products through third countries that are also covered by bilateral quotas. In other words, the Chinese substitute their products for the unfulfilled quotas of third countries. A U.S. Customs Service study put the value of these transshipments at $2 billion, or about one third of China's official exports of textiles and apparel.[23] The main transshipment points are the high-wage locations of Hong Kong, Taiwan, Macau, and Singapore. Textile and apparel imports from these four countries were $8.5 billion in 1993. In other words, the Treasury figure implies that nearly 25 percent were transshipped.

A bilateral agreement on this issue was signed in January 1994. Government sources indicate that the problem appears to be getting worse, however. According to the Customs Service, there appears to be roughly $10 billion in Chinese textiles and apparel floating around the world not properly accounted for. For example, Chinese customs officials reported $13 billion in exports to 120 countries in 1992. But just 81 of these countries alone reported $23.7 billion of imports from China in the same year. (Ministry of Foreign Trade and Economic Cooperation [MOFTEC] reports $7.7 billion in textile and apparel exports in 1992, making the discrepancy even bigger.)

China reports $6.4 billion of textile and apparel exports to Hong Kong in 1992. Hong Kong reports $8.6 billion in consumption imports (more than $1,000 per person—an enormous figure), and $9.7 billion in reexports. Even allowing for high reexport markups, these discrepancies are huge.

The U.S. Customs Service found that half of the thirty-six fastest-growing apparel suppliers to the U.S. market had no significant domestic production for export, but report a significant increase in imports from China. Kenya, for example, has recently experienced a 790 percent growth rate in apparel imports from China, and a 212 percent growth in exports to the United States. Other countries, including Belize, the Czech Republic, Ecuador, and Qatar, exhibit similar triple-digit growth rates. All in all, the Customs Service estimates that at least $200 million of illegally transshipped apparels is coming into the United States through these countries.

Transshipping is currently subject to criminal prosecution, and Customs and the Justice Department have launched a major campaign to prosecute transshippers. There was recently a major conviction involving a Chinese state-owned firm. In May 1995 the United States cut China's cotton underwear quota by 35 percent and also reduced some other quotas because firms were illegally transshipping textiles through Hong Kong, mislabeling them as video rewinders and metal furniture.[24] In September 1996, the U.S. government announced "triple charges" in a circumvention case, and in November the Chinese government threatened sanctions on $1.5 billion in U.S. exports if the "triple charges" were implemented.

To head off this potential flare-up a new agreement was signed in February 1997, which provided for some changes in China's quota levels and growth rates. The core of the agreement, however, is the reduction in quota levels for fourteen product categories that were subject to repeated violations of the 1994 agreement, and the introduction of a provision to "triple charge" quotas in case of repeat violations. The agreement also contains new monitoring and bilateral consultative mechanisms. It remains to be seen if this new agreement will prove more effective than its predecessor.

The obvious question arises as to whether imports from China primarily displace domestic production (thereby exerting significant downward pressure on the wages of low-skilled workers employed in these industries) or whether these imports simply replace imports from elsewhere. To investigate this question a constant market share (CMS) analysis was undertaken.

The CMS approach is based on the idea that a particular country's share of world production is a function of its "competitiveness"

$$s \equiv \frac{q}{Q} = f(\frac{c}{C}), \ f'(.) > 0 \tag{1}$$

where s denotes share, q production quantity, and c "competitiveness"; lowercase letters indicate reporting country values, uppercase world values.[25] Rearranging and differentiating with respect to time, Equation (1) yields

$$\dot{q} \equiv s\dot{Q} + Q\dot{s} \tag{2}$$

$$= s\dot{Q} + Qf' \left(\frac{\dot{c}}{C}\right)$$

where dotted variables indicate time derivatives. Thus, in Equation (2), changes in the reporter country's production are decomposed into two terms—the first indicating what the country's production would have been if it simply maintained its share of world production, and a second indicating gains or losses due to changes in share (competitiveness).

Production, in turn, is also a function of the pattern of domestic consumption, exports, and imports, and changes in production will be affected by the commodity and geographical market (partner) composition of trade. So, for example, countries specializing in exports to rapidly growing product markets or partner countries would experience faster export growth than competitors concentrated in slowly growing markets for a given level of relative competitiveness. Their *shares* in those markets, however, would be constant as long as the underlying competitiveness factors remained unchanged. Thus a more sophisticated model can be constructed by decomposing production into consumption, exports, and imports, and redefining the relationships in Equations (1) and (2) in terms of commodity- and geographic-specific markets

$$s_{ij} \equiv \frac{q_{ij}}{Q_{ij}} = f_{ij}(\frac{c_{ij}}{C_{ij}}), \; f'_{ij}(.) > 0 \tag{3}$$

$$\dot{q} \equiv \Sigma_i \Sigma_j s_{ij} \dot{C} + \Sigma_i \Sigma_j C_{ij} \dot{s}_{ij} - \Sigma_i \Sigma_j s_{ij} \dot{M} -$$
$$\Sigma_i \Sigma_j M_{ij} \dot{s}_{ij} + \Sigma_i \Sigma_j s_{ij} \dot{X} + \Sigma_i \Sigma_j X_{ij} \dot{s}_{ij} \tag{4}$$

where i and j indicate product and partner respectively. The first term on the rhs of Equation (4) is the CMS rate of consumption growth—the rate of production growth that would have occurred if the country simply maintained its market share in domestic consumption in each commodity market. The second term gives the change in production for domestic consumption due to changes in share—that is, changes in competitiveness. The remainder of the terms in Equation (4) can be defined analogously.[26]

This approach has been applied to data on U.S. production, exports, and imports for the years 1988 through 1994. At the sectoral level the data were disaggregated to 460 product categories at the four-digit SIC level and three geographical markets—the U.S., China, and the rest of the world—were distinguished.

The results indicated that in 1994 the Chinese share in U.S. consumption was approximately $10.9 billion higher than would be expected if China had simply maintained its competitiveness in the U.S.

market since 1988.[27] However, the vast majority of this gain—$10 billion—was at the expense of third-country imports, so larger-than-expected Chinese imports only displaced around $900 million of U.S. production bound for domestic consumption.

U.S. exports to China were also approximately $700 million higher than expected, so at the end of the day, Chinese trade with the United States reduced U.S. industrial production by about $200 million over what would have been expected if the United States and China had maintained their relative competitiveness. Applying the Department of Commerce figure for average labor productivity across the industrial sector, this would amount to a loss of less than 1,000 jobs.

This is not the end of the story, however. Export jobs pay on average 13 percent more than nonexport jobs. Applying the export-related wage premium to the jobs figures one finds that the higher pay of the export jobs more than compensated for the slight reduction in total employment, and total compensation in the industrial sector was higher than expected, even with the Chinese competitiveness gains.

Whatever the Chinese gains in competitiveness, these gains have come almost exclusively at the expense of third-country exporters, and the direct impact on the U.S. economy has been minor.

Export Controls

U.S. policy discourages exports to China. This discouragement takes the form of both generic export disincentives such as unfavorable tax treatment (most notably lack of border adjustment, that is, the inability of U.S. exporters to rebate direct taxes on export sales as is commonly done elsewhere), and specific disincentives such as restrictions on the export of militarily sensitive products or the refusal of the Exim Bank to support participation of U.S. firms in the Three Gorges Dam project. Richardson (1993) uses a gravity model (similar to the one used to generate the bilateral trade volume estimates of Table 4.7) to estimate the impact of export disincentives. His estimates for all merchandise trade for 1989 ranges between $5.1 billion and $10.7 billion, on a base of $5.7 billion in U.S. exports to China. In other words, U.S. exports to China for 1989 would have been something like twice their actual volume had it not been for export disincentives. For the more narrowly defined categories of chemicals and machinery the export shortfall ranges between $2.8 billion and $6.2 billion. Using a somewhat different data set, Richardson obtained estimates of the export shortfall of $6.1 billion to $13.4 billion for 1991.

These estimates are subject to considerable uncertainty, the U.S. export control regime has changed with respect to China since Richardson's sample period, and the Chinese economy has grown by approximately one half.[28] Nonetheless, even if they are remotely accurate, they suggest that self-inflicted U.S. export disincentives dwarf the impact of Chinese policies on U.S. trade.

Intellectual Property Rights

Bilateral trade disputes between the United States and China have not only involved merchandise trade. An important, possibly preeminent, source of conflict has been over the lack of intellectual property rights (IPR) protection in China. Early in its reforms, China proclaimed its commitment to protecting copyrights, patents, and trade secrets by signing the U.S.-China Bilateral Trade Agreement of 1979. Throughout the 1980s, the two countries used the Joint Commission on Commerce and Trade as a forum to discuss issues of compliance, and China even joined the Paris Convention for the Protection of Intellectual Property.

Frictions resurfaced in 1991, when the U.S. government instigated a Special 301 investigation of Chinese IPR violations.[29] After a series of negotiations aimed at heading off retaliatory tariffs, the two countries signed a memorandum of understanding in 1992 under which China agreed to strengthen its IPR laws. It pledged to treat computer software as literary works: subject to copyright protection for fifty years. It also promised to expand the definition of and increase the protection for pharmaceutical patents, an issue that had proved to be a major sticking point in the negotiations. Later that year China joined the Berne Copyright Convention and the Universal Copyright Convention, and in 1993 it took on additional responsibilities under the Geneva Phonogram Convention.[30]

Although China carried out most of the institutional and legal changes required by the memorandum, the incidence of piracy continued to skyrocket. Concern over lax enforcement prompted the USTR to launch another Special 301 investigation in 1994. U.S. Trade Representative Mickey Kantor threatened a 100 percent tariff on $1.08 billion worth of Chinese imports. In February 1995, after a flurry of consultations, negotiators reached an agreement on the day before the tariffs were to be imposed. China agreed on specific enforcement measures to crack down on IPR infringement, to conduct frequent bilateral consultations, and to establish task forces to raid illegal manufacturers and improve border control. China also promised to increase market access for U.S. products by banning quotas on several goods and allowing U.S. companies to set up new joint ventures. This last move was seen as important to counteract the implicit trade barrier to U.S. goods caused by China's domestic sales of pirated goods.

China's efforts focused on curbing sales of pirated goods at the retail level. Yet production, distribution, and exports have continued. Not only does domestic sales of pirated goods act as a barrier to U.S. goods, China exports them to third-country markets (mainly Hong Kong, but also Southeast Asia, Eastern Europe, and Latin America) inflicting losses on American exporters to those markets as well.[31] Industry trade associations argue that the losses associated with piracy of computer software, compact discs (CDs), films, and trademarks cost American companies $2.3 billion in 1995 alone (IIPA, 1996). For its part, Beijing has pointed out that in the last year it closed seven CD plants that violated copyright laws and confiscated hundreds of thousands of bootleg CDs. It has also installed new government inspectors at CD factories.

The trade associations that make up the International Intellectual Property Alliance (IIPA) use different methodologies to estimate losses to piracy in their respective markets. Most share a common defect, however, in that they assume that the number of units sold in China would be the same regardless of price; in other words they assume that the price elasticity of demand is zero, as illustrated in the top panel of Figure 4.3.[32] This is ludicrous for luxury items in China such as computer software, videos, and CDs. In this case industry losses are given by the rectangle EFGH, which the industry claims is $42.3 billion. A more conventional set of assumptions is shown in the lower panel of Figure 4.3. Here, demand has some negative price elasticity so that it is downward-sloping. Supply is upward-sloping rather than infinite as the IIPA assumes. In the initial case, the producer surplus (the area above the supply curve below the price line) is triangle IJK. If the price is increased because of royalty payments, the supply curve shifts back along the demand curve to the new high price and low quantity combination P2, Q2. Producer surplus is the triangle LMN.

Figure 4.3.

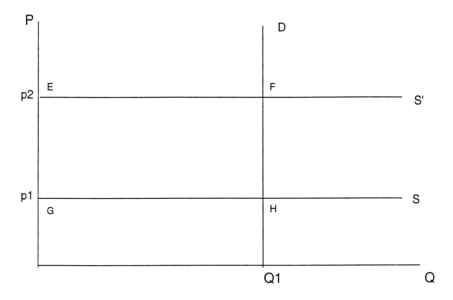

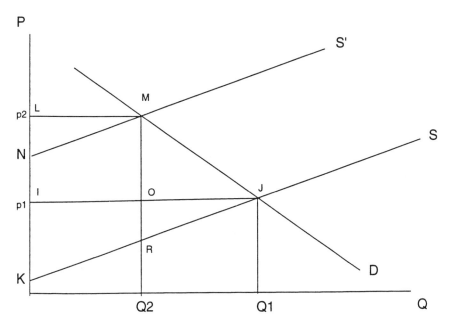

The industry might argue that in this case, the supply does not really shift, rather protection of intellectual property rights in the form of royalties is like a tax, with the revenues going to the producing firms. In this case producer surplus would be the trapezoid LMRK. Either way, the true loss of producer surplus associated with piracy is far lower than the $2.3 billion asserted by the industry.[33]

The IPR issue appears to be a quintessential case of domestic special interest groups successfully capturing government policy—in both countries.[34] In the United States, the intellectual property producers appear to have an influence of policy completely out of proportion with the actual impact on the U.S. economy.[35] The administration stated its determination to impose a 100 percent tariff on $2 billion worth of Chinese goods unless China clearly demonstrated it lived up to its 1995 commitment, and has published a proposed retaliation hit list for public comment.[36] The Chinese reacted sharply to the attack, threatening to retaliate with a package of tariffs of even greater value.

In keeping with past history, Chinese negotiators engaged in brinkmanship, waiting until the final possible moment before reaching the June 1996 accord. Since then, China has shut down a number of pirate factories and imposed $491 million in fines (USTR 1997). Yet despite the emphasis on enforcement, the suspicion remains that shutting down politically well-connected pirates will prove elusive. Although China often agrees to U.S. conditions, its track record of effective enforcement belies its procedure of superficial compliance.[37] Moreover, the technology and equipment necessary to engage in piracy is relatively inexpensive, lending itself to a pattern of rapid relocation in response to legal enforcement pressure. (Indeed, the Chinese industry has its origins in Taiwan.) Thus it is likely that successful prosecution of piracy is going to prove relatively difficult both in China and around the world.

Ultimately, the Chinese IPR regime will be strongly shaped by its entry into the WTO and the pressures of international enforcement. As it now stands, China provides far less statutory IPR protection than required under the Trade-Related Intellectual Property (TRIP) provisions of the WTO single undertaking. Its enforcement mechanisms are also less than required under the WTO both with respect to border measures and general procedures and remedies (Subramanian 1995).[38] Entry into the WTO would require China to strengthen both legal protections and their enforcement. Presumably these costly actions are more likely to occur if China undertakes them in the context of an overall package in which China obtains significant benefits in other areas. WTO entry would also move resolution of disputes from bilateral negotiations to an arguably less politicized multilateral setting.

Multilateral Issues in U.S.-China Relations

While the U.S. government has little direct influence on China's internal reforms, it has substantial ability to influence the terms on which China is integrated into global economic institutions, most notably the World Trade Organization (WTO). The United States (and other countries) is understandably cautious on this issue because of China's enormous size and the likely precedential effect that the terms of China's accession will have on the protocols of approximately twenty other economies in transition that wish to join the WTO.

The World Trade Organization

To join the WTO a signatory must agree to uphold the basic requirements of membership: transparency of the trade regime; uniform, nondiscriminatory application of trade rules; and national treatment for goods and, to a more limited extent, service providers. In the case of China, foreigners have encountered significant difficulties in a lack of transparency in the application of trade restrictions, as well as nonuniform application of trade policy in different parts of China.

In these negotiations the United States has tended to put more emphasis on obtaining access to the Chinese market (this would be consistent with the U.S. domestic political emphasis on exports), while the EU has put more emphasis on securing liberal safeguard provisions to protect against imports from China.[39] (During most of the negotiations Japan tended to align itself more closely with the U.S. position. However, in September 1997, Japan apparently unilaterally softened its position on market access significantly, much to the chagrin of its erstwhile U.S. and EU allies who expressed some bitterness about the Japanese action.) Ironically, the U.S. insistence on market access (which is, after all, trade-expanding and welfare-enhancing) has been criticized in China, while the EU's demand for safeguards (which restrict trade and reduce welfare) has received less opprobrium.

Beyond these fundamental issues, the main points of contention regarding China's application to join the WTO have been whether China will enter as a developed or developing country (which determines the length of the transitional period granted for bringing domestic practices into compliance with WTO obligations) as well as the issue of trading rights and state trading monopolies and the subsidization of state-owned firms.

China has argued that it should be allowed to enter the WTO as a developing country, and China is a developing country on any measure of per capita income. The United States has argued, however, that since significant parts of China are sufficiently developed it would be folly to permit China the additional leeway granted developing countries. (China's case is complicated by the fact that Taiwan has indicated that it is prepared to join the WTO as a developed country.) The likely outcome will be to classify China as a developing country for some WTO obligations and a developed country for others.

China maintains state trading monopolies, and unless foreigners are freely allowed to import and export, concessions on tariffs and other impediments to trade would be meaningless.[40] The current negotiations center on the dismantling of these monopolies and foreign monitoring of the operations of state-owned firms to ensure that they do not run afoul of the WTO's antisubsidy provisions. U.S. firms also argue that the "trade balancing requirement" of the current foreign exchange allocation system is in effect a nontariff barrier and a clear violation of the TRIPs agreement.

Historically Chinese tariffs have been quite high—as of 1996 some most favored nation levels were as high as 120 percent, and the simple average tariff was 23 percent.[41] (In point of comparison, average U.S. or other developed country tariffs are typically in the low single digits.) In the market access talks, the United States has asked China to join the "zero for zero" group, which eliminated tariffs on construction equipment, medical equipment, steel, beer, distilled spirits, pharmaceuticals, paper, toys, and furniture, and which greatly reduced tariffs on chemicals and electronics. The European Union has requested that China bind industrial product tariffs at 20–25 percent. Although neither demand is likely to be satisfied, China will undoubtedly increase market access as part of its WTO accession, and has signaled some willingness to do so as noted in the following discussion of APEC.

With regard to investment, foreign investors have to go through a protracted administrative approvals process, which is subject to corruption, and the United States has requested a streamlining of this process. The United States has also insisted that China accept international standards on expropriation and compensation and avail investors with international binding arbitration for settlement of disputes with the state (Cheng 1997).

The situation in services is more complicated. As part of its effort to join the WTO, China has begun some very limited opening of service markets to foreign participation. In the banking sector, for example, a few foreign banks in Shanghai have been granted on a trial basis the right to engage in domestic currency transactions. Likewise, a few foreign law firms have been allowed to open offices, though their activities remain extremely circumscribed. In insurance, only three foreign firms have been granted licenses, and again, their permitted activities remain highly circumscribed in both geography and function. A similar pattern of geographically and functionally limited opening has been replicated in other service sectors (USTR 1997). In other cases, Chinese policy has either required or effectively forced foreign firms to adopt joint venture partners that can foreclose commercial strategies available to U.S. firms.[42]

China has resisted opening up its telecommunications services market to foreign providers on national security grounds. However, without a modern telecommunications system, concessions in other areas, such as banking, are less valuable. Again, the most likely outcome is a highly detailed set of provisions specifying which forms of telecommunications are open to foreign participation. This has led some foreign observers to wonder if the timidity exhibited by the Chinese negotiators is not evidence of the great deal of uncertainty surrounding policy in the post-Deng era and the unwillingness of the Chinese negotiators to "stick their necks out" until some of this uncertainty is clarified. If this is the case the recent consolidation of power by Jiang Zemin may signal the possibility of more rapid reform and progress on WTO accession. The U.S. should seize this opportunity.

The stakes appear to be high. Recent modeling work by Mai and Adams (1996) suggests that the pay-off to China of joining the WTO could be on the order of 1.1–4.6 percent of GDP (depending on the form of the agreement and the underlying modeling assumptions). The United States too would benefit substantially from Chinese accession (0.5–1.8 percent of GDP) according to this work.

Asia-Pacific Economic Cooperation

China is also a participant in the Asia-Pacific Economic Cooperation (APEC). The major achievements of APEC thus far have been the holding of the first pan-Asian meeting of heads of government (ironically held in the United States in November 1993) and the declaration a year later of a commitment by the leaders to free trade and investment in the Asia-Pacific region. Concrete progress toward this goal has been less evident, however, and observers looked to the 1995 Osaka meeting to see if APEC would develop into more than a talking shop. Were the APEC countries to actually implement free trade and investment in the region, the results could be quite impressive. One recent study put the income gains to China at 1.9 percent of GDP (Mai and Adams 1996) while another concluded that the static income gains alone to China of such an agreement would be 2.2 percent of real GDP, with dynamic gains even larger (Lewis, Robinson, and Wang 1995). (Interestingly China is shown to experience an income gain even if it were excluded from any such arrangement—the impact on the other Asian economies would be sufficiently large that China itself would gain through the spillover from the others' income boost.) Another study, undertaken by the Australian government, put the gains to China of an APEC free trade agreement at 4.2–5.5 percent of GDP depending on model and specification (Office of National Assessment 1994).

Countries brought to the table "downpayments" or "deliverables" intended to establish the credibility of the liberalization process to the Osaka meeting. While some countries, notably Japan, agreed to accelerate their scheduled Uruguay Round tariff cuts, other countries, including the United States, brought little to the table. China tabled a package of tariff reductions, though given the questions of trading rights noted earlier its significance was questionable. The proposal included a commitment to cut tariffs on 4,000 products and to eliminate quotas and licensing requirements on 170 others. Shanghai and other cities would be designated "pilot bases" for joint ventures oriented toward foreign trade.

On April 1, 1996, China cut the average import tariff from 35.9 percent to 23 percent and scrapped one third of its import quotas. Tariff cuts were the largest on raw materials and high-tech items that China needs to import in order to sustain its economic growth. Tariff reductions on consumer goods and processed manufactured goods were much smaller. For example, tariffs on cars, which China protests is still an infant industry in need of protection, were only reduced from 110 percent to 100 percent.[43] At the Subic Bay APEC leaders' meeting in November 1996, China announced that it would reduce its simple average tariff rate from 23 percent to 15 percent over four years and make additional tariff cuts in the medium to long term to attain APEC's goal of free trade in the region by 2020.

Conclusions

Integrating large, rapidly emerging countries into the international order is always problematic. In the case of China, this is made more difficult by differences in political values, as well as its large bilateral surplus with the United States, which acts as a political lightning rod. As a consequence, one must expect that China will be involved in intermittent trade conflict with the United States and others for the foreseeable future. Moreover, due to China's size, the inevitable mishaps that may accompany the process of reform could well have international ramifications.

From this perspective it becomes highly important that China be brought into international bodies such as the WTO to try to contain and intermediate these prospective frictions. At the same time, China must assume the obligations that come with membership—otherwise China's entry may eviscerate these groups. And indeed, China stands to be the primary beneficiary if it does undertake these obligations, in effect adopting international legal norms and procedures in the absence of an effective domestic legal system. Under these circumstances the benefit to China could be enormous.

Four actions could be taken in the United States to facilitate this process. First, the United States needs to recognize that China is not the source of its economic problems—although Chinese economic policy leaves much to be desired, trade with China is not an important source of job displacement in the United States. If the United States is worried about the trade deficit, it should first reduce its own government budget deficit to close the saving-investment gap.

With respect to trade at the industry level, Chinese imports largely displace third-country imports in light manufacturing industries, not domestic production. When the compensation premium on export-related employment is considered, total worker compensation is higher because of trade with China than it would have been in its absence. Indeed, self-imposed U.S. export disincentives probably have a bigger impact on U.S. exports to China than Chinese policies have.

Second, the United States needs to find some way of extricating itself from the annual Jackson-Vanik certification process, which has become increasingly unproductive. One possibility is to scrap Jackson-Vanik altogether, though this is unlikely. A more feasible approach might be to conclude a nondiscriminatory bilateral trade agreement with China and extend open-ended MFN (as has been done in the cases of a number of Eastern European countries) at the time of its entry into the WTO.

Third, the United States needs to be more careful defining national interests and resisting political capture by special interests. The USTR, the negotiating arm of U.S. trade policy, does not have the analytical capability to ascertain the true impact of various foreign practices. It would be desirable to establish a formal interagency group including officials from the Council of Economic Advisers, the Office of Management and Budget, and the Treasury, which tend to have far stronger analytical capabilities than USTR, to scrutinize industry claims and develop some sense of priorities in setting the trade policy agenda.

Last, the United States needs to do a better job of cultivating relationships with subcentral government officials. In cases such as the IPR dispute, the central government signs agreements that it is either unwilling or unable to carry out. The United States needs to do a better job of identifying key local officials who can get the job done. A reorientation of engagement to the local level could also prove quite useful if political power devolves in a less centralized way in the future.

Notes

I would like to thank Chi Zhang and Dan Magder for research assistance, and Geoff Carliner, Kim Elliott, Robert Ross, Jeff Schott, and participants at the workshop at the Fairbank Center, Harvard University, for helpful comments.

1. Professor Li Jingwen of the Chinese Academy of Social Sciences recently concluded that on current trends, measured on a purchasing power–adjusted basis, the Chinese economy would be the world's largest by 2030 (*Financial Times*, 7 August 1997).
2. One consequence of these difficulties is that growth may be overstated.

Inflation was officially 24.2 percent in 1994, but many observers believe the true figure is higher. The basket of goods and their weights in the price index are not reported and apparently are subject to change, and the sampling techniques used to assemble the underlying data are poor. The industrial and producer price deflators diverge significantly after 1992, and an unofficial recalculation puts real GDP growth at 9.0 in 1993 and 7.8 in 1994, significantly below the official values reported in Figure 4.1.

3. Purchasing power–adjusted income figures take into account differences in national price levels, especially for nontraded goods. These figures are superior to those based on converting different national incomes to a common currency using market exchange rates that do not capture the large international differences in nontraded prices.

4. Lardy (1994, Table 1.3) cites estimates of purchasing power–adjusted per capita income for 1990 that range from $1,000 to nearly $2,600. The World Bank's recent report on poverty in China concluded that Chinese per capita income in 1994 was between $2,500 and $1,800 in 1994 dollars or between $2,200 and $1,600 in 1990 terms (World Bank 1996). Madison (1996) reaches an estimate of $2,047 in 1990 dollars. The estimate of $1,910 used in the construction of Tables 4.1 and 4.7 is well within the range of these alternative estimates.

5. Note that the subtotals for the high and low shares are calculated on the assumption that the particular unit experiences high (low) growth while the rest of the world experiences low (high) growth. Thus Table 4.1 is not based on three scenarios, but rather forty-one scenarios—the medium scenario, and one for each entry into the high and low columns. See Noland (1994) for further details on the underlying scenarios and the derivation of the projections.

6. Chinese access to the Asia Development Fund, the soft loan window of the Asian Development Bank is a different issue. Like the case of IDA, relatively stingy support by the United States has undercut its position, and China may be able to maintain its access to concessional funds for some time.

7. In an interesting survey of managers of foreign invested enterprises, Rosen (1997) found that the four most frequently cited problems of foreigners doing business in China were distribution-related conundrums; human resource shortages; anxieties about the changing balance of obligations and incentives; and strategic difficulties arising from partnering or relationship choices. Although some of these problems are endemic to poor countries, Rosen's survey makes clear that much of these difficulties is intimately related to China's status as an economy in transition from the plan to the market.

8. Ironically, the recent intellectual property rights disputes between the United States and China can at least in part be attributed to Taiwanese entrepreneurs moving their pirating factories to mainland China.

9. The mechanism by which this occurs is that imports push down the prices of competing domestic products, which is then translated into reduced wages for workers in those sectors. The impact may go far beyond the immediately affected sectors, as reduced wages in the import-competing sectors may be translated into lower wages in other sectors (including low-skill activities such as janitorial services or fast-food provision), which do not compete directly with imports but which do hire workers from the same pool of prospective employees. There is considerable academic debate in the United States as to whether this indeed has

been occurring and little consensus as to its significance. See Lawrence and Slaughter (1993) and Leamer (1995) for opposing views,.and Richardson (1995) for an accessible survey of the literature.

10. The term *foreign affiliate* refers to any Chinese firm in which a U.S. parent company or individual owned more than 10 percent of the voting securities or the equivalent. A majority-owned affiliate is a Chinese firm in which U.S. individuals or parent companies collectively owned more than 50 percent of voting securities or the equivalent. In the case of China, majority-owned affiliates account for most of assets, sales, earnings, employment, and compensation.

11. Some argue that corruption, at least partly a function of the incomplete nature of China's reforms, affects both the path of future reforms and makes conflicts that arise more difficult to resolve. China was ranked fiftieth out of fifty-four countries in the 1996 corruption perception index published by Transparency International. The United States ranked fifteenth.

12. The one notable exception to the pattern of trade conflict driven by the particularistic demands of U.S. special interests is the U.S. Treasury's condemnation of Chinese exchange rate practices. Beginning in May 1992 and four times since, the U.S. Treasury has cited China for manipulating its currency "to prevent balance of payments adjustment and gain unfair advantage" under Section 3004 of the 1988 Trade Act. A positive interpretation of this would be action on the exchange rate could forestall more politically damaging sectoral trade disputes that could arise from exchange rate misalignment.

13. Again, see Noland (1994) for details of this estimation.

14. Deng Xiaoping graciously offered to permit 10 million Chinese to emigrate to the United States, in order to prove there was no restriction on emigration. (As a point of reference, the Immigration and Naturalization Service only allows 20,000 immigrants from any given country each year, although family members, political refugees, and some others may be exempted from this restriction.)

15. President Clinton did impose one minor sanction, a ban on $200 million worth of Chinese weapons and ammunition, a cursory nod capable of pleasing everyone from the gun industry to opponents of trading with the military enterprises who produce the weapons.

16. The vote in the House of Representatives was 396 to 0, and the tally in the Senate was 97 to 1. The sole senator voting against the resolution had previously announced that he would not stand for reelection, and reportedly had two sons doing business in Shanghai.

17. A recent public opinion survey found that both elites and the general public believe by substantial majorities that the United States has vital national interests at stake in China (Reilly, 1995). However, China's ranking was in the lowest quartile of countries, below the EU, Japan, and Russia, and just above the Cedras dictatorship in power in Haiti at the time of the poll.

18. In a widely publicized speech in May 1996 Dole argued that "denying MFN would not free a single dissident, halt a single missile sale, prevent a single threat to Taiwan, or save a single innocent Chinese life."

19. One study funded by a Washington business lobby concluded that withdrawal of MFN would cost consumers $27–29 billion annually with the bulk of these losses coming in footwear, toys, dolls, and apparel. The study also concluded that approximately 190,000 U.S. jobs would be put at risk by China's threatened retaliation.

20. Admittedly the Uruguay Round deal was completed under the assumption that Chinese textile and apparel exports to the United States would remain constrained under the bilateral quota system.

21. Politics surely makes for strange bedfellows. A formal coalition of groups that formed to oppose MFN renewal included the conservative Family Research Council, the AFL-CIO, the U.S. Catholic Bishops Conference, the International Campaign for Tibet, the Robert F. Kennedy Memorial Center for Human Rights, the U.S. Business and Industrial Council, the Wisconsin Project on Nuclear Arms Control, and the right-wing Christian Coalition.

22. This suit follows the imposition of antidumping duties on Chinese bicycles in Canada, Mexico, and the EU (*Financial Times*, 7 April 1995).

23. Another published estimate put them at $10 billion (Mastel and Szamosszegi, 1996).

24. This sort of problem is not limited to the United States. In April 1995 the EU announced that it was deducting 9.3 million garments (less than 1 percent of the Chinese quota) for three years because of illegal transshipping through Hong Kong, Dubai, Morocco, Bangladesh, and Kenya (*Financial Times*, 19 April 1995).

25. This discussion follows Richardson (1971).

26. Two problems arise though, in the application of this method. The first is an index number problem. In the discrete time application of Equation (4), the values of the share weights (s_{ij}) may change over time. Use of initial year weights (the Laspeyres index) will tend to underestimate hypothetical export growth, while the use of terminal year weights (the Paasche index) will tend to overestimate it. A continuous time Divisia index would be preferable to either. The second problem is that while CMS analysis is typically performed on value share data, it is quantity share that will vary directly with competitiveness.

In this application U.S. production data was obtained from the Annual Survey of Manufacturers and deflated to December 1984 dollars using price indices from the Bureau of Labor Statistics. Chinese and world imports were obtained from the Bureau of the Census and deflated to 1985 dollars using import and export indices also from the Bureau of Labor Statistics. U.S. consumption was then calculated as production plus imports minus exports.

CMS weights were calculated by taking the geometric means of initial and terminal year weights, approximating the Divisia index.

27. These figures should not be compared to the trade balance—they are measuring something conceptually different. Specifically, the CMS analysis does not indicate that Chinese imports were only predicted to rise by $10.9 billion. It indicates that Chinese imports were $10.9 billion higher than expected based on the maintenance of constant market shares.

28. Most of the China-specific restrictions in place in 1989 have since lapsed or have been rescinded. The range of products covered under generic national security provisions has narrowed since 1989, though government officials indicate privately that the strictness of enforcement of remaining controls has grown. All in all, it is not clear whether the aggregate impact of these restrictions has grown or lessened since 1989.

29. The Omnibus Trade and Competitiveness Act of 1988 gives the United States the ability to conduct Special 301 investigations and to unilaterally impose tariffs on countries found to be violating intellectual property.

30. The presumption in this discussion is that China ought to adhere to the international norms. It should be noted, however, that these norms by and large reflect the interests of intellectual property producers—not consumers. There is little consensus in the economics profession as to the optimal regime from a global welfare standpoint, and it is even less evident that the status quo is optimal for all countries. (To make this concrete, it may be in a low-income country's interests to permit the copying of pharmaceuticals if this would greatly reduce the cost of medicines to consumers.) More generally, it may be in the interests of a low-income, net intellectual property–consuming country to try to avoid the provision of intellectual property rights while in a catch-up phase.

31. According to the Brussels-based International Federation of the Phonographic Industry (IFPI), China has increased CD production capacity to around 150 million units, though the domestic market can only absorb around 5 million units annually. The International Intellectual Property Alliance (IIPA), a Washington-based industry lobby, estimates that China has more than twenty-nine factories with a combined annual production capability of around 100 million CDs yet domestic consumption is only 5–7 million CDs a year. In both cases, the estimated domestic demand of CDs appears quite low—implying an annual demand of 1 CD for roughly every 250 people. A higher estimate of domestic demand would decrease the estimates of pirated exports.

32. U.S. government officials privately indicated that the IIPA's estimate was not the basis of the $2 billion retaliation figure arrived at by the U.S. government, but could provide no information on how this figure was determined.

33. To get a sense of how the numbers might change, figures released by the IFPI suggest that the piracy rate in China is 88 percent and that the losses are approximately $4 per disk. If these parameters are applied to the IIPA's estimate of 150 million units produced, one gets an industry methodology loss estimate of $528 million. However, if one assumes that the payment of royalties would increase the price of a CD at the retail level from $8 to $12, and that the price elasticity of demand is −1 and the price elasticity of supply is 1, the producer surplus loss would be $160 million, or around 30 percent of the industry's estimate. If the price elasticity of demand is −2, producer surplus falls to $44 million, or less than a tenth of the industry's estimate.

Moreover, it should be noted that this loss calculation is for all foreign producers—estimates of losses suffered by U.S. producers would be even smaller.

Lastly, it should be emphasized that this calculation is highly speculative and is presented for heuristic purposes only.

34. A large academic literature is devoted to examining the characteristics of industries that successfully lobby for import protection or export assistance. On the import side, successful lobbying appears to be strongly associated with high seller concentration (which reduces organizing costs and free rider problems) and low buyer concentration (which conversely inhibits the development of opposing lobbies). Success also appears to be positively correlated with employment of high-skilled labor. See Trefler (1993).

35. One can only speculate as to why the IPR industry would be so successful in pressing its case. One argument is that the administration felt a need to compensate the entertainment industry for the less than satisfactory outcome (from its standpoint) in the Uruguay Round. Others point to the importance of the industry

in Democratic Party fund-raising activities. Shortly after the last IPR agreement with China was concluded, Hollywood mogul Steven Spielberg hosted for President Clinton the highest revenue per person ($50,000 per couple) fund-raiser in U.S. political history. Moreover, both the entertainment and computer industries are concentrated in California, a politically critical state for the Democrats. However, the IPR industries appear to have been as successful in pressing their case in the Bush administration, casting some doubt on both these explanations.

36. The recently announced retaliation list appears to depart from previous practice of trying to maximize the impact on politically influential groups in the target country while minimizing the impact on U.S. consumers, while trying to avoid conflating market-opening and domestic protection—that is, where possible they have tried to avoid import-sensitive products.

The predominance of textiles and apparel on the list may set an unfortunate precedent for the opportunistic use of 301 sanctions in the future. The Committee for the Implementation of Textile Adgrements (CITA), the interagency group on textiles and apparel protection with a reputation for being completely captured by the domestic industry, was reportedly very involved in the discussions and wanted the retaliation list to include nothing but textiles and apparel.

37. China's record on other issues suggests that there is a gap between what it will agree to under pressure and its compliance with those commitments. Since the McKinley tariff of 1890, the United States has prohibited imports of goods produced using prison labor (a practiced explicitly authorized in the GATT/WTO agreement). In the late 1980s evidence surfaced that Chinese exports to the United States were produced in prison-run factories. The two countries signed a memorandum of understanding in 1992, under which the Chinese agreed to take steps to halt any exports of goods produced by prison labor. In order to ensure proper enforcement, the Chinese further agreed to allow a U.S. Customs official, based in Beijing, to conduct routine inspections of Chinese facilities suspected of using prison labor. However, a Human Rights Watch/Asia report published in 1994 reported on the continued use of political prisoners in export industries. Furthermore, following the deterioration of U.S.-China relations in 1995, China suspended inspections and did not allow a Customs official visit for a full year.

38. For example, China has not signed the Rome Convention (the International Convention for the Protection of Performers, Producers of Phonograms, and Broadcasting Organizations) nor is a signatory to UPOV (the Convention for the Protection of New Varieties of Plants), which are incorporated into the WTO TRIPs agreement. It also does not have in place a number of enforcement mechanisms required under TRIPs. See Subramanian (1995).

39. The United States also faces a legal issue on the apparent conflict between U.S. application of the WTO agreement to China and the Jackson-Vanik amendment, which inhibits the extension of unconditional MFN treatment to nonmarket economy countries that restrict emigration. (Although MFN is a basic tenet of the GATT system, Article XIII of the Marrakesh Agreement establishing the WTO allows signatories to suspend the application of the WTO agreements to new members.) China will undoubtedly seek some reassurance that the United States would not invoke this article to withhold nondiscriminatory treatment. The USTR maintains that only an explicit change in the law would resolve the issue, but many legal observers in the United States believe that this conflict can be finessed when the time comes.

40. Under current practices, foreign-funded enterprises can only export goods produced by themselves and import equipment and raw materials needed for their own production. China, which only grants trading rights to a limited number of domestic firms, fears that if trading rights were generally available, the resultant competition would cause a deterioration in China's terms of trade and a spate of dumping suits in foreign markets.

41. These statutory rates are much higher than actual collected rates, because the Chinese government has provided generous duty-drawback schemes for the importation of capital goods and intermediate inputs for foreign invested enterprises (FIEs). These duty-drawbacks (which effectively allowed the FIEs to import duty-free were scaled back in 1996, though the resulting fall in foreign direct investment (FDI) has spurred a reconsideration of their reintroduction.

42. The Rosen (1997) survey of managers of foreign invested enterprises identifies "strategic difficulties arising from partnering or relationship choices" as one of the principal problems facing foreign businesses in China. Likewise the trend toward the formation of huge conglomerates out of existing state owned enterprises (SOE) may begin to pose anticompetitive behavior problems similar to those observed with respect to the Japanese *keiretsu* and the Korean *chaebol*.

43. China also did away with preferential tariff rates for foreign investors importing capital equipment and raw materials. The impact of these changes on foreign companies is mixed. They will find it cheaper to import components into China but more expensive to build materials for factories.

References

Cheng, Leonard K.H. 1997. "US Attitudes and Policy Towards Investment in China," in Y.Y. Kueh, ed., *The Political Economy of Sino-American Relations,* Hong Kong: Hong Kong University Press.

Fung, K.C. 1995. "Accounting for Chinese Trade: Some National and Regional Considerations," paper presented at the Conference on Research in Income and Wealth, *Geography and Ownership as Bases for Economic Accounting,* Washington, D.C., May 19–20.

Fung, K.C., and Lawrence J. Lau. 1996. "The China-United States Trade Balance: How Big Is It Really?" Asia/Pacific Research Center, Stanford University, Stanford, CA, April.

Lardy, Nicholas R. 1994. *China in the World Economy,* Washington, DC: Institute for International Economics.

Lawrence, Robert Z., and Matthew J. Slaughter. 1993. "International Trade and American Wages in the 1980s: Giant Sucking Sound or Small Hiccup?" *Brookings Papers on Economic Activity* 1993:2, 161–226.

Leamer, Edward E. 1995. "A Trial Economist's View of U.S. Wages and 'Globalization'," paper presented at the Brookings Institution Conference on Imports, Exports, and the American Worker, Washington, D.C., February 2–3, 1995.

Lewis, Jeffrey D., Sherman Robinson, and Zhi Wang. 1995. "Beyond the Uruguay Round: The Implications of an Asian Free Trade Area," Washington, DC: World Bank, mimeo.

Madison, Angus. 1996. *Chinese Economic Performance in the Long Run,*

Gronigen: Gronigen Growth and Development Center, University of Gronigen, The Netherlands.

Mai, Y., and M. Adams. 1996. "Modelling the Benefits of Trade Liberalization," East Asian Analytical Unit, Department of Foreign Affairs and Trade, Government of Australia, Canberra, processed.

Mastel, Greg, and Andrew Szamosszegi. 1996. "America's New Trade Nemesis," *International Economy*, May/June, pp. 24–27.

Naughton, Barry. 1997. "The United States and China: Management of Economic Conflict," this volume.

Noland, Marcus. 1994. "Implications of Asian Economic Growth," *Working Papers on Asia Pacific Economic Cooperation* 94–5, Washington, DC: Institute for International Economics.

————. 1996. "Trade, Investment, and Economic Conflict Between the US and Asia," *Journal of Asian Economics,* 7:3, 435–458.

————. 1997. "Chasing Phantoms: The Political Economy of USTR," *International Organization,* 51:3 365–388.

Office of National Assessments. 1994. "APEC Liberalization Gains," Canberra, mimeo.

Reilly, John E. 1995. *American Public Opinion and U.S. Foreign Policy 1995*, Chicago: Chicago Council on Foreign Relations.

Richardson, J. David. 1971. "Constant-Market-Share Analysis of Export Growth," *Journal of International Economics,* 1:2, pp. 117–133.

————. 1993. *Sizing Up U.S. Export Disincentives,* Washington, DC: Institute for International Economics.

————. 1995. "Income Inequality and Trade: How to Think, What to Conclude," *Journal of Economic Perspectives,* 9:3, 33–55.

Rosen, Daniel H. 1997. "Priority Concerns of Foreign Invested Enterprises in China: Insights from Business Professionals," Washington, DC: Institute for International Economics, processed.

Subramanian, Arvind. 1995. "Trade-Related Intellectual Property Rights and Asian Developing Countries: An Analytical View," paper presented at the Asian Development Bank, Manila, May.

Trefler, Daniel. 1993. "Trade Liberalization and the Theory of Endogenous Protection: An Econometric Study of U.S. Import Policy," *Journal of Political Economy,* 101:1, 138–160.

USTR. 1997. *National Trade Estimates.* Washington, DC: Government Printing Office.

World Bank. 1994. *China Foreign Trade Reform.* Washington, DC: World Bank.

————. 1996. *Poverty Reduction and the World Bank,* Washington, DC: World Bank.

5

The United States and China

Management of Economic Conflict

Barry Naughton

The economic relationship between China and the United States has grown rapidly over the past twenty years. The current relationship is bigger, much more important, and more mutually beneficial than ever before. The paradox of U.S.-China relations is that despite the growth of mutually beneficial interaction, economic disputes and misunderstandings have repeatedly contributed to strained relations between the two countries. Given the enormous differences between these two large and important economies, some level of friction is inevitable. Moreover, the improvised institutional framework that has evolved in China as part of its transition to a market economy is complex and sometimes inconsistent, and creates a fertile soil for misunderstanding and conflict. Given the underlying mutuality of economic interests between China and the United States, though, there is reason to hope that a better understanding of the institutions and interests on the Chinese side may help to reduce the frequency of conflict.

Many of the economic conflicts that disturb U.S.-China relations ultimately can be traced to China's ambiguous relation to the world market. China is currently deeply involved in the international division of labor, because it is now the favorite site for the relocation of labor-intensive manufacturing industries pioneered by other East Asian economies. But on the other hand, China's domestic economy still has a fairly high degree of protection from imports and from world market forces in general. Indeed, China's current trade institutions evolved precisely because China sought to begin expanding trade quickly, while minimizing disruption to domestic industries early on. During the 1980s and early 1990s, China developed a dualistic trading regime that encouraged foreign investment, particularly in export-related activities, while maintaining significant restrictions on access to the domestic market.

The rapid growth of Chinese exports to the United States has come primarily from foreign-owned firms operating in the highly liberalized and open section of the Chinese economy. This rapid growth creates anxiety in the United States, particularly when individuals extrapolate continued rapid growth into the future. At the same time, U.S. businesses seeking to sell to Chinese customers frequently find themselves trying to sell into a trading regime that remains relatively closed and difficult to penetrate, despite significant reforms. On the United States side, the frustrations born of trying to sell to the least reformed parts of the Chinese economy merge with the anxieties born of receiving a flood of imports from the most reformed part of the Chinese economy. Frustration and anxiety together create a nightmare vision of a neomercantilist Chinese trading state manipulating and abusing the world trading regime.

In fact, neither the present nor the future of the U.S.-China economic relationship corresponds to these nightmare visions. More important, both China and the United States have an interest in moving beyond the current dualistic regime and toward significantly more liberal and uniform institutions. China, in order to consolidate the gains of opening and reform, needs to extend the provisions pioneered in the open trading regime to the whole of the domestic economy. This is not only in China's interest, it is also a requirement of membership in the World Trade Organization (WTO). China has already recognized this in principle and has begun to take steps in this direction: U.S. interests are fundamentally consistent with these moves.

The first section of this chapter lays out the basic facts about this important and mutually beneficial relationship. The second section describes China's unique trading regime, stressing the difference between the rules that govern the foreign-investor-dominated export sector and those that govern the domestic economy. The third section discusses the implications of the Chinese trading regime for U.S. interests. The fourth section discusses the potential future of the Chinese trading regime, in particular addressing the question of whether

China is likely to develop into "another Japan," a country with a chronic global surplus. The fifth section describes some of the fundamental issues that underlie differing views about China's WTO membership. The last section provides a brief conclusion.

The U.S.-China Trading Relationship

The United States and China first developed friendly diplomatic relations in the 1970s in an economic vacuum. Trade and investment were literally zero when the diplomatic opening began. The limited economic interaction that developed during the 1970s was managed by the central government on the Chinese side and seen as subordinate to strategic interests by both sides. Since the 1980s, U.S.-PRC economic ties have grown into a web of complex relations carried out by thousands of independent agents. In a sense, the U.S.-China relationship has grown from a narrow, unbalanced but warm relationship between two distant partners into a broad, important and in many ways "normal" relationship, that is nevertheless troubled by serious chronic disputes and misunderstandings. The economic relationship brings significant benefits to both sides, but it also creates opportunities for friction and misunderstanding, and increases the expectations and demands that each side places on the other.

China's role in the world economy has grown rapidly since economic reforms began. Between 1978 and 1995, China went from being the thirtieth largest exporter in the world to being the tenth largest, and its share of world exports increased from 0.75 percent to 3.0 percent over the same period. China and the United States are very important to each other, and each country's exports to the other are growing more rapidly than their overall exports. In 1996, the United States imported $51.5 billion worth of goods from China, making China the U.S.'s fourth largest supplier of imports, surpassed only by Canada, Japan, and Mexico. Moreover, the growth rate of United States imports from China between 1979 and 1994, at 32 percent *per year*, was much higher than that of imports from any other major supplier. Growth has slowed in recent years; it was only 17 percent in 1995 and 13 percent in 1996, but it rebounded to 21 percent in 1997. The United States now buys more from China than from Germany, the United Kingdom, or all of South America, and almost as much as from all the ASEAN countries combined.

U.S. exports to China are also large, but significantly smaller than imports. According to official U.S. statistics, the U.S. exported $12 billion worth of goods to China in 1996, making China the U.S.'s fourteenth biggest customer. The Chinese figure for U.S. exports is larger, at $16.2 billion, which would make China the U.S.'s tenth largest customer (leapfrogging France, Belgium, Brazil, and Hong Kong in the rankings). U.S. exports to China are growing rapidly, but not as rapidly as Chinese exports to the United States. U.S. figures show its exports growing at 12 percent annually from 1979 to 1994. This is the second fastest growth of U.S. exports to any major market, second only to Malaysia, and substantially more rapid than the overall growth of U.S. exports during the same period, at 7 percent annually. However, since 1995, China's imports from *all* sources—including the U.S.—have slowed markedly, to annual rates of 5 percent in 1996 and below 3 percent in 1997.

The published figures of China and the United States appear initially to present very different quantitative pictures of trade between the two, and the difference is particularly great with regard to the size of the total bilateral trade deficit. However, the apparent difference between the two melts away once agreement is reached about what is being measured. Both sides have agreed in principle to classify imports according to the "country of origin." Goods transshipped or reexported through an entrepot such as Hong Kong should not be classified as imports from the entrepot, but rather as imports from the country of origin. Both China and the United States—like most countries in the world—do a fairly good job of recording the country of origin of their imports, but neither country effectively monitors the ultimate destination of their exports.[1] As a result, both countries undercount their exports to the other because they show significant exports to Hong Kong, which are in fact ultimately reexported to the other.

This discrepancy between measured and actual exports is significant for U.S. exports to China, but enormous for Chinese exports to the United States. The principle involved in both cases, however, is exactly the same. Table 1 shows that the national statistics of each side are compatible once Hong Kong reexports are taken into account. Each country's imports (by their own count) are approximately equal to the other country's declared exports plus goods reexported through Hong Kong.[2] It is true that the numerical relationships become a bit less neat from 1993, because beginning in that year, China made a

Table 5.1

US-China Trade: Reconciling National Statistics (in billions of dollars)

	(a) U.S. imports from China (U.S. data)	(b) U.S. imports from China (PRC data)	(c) Hong Kong reexports to U.S. (HK data)	(d) Sum of (b) and (c)	(e) Percentage difference (d–a)/a
1989	12.0	4.4	8.5	12.9	7.5
1990	15.2	5.2	10.5	15.7	3.3
1991	19.0	6.2	13.4	19.6	3.2
1992	25.7	8.6	18.1	26.7	3.9
1993	31.5	17.0	21.8	38.8	23.2
1994	38.8	21.5	25.3	46.8	20.6
1995	45.6	24.7	27.6	52.3	14.7
1996	51.5	26.7	29.2	55.9	8.6

	(f) PRC imports from the U.S. (PRC data)	(g) PRC imports from the U.S. (U.S. data)	(h) Hong Kong reexports to PRC (HK data)	(i) Sum of (g) and (h)	(j) Percentage difference (i–f)/f
1989	7.9	5.8	1.3	7.1	−10.1
1990	6.6	4.8	1.3	6.1	−7.6
1991	8.0	6.3	1.7	8.0	0.0
1992	8.9	7.4	2.4	9.8	10.1
1993	10.7	8.8	3.2	12.0	12.1
1994	14.0	9.3	3.7	13.0	−7.1
1995	16.1	11.7	5.0	16.7	3.7
1996	16.2	12.0	5.9	17.8	10.3

Source: Fung and Lau (1996); updated with country statistical sources.

half-hearted effort to count as exports to the United States goods shipped to Hong Kong that were known to be destined for the United States. The Chinese were unable to sustain this rather difficult effort and it has, in fact, tailed off in recent years, as column (e) of Table 5.1 indicates.

The numerical exercise is important because it shows that China and the United States really do not disagree on *what* the numbers show; they simply disagree on how they should be interpreted. The figures also show that each country's import figures are approximately correct, and that each country's export figures are roughly compatible with the other's import numbers. For simplicity, it is acceptable to just use the import figures of each side. These show the United States exporting $16.2 billion to China and importing $51.5 billion. The United States exports to China less than one-third of what it imports, and the U.S. trade deficit with China, at $35.3 billion, amounts to over half of the total volume of trade ($67.7 billion). This figure is smaller than the official U.S. government figure for the deficit ($39.5 billion), but it is still large, both in relation to the total volume of U.S.-China trade and in relation to other U.S. trading relationships. Since mid-1996, the monthly U.S. trade deficit with China has on a number of occasions surpassed that with Japan, which was declining until early 1997. In short, the overall pattern of trade between the United States and China is extremely unbalanced. This imbalance is directly or indirectly responsible for many of the economic tensions between the United States and China.

From an economic standpoint, there is no basis to condemn bilateral trade deficits. Consumers benefit from importing low-cost goods from a foreign partner, and the overall trade balance of any country—including the United States—is determined by overall saving and investment in that country. Moreover, in a world of multilateral trading, it is natural that between any two nations trade will be "unbalanced," in the sense that one side or the other will be in deficit, at least temporarily. China shows no tendency toward running consistent global trade surpluses: since reform began, China's current account has been approximately in balance (Lardy 1995). Thus, China's surpluses with the United States are offset with deficits it runs with other trading nations. This is a clear difference from Japan, which has consistently maintained overall trade surpluses since 1974.

More fundamental is that the existing trade between China and the United States overwhelmingly fits the pattern of "comparative advantage" trade. That is, each side imports from the other goods that embody resources or factors of production that are scarce in its home economy. Since 1985, China's exports of labor-intensive light manufactures have grown very rapidly. Thus, China now exports goods that embody its most abundant factor of production, labor.[3] Toys, shoes, and clothing accounted for half of U.S. imports from China. Another 22 percent of 1996 imports were in the categories of telecommunications equipment, appliances, and office equipment. While potentially "high tech," these categories are actually dominated by simple labor-intensive assembly operations, which at most incorporate a few imported high-tech components. This can be confirmed by a visit to any U.S. department store, which displays shelves of inexpensive telephones, fans, and light fixtures, all assembled in China. Conversely, China imports substantial amounts of capital goods and technology. The three most important U.S. exports to China—airplanes, fertilizers, and industrial machinery—are all capital and technology intensive. Moreover, these goods are often substitutes for land resources: the fertilizer the United States supplies embodies capital and technology, and substitutes for land.

The fact that U.S.-China trade corresponds so well with comparative advantage ought to make it economically more advantageous and politically less sensitive than the kind of trade the United States conducts with, say, Japan, Canada, or Germany. U.S. trade with other developed economies is dominated by "intraindustry trade," in which the two countries exchange essentially similar goods (such as automobiles) with slightly different attributes. In some types of intraindustry trade, rivalry among nations to dominate "strategic" sectors can be intense. Thus, the U.S. deficit with Japan was especially sensitive politically because much of the deficit was concentrated in automobiles and electronics, sectors in which the United States was struggling to protect initial technological dominance and maintain future competitive advantage. By contrast, China-U.S. comparative advantage trade is founded on mutually beneficial exchange in which suppliers in the respective countries are rarely in direct competition. If China exported fewer toys to the United States, U.S. toy production would not increase. Instead, U.S. retailers would simply source their toys from alternative low-wage sites.[4]

The rapid growth of China's exports to the United States has come about largely as the result of investment in China from Hong Kong and Taiwan. The People's Republic of China (PRC), Hong Kong, and Taiwan are sometimes linked together as a "Greater Chinese Economic Region," or "China Circle" (Naughton 1997). If we consider the growth of trade between the United States and this entity, we discover some interesting patterns. First, as Figure 5.1 shows, the United States began to run a large deficit with the region as far back as 1987, when it reached $26 billion. The deficit dropped back slightly in 1988, but since 1988 U.S. exports, imports, and its deficit with "Greater China" have all increased at about 10 percent per year. By 1996, the combined deficit had grown to $46.9 billion, while U.S. exports had grown to $44 billion. Since 1987, there has clearly been a long-term structural deficit in U.S.–Greater China trade, growing steadily, though at a mod-

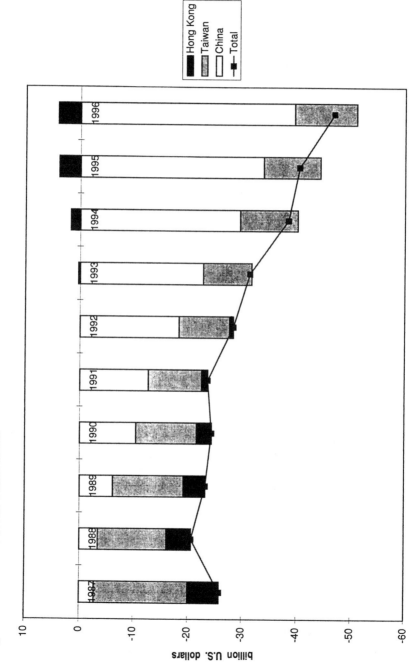

Figure 5.1. U.S. Deficit with China Circle

Table 5.2

The U.S. Deficit with Greater China

	Total	Taiwan	Hong Kong	PRC
1987	25.9	17.2	5.9	2.8
1996 official	46.9	11.5	−4.1	39.5
1996 adjusted	46.9	11.5	0.1	35.3

Source: U.S. Department of Commerce.

erate pace. The deficit has not changed much in relation to total trade between the two regions. But total trade with Greater China is growing more rapidly than U.S. trade overall, and thus the deficit is becoming larger in relation to overall U.S. trade and to the U.S. economy.[5]

Table 5.2 shows that the share of this deficit that is attributed to the PRC has increased sharply. In 1987, two thirds of the U.S. deficit was incurred vis-à-vis Taiwan, whereas in 1996, three quarters of the U.S. deficit was incurred vis-à-vis the PRC (according to our adjusted figures: even more if official U.S. figures are used). The U.S. trade deficit—a long-standing stable phenomenon—is being redistributed among the members of the Greater Chinese economic region. U.S. official figures overstate the degree to which the deficit has been redistributed to China; adjusting those figures slightly reduces the degree of redistribution but does not change the size of the overall U.S. deficit with "Greater China." Another equally revealing symptom of the continuity between past Hong Kong and Taiwan surpluses and current PRC surpluses is that an identical process can be traced for individual commodities. For a whole series of commodities such as footwear, toys, and bicycles, declining U.S. market share for Taiwan or Hong Kong has been matched by increasing market share for the PRC. (See Noland 1996 and Chapter 4 in this volume.) Underlying the dramatic growth in U.S.-PRC trade is the substantial continuing role of Hong Kong and Taiwan businesses as intermediaries in this trade.

There are thus many reasons to believe that the current U.S. bilateral deficit with China should not be an important political issue. It is not merely that economists, arguing from fundamentals, tell us that bilateral deficits should not matter. In addition, two of the most important issues that are at the center of most trade disputes are basically irrelevant to the U.S.-China deficit. That is, rivalry over position in strategic industries of the future is not an issue in U.S.-China trade, at least not in the immediate future; and painful adjustment of domestic industries to competing imports has also not been an important factor, since the United States was already importing similar goods from East Asia anyway. It is impossible to argue that U.S. jobs are lost to Chinese imports on any significant scale. And yet despite these factors, the bilateral trade deficit is an important irritant in U.S.-China relations. This is because U.S. firms continue to face substantial obstacles in their attempt to export to the Chinese market, and to the extent the Chinese market is "closed," a large trade deficit will inevitably lead to tension. Trade barriers plus deficits equal conflict.

The Chinese Trading Regime

Chinese foreign trade and foreign investment in China have grown rapidly since the beginning of economic reform. Yet China's economy has not become as open to foreign trade as the numbers might suggest. In essence, China has created two separate trading regimes. The first regime is an export promotion regime, dominated by foreign invested enterprises (FIEs). FIEs (and some domestic export-oriented enterprises) are able to import raw materials, components, and (until 1996) production machinery duty-free, as long as they are engaged in export production. Export-oriented FIEs experience little interference with specific import and export decisions, and enjoy very favorable tax and regulatory treatment. They thus operate in an overall environment that is extremely open to the world market. The second regime is an import substitution regime, that applies to the bulk of the domestic economy. Imports are restrained by a wide variety of tariff and nontariff barriers, and import trade is dominated by state-owned enterprises (SOEs). Foreign companies are encouraged to invest in the domestic economy and are given access to the market, provided they bring in substantial "technology," broadly interpreted. Thus, the import substitution regime is quite open to foreign investment (as many traditional import substitution regimes have been), even while it is restrictive of imports.

China created its liberal trading regime during the 1980s for the benefit of export-oriented FIEs, particularly those in southern coastal China. The policy worked well. Table 5.3 shows the rapid growth both of Chinese exports and of exports generated by foreign invested firms. During 1996, foreign invested firms generated 41 percent of

Table 5.3

Share of Exports Through FIEs and Processing Arrangements

	FIE share	Processing share
1985	1.1%	
1986	1.9%	
1987	3.1%	
1988	5.2%	27.2%
1989	9.4%	
1990	12.6%	40.9%
1991	16.8%	45.1%
1992	20.4%	
1993	25.8%	48.2%
1994	28.7%	47.1%
1995	31.5%	49.5%
1996	40.7%	57.6%
1997–first half	40.7%	54.2%

Sources: World Bank 1994, p. 12. *China Custom's Statistics,* 1993:12, 1994:12, 1995:12, 1996:12; 1997:6, p. 12. 1990, 1991: SSB 1992 *Zhongguo Fazhan Baogao*, p. 218.

China's total exports. Experimentation began at the end of the 1970s, when the PRC government began to allow Hong Kong businesses to sign contracts for "processing materials" (*lailiao jiagong*: also known as "processing and assembly" or "outward processing" from Hong Kong). In these contracts, raw materials and components were shipped into China duty-free, with Hong Kong businesses maintaining ownership. Chinese enterprises were paid "processing fees," and the completed goods were then shipped back to Hong Kong for final processing, packaging, and reexport. In 1987, these and similar provisions were broadly extended in an effort to attract additional export-oriented investment. As part of Zhao Ziyang's "Coastal Development Strategy," related provisions were made available to almost any foreign investor. By the late 1980s, foreign investors were able to control and manage their own imports and exports, and bring in materials and equipment duty-free, so long as they were engaged in export production.

This policy was a constructive adaptation to China's economic challenges at that time. On the one hand, the success of the East Asian newly industrializing economies was creating an immense opportunity for China. Both Hong Kong and Taiwan had become established as major exporters to the U.S. market, and by the mid-1980s, export success had created new economic pressures in both Hong Kong and Taiwan. Domestic costs were rising while persistent export surpluses were creating upward pressure on their currencies, which intensified the effects of increased domestic costs. Exporters in Hong Kong and Taiwan began to search for alternative production sites with lower costs, and particularly lower labor costs. A liberal trade regime allowed China to quickly emerge as an attractive alternative site for export-oriented production. At the same time, given the semireformed nature of its economy during the mid-1980s, the PRC government had to allow exporters exceptional latitude to import components and raw materials. The Chinese domestic supply system was unreliable and unlikely to adapt to the needs of foreign investors. Chinese policy, sometimes called "both ends outside" (*liangtuo zaiwai*) because it implied FIEs would find both suppliers and markets abroad, allowed exporters maximum freedom in importing and exporting, and at the same time minimized the links between these new export-oriented factories and existing supply capacity in the Chinese economy. Hong Kong and Taiwan businesses were able to maintain control of lucrative packaging, marketing, and distribution activities in their traditional locations. Low transactions costs made it possible for them to move only the low-skilled labor-intensive stages of production onto the mainland, while retaining other activities in Hong Kong or Taiwan. Production chains were quickly created that crossed political boundaries and which allowed Hong Kong and Taiwan to specialize in high-value services and technology-intensive production, while much of the ordinary manufacturing moved to the PRC. It would not be too extreme to call this an enclave economy: based on foreign investment, strongly integrated into neighboring political jurisdictions and existing export markets and weakly integrated into the remainder of the domestic economy.

Today, most FIEs import and export under provisions for "processing imports" (*jinliao jiagong*). It differs from the "processing materials" contracts in two ways: first, the imported materials are purchased by the enterprise within China instead of being "loaned" by the foreign business; second, the manufacturer is almost always an FIE. As Table 5.4 shows, in the first half of 1997, 38 percent of all exports fell under the "processing imports" provisions, and more than 80 percent of these were produced by FIEs. "Processing materials" provisions covered another 16 percent of exports, and almost 80 percent of these were pro-

Table 5.4

Chinese Trade by Regime and Ownership: First Half of 1997

	Imports (billion $US)			Exports (billion $US)		
		Percentage share			Percentage share	
		SOEs	FIEs		SOEs	FIEs
Total	63.05	43	54	80.82	57	41
Ordinary trade	17.38	77	21	34.97	85	12
Processing materials	9.48	75	22	12.78	77	20
Processing imports	22.95	13	86	31.06	17	82
FIE investment	7.18	0	100	0.00	0	0

Source: China Customs Statistics, 1997: 6, pp. 14-15.

duced by domestic SOEs. Put together, these two provisions accounted for 54 percent of China's exports and 85 percent of FIE exports.

The contrasting import substitution trade regime is labeled "ordinary trade" in Chinese classifications. As Table 5.4 shows, ordinary trade accounts for 43 percent of China's exports but only 28 percent of imports ($17.38 billion out of $63 billion).[6] But ordinary trade is the only one of the major trade forms shown in Table 5.4 that permits sales of imported goods to Chinese customers—the other trade forms require that the imports be used only by the importing enterprise, either as investment or as inputs into export production. China's ordinary imports have fallen below 6 percent of GDP since 1995, converted at exchange rates. In some respects, this would be an appropriate measure of the degree of openness of China's economy. While 6 percent is not a trivial import ratio for a large, continental economy, it is certainly modest compared to other economies. Correspondingly, this means that the Chinese market for ordinary U.S. exports is also not terribly large.

More important, most ordinary trade transactions are controlled by state enterprises, usually foreign trade companies (FTCs), which accounted for 92 percent of ordinary trade exports and 86 percent of ordinary trade imports in 1995. Many ordinary import trade transactions remain under the control of state-run trading organizations that are direct descendants of the former national monopoly trade companies. Thus, in 1993, the most recent year for which such a breakdown exists, ordinary imports were $38 billion, and FTCs directly subordinate to central government ministries accounted for exactly half, $19 billion.[7]

Locally controlled FTCs have undergone substantial change in recent years. Under enormous pressure to earn foreign exchange and make a profit, many of these corporations have become real trading companies, procuring export commodities from a variety of domestic producers at the most advantageous possible price. Trade corporations have aggressively expanded commercial relations with township and village enterprises (TVEs), and in 1995, purchased RMB 242 billion (U.S. $29 billion) of exportables from TVEs.[8] That was equivalent to about 40 percent of ordinary trade exports, and TVEs exported on their own another RMB 105 billion (U.S. $12.5) or another 18 percent of ordinary trade exports. The proliferation of state-owned FTCs has played a constructive role in promoting exports via stronger incentives, greater competition, and improved access to export markets. But central government trading companies continue to play a much greater role in ordinary trade imports, and there is less evidence of competition and reform with regard to imports. Indeed, central government FTCs run a large trade "deficit," since in 1993 they exported only $5.6 billion worth of goods and imported $19 billion. Many of these central government trading companies ferociously guard their monopoly over imports. If you are an American exporter selling goods to China, the odds are good that you are selling directly to an FTC run by the central government.

Nontariff barriers (NTBs) are also extremely important to businesses that try to sell to China. Fifty-one percent of all imports were subject to one or more of four different overlapping NTBs in 1992. These included compulsory import planning, canalization, licensing, and a separate system of import controls for machinery.[9] Since that time, two of the four (import planning and machinery import controls) have been eliminated, and the coverage of import licensing and canalization has been reduced. Following commitments made initially to the United States, China has reduced the coverage of its import licensing in annual increments. By mid-1996, twenty-eight categories of commodities were still subject to quota licensing, and another eight categories were subject to compulsory canalization.[10] Roughly 20 percent of China's imports are today subject to formal quantitative controls, including most important raw materials and virtually all transport equipment. There has clearly been a significant reduction in overall NTB coverage since 1992.

Nevertheless, it is not clear that the reduction in formal NTBs has significantly opened the Chinese market. Ambiguity persists because of the continuing gatekeeper position of the state-owned FTCs, and because after abolishing some NTBs, the Chinese government introduced new procedures like "automatic registration," that have the potential to restrain trade in the same commodities. The problem is that as long as control of imports is restricted to a small number of state-run FTCs—many of which have local monopolies in a given product—those FTCs have strong incentives to accept government guidance over permitted import quantities.[11] The institutions that restrain imports are still in place, even though the formal authorization for them to do so has been repealed.

In contrast to the situation with regard to the "ordinary" trade regime, the export promotion trade regime is largely outside direct government control or surveillance. Foreign invested firms manage their own imports and exports with little interference from the Chinese government. One reflection of this dual trade regime is that there is currently a huge gap between the nominal level of tariffs in China and the actual collection of tariffs by the government. The World Bank has analyzed the Chinese legal tariff structure prevailing in 1992. According to the bank, China in 1992 had one of the highest number of different tariff rates of any developing country (69), as well as a relatively high average tariff level. The unweighted mean tariff was 43 percent, and the trade-weighted mean tariff was 32 percent, meaning that total tariffs collected should theoretically equal about 32 percent of the value of imports. In fact, the value of duties actually collected in 1991 was only 5.6 percent of the value of imports.[12] Import duties are only collected on about one sixth of China's imports. The largest part of this discrepancy is due to the large share of duty-free imports of components and materials destined for export production, as well as duty-free import of investment goods by foreign invested enterprises, discussed earlier. But even after accounting for this factor, actual duties collected are a small proportion of legal stipulations. In 1991, 50.4 percent of China's total imports came in under some kind of import duty concessional provision, so if concessional imports had the same commodity composition as all imports, we would expect the actual value of duties collected to be approximately 16 percent of the value of imports: the actual value of 5.6 percent is only a third of this.

The export processing regime is in fact even more open than is indicated by the liberal legal provisions on which it is based because the regulations are easily abused. Goods can be moved into China under concessional provisions even when they are not strictly eligible for coverage. Such goods can then be diverted to other enterprises or sold on the open market. Many foreign businessmen have reported their surprise at seeing goods produced by their own companies for sale in China, through unauthorized distributors, at prices substantially below the international price plus nominal tariff duty of the good. There are even businesses in Hong Kong—called "channel providers"—who specialize in providing these services. Thus, the Chinese statistics on imports of materials and components for processing are probably substantially overstated and include a significant amount of goods subsequently diverted to other uses.

Probably equally important is the impact of outright smuggling. An official Hong Kong government estimate from the early 1990s was that goods smuggled into China equal about 15 percent of the value of legal trade from Hong Kong to China.[13] Given that legal exports from Hong Kong to China in 1995 totaled U.S. $58 billion, that would imply a smuggling trade of over $8 billion. Some of this is directly relevant to U.S. interests. Two U.S. commodities that are widely available for sale in Chinese cities are cigarettes and apples. According to Chinese customs statistics, neither is legally imported into China in significant quantities, implying that virtually the entire supply is smuggled in (Smith 1996). One reasonably well-educated guess of the value of smuggled cigarettes in 1990 was $500 million. A similar situation prevails for VCRs. In the first half of 1991, China produced 60,000 VCRs, none were legally imported, and 1.19 million were sold domestically.[14] Other consumer electronics products, as well as vehicles, are also often smuggled.

The separation between the trading regime for domestic enterprises and that for foreign invested enterprises is not, of course, absolute. There is substantial leakage from the open "enclave" economy to the remainder of the domestic economy. Indeed, one of the strongest incentives Chinese domestic enterprises (including SOEs) have for engaging in joint ventures with foreign businessmen is that the joint venture will immediately obtain privileges not accorded to the domestic enterprise. These include favorable financial treatment and the ability to import and export fairly freely. One example is provided by a domestic garment factory the author visited in 1995. Although the (state-owned) factory had export authority, it was subject to obstacles and delays in importing nice-quality zippers for its export clothing. After establishing a joint venture subsidiary, the domestic enterprise used the joint venture to freely import zippers, which it then diverted to the parent enterprise. The flexibility provided to the enclave economy unquestionably enhances the flexibility and productivity of the economy as a whole. Domestic enterprises learn to "work the system" and obtain many of the benefits.

Relevance to U.S.-China Trade Issues

The dual trading regime described earlier confronts American businesses and policymakers with a very frustrating situation. On one hand, it is still quite difficult to sell goods directly to the Chinese domestic economy. If you do not qualify for some kind of special treatment, tariffs are high and nontariff barriers are still significant. Most crucially, exporting to China often means selling to central government agencies that are actively engaged in restricting trade within certain parameters. American businesses are strongly encouraged to invest in productive facilities in China rather than to contemplate exporting to China for a prolonged period. It is clear that this is in accord with Chinese policy objectives. The most frustrating situation comes when U.S. businesses invest in China to get under tariff barriers, only to find themselves competing with their own products imported tariff-free by Hong Kong "channel providers." However you look at it, the Chinese market is difficult.

On the other hand, Chinese exports continue to flood into the U.S. market. Most U.S. imports from China are produced by firms in the export processing regime, which is dominated by FIEs. In 1994, processing trade (of both types) accounted for 47 percent of China's total exports, and fully 69 percent of China's exports to the United States, according to Chinese data (Ma and Zheng 1996: 48). Moreover, the *majority* of U.S. imports from China were reexported through Hong Kong.

In fact, the existing trade statistics, even after adjustment, give a profoundly misleading sense of the PRC's role in the growing U.S. trade deficit with Greater China. The numbers are *correct*, in the sense that they accurately reflect the fact that the main stages of production—assembly or manufacture—of the completed goods take place in the PRC. And this is in fact the commonly accepted convention for trade statistics. But they are extremely inaccurate in that they reflect very poorly the way in which the value created—and thus the income earned—is distributed among the different locations within greater China. At both ends of the chain of production—or of the "value added chain"—the contribution of economic agents outside the PRC is large. On the input or "upstream" side, precisely because the enclave economy is very open to imported inputs, the import content of Chinese exports is quite large. Chinese factories make toys with fabric and material imported from Hong Kong, and electronic devices are assembled from components imported from Taiwan. For example, in the first half of 1994, two thirds of Taiwan's exports to the mainland (transshipped through Hong Kong) consisted of man-made fibers and cloth, plastic materials, mechanical equipment, or electronic parts, all of which were inputs or materials for factories on the mainland. Most went to Taiwan-owned firms producing primarily for export, often to the United States.[15] Overall, the value of production inputs imported duty-free into China in any given year is about 80 percent of the value of exports in that year produced with duty-free inputs.[16]

On the output or "downstream" side, once exports leave China, substantial additional value is added in Hong Kong. The postmanufacture activities, such as packaging, marketing, insurance, and shipping of China's exports are almost invariably controlled by Hong Kong and Taiwan businesses. In fact, Hong Kong in 1995 imported a total of approximately $70 billion of PRC goods, kept some, and then reexported $82 billion of PRC goods![17] Of course, "underinvoicing"—understating of the value of shipments from China to Hong Kong—may skew this comparison as well. In any case, it is clear that substantial increments to the value of goods destined for the United States occurs in Hong Kong. Relying on survey data, Yun-wing Sung suggests that average mark-ups are on the order of 25 percent. Ma and Zheng (1996: 41) report a Chinese study of all exports for which price and quantity data were available and found an average 40 percent mark-up in Hong Kong. It is difficult to settle on any average figure given the variability and unreliability of the data. But it is certainly true that when imports labeled "Made in China" arrive at the port in Long Beach, California, it would not be unusual for the value-added within China to be 20 to 30 cents or less per dollar of CIF imports.[18]

Another approach to understanding the relationship among these economies is to look at Hong Kong's overall trade statistics. Some of the U.S. deficit with China ought to be offset by the U.S. surplus with Hong Kong. But, in addition, China and Hong Kong run a very large deficit with Taiwan. According to official Taiwan data, in 1995 Taiwan ran an export surplus of $24.3 billion with Hong Kong and China combined.[19] Of course, some of this surplus represents goods sold to end-users in Hong Kong and China. But some unknown proportion also represents inputs into production in China destined for export to the United States. Thus, there is a chain of deficits. If the United States has a "structural deficit" with the PRC, it is equally true that the PRC has a large structural deficit with Taiwan.[20] Neither Hong Kong nor Taiwan nor the PRC maintain chronic large global trade surpluses. Instead, they run chronic surpluses with some countries that are offset with deficits to other countries or regions.

As these relations amply demonstrate, the basic reason behind China's rapid emergence as an export power has been its ability to attract existing Asian exporters to relocate manufacturing facilities to the China mainland. As China emerges as the "factory" of Asia, the process pioneered by Hong Kong and Taiwan is now becoming an Asia-wide process. As the Japanese economy matures and restructures, Japan has been moving production facilities abroad. Shifts in national saving and investment have led to declining Japanese trade surpluses at the same time as production facilities move abroad. China has emerged in recent years as the beneficiary of Japanese and Korean production relocation. FIE exports from China have moved north: in 1993, 10.5 percent of Chinese FIE exports were from the northern coastal Bohai gulf area, where Japanese and Korean investment are most important; by the first half of 1997, 17 percent were from this region (FIE exports from Guangdong and Fujian, while growing steadily, have declined from 67 percent to 57 percent of the total during this period). (*Chinese Customs Statistics*; see also Seki 1994). These changes ensure that the volume of U.S. imports labeled "Made in China" will continue to increase, even as the economic significance of this fact dwindles.

Will China Become Another Japan?

American policymakers look at the statistics showing rapid growth of imports from China and much slower growth of exports to China. They hear complaints from American businesses about the difficulties of selling to China. These problems, combined with China's rapid economic growth, feed into fears that China will become "another Japan." That is, there is a fear that China will continue to grow while following policies of "techno-nationalism" or "neomercantilism." (Mastel 1995) In this framework, China will systematically restrict access to its own market while promoting its own exports. The Chinese surplus with the United States will continue to grow, becoming a chronic "structural deficit."[21] The Chinese will not be willing to play by impartial rules, and the result will be escalating economic conflicts. In a superficial reading of the evidence, these fears are not unfounded. However, upon further analysis, it emerges that the parallels are superficial. There are many important differences between the emerging Chinese "model," and that of Japan and subsequently Taiwan and Korea, three of which emerge as most important.

First, in Japan, Taiwan, and Korea, government policy aimed at the establishment of domestically owned enterprises as the chief instruments (and beneficiaries) of an export promotion policy. During their peak growth periods, foreign investment was severely limited in all three countries. In none of these countries did FIEs play a major role in export expansion. The situation in China is quite different. China is already more open to foreign investment than Japan, Korea, or Taiwan ever were during their peak growth periods. In this sense, China resembles the ASEAN countries more than Japan, Taiwan, or Korea.

This generalization holds not only with respect to producers of export commodities but also with respect to the firms that managed the actual export and import of commodities. In both Japan and Korea, the bulk of exports and imports have always been managed by domestically owned trading companies, the *soga sosha* in Japan and the *chaebol* in Korea. The situation in Taiwan is more complex: there are no large trading companies, and developed country procurement agents played a major role in Taiwan's export success. Nonetheless, Taiwan's thousands of smaller domestic trading companies have played the dominant role in export and import transactions. In all three economies, trade was not only closely watched by government agencies, it was also directly managed by domestic enterprises. Again, China is already different. Half of all imports and almost half of all exports are generated by firms with a foreign ownership stake.

Second, Japan and Korea, and to a much lesser extent Taiwan, carried out a government "industrial policy" that was designed to

strengthen domestic firms into "national champions" that would compete effectively in international markets and control significant advanced technology. China, undoubtedly influenced by its perception of
the success of these policies in Japan and Korea, is also carrying out
"industrial policy," even as it ends the era of planned economic
growth. But there are important differences. The most visible Chinese
industrial policies are precisely in those emerging areas that are dominated by foreign investors. The only really coherently elaborated industrial policy the Chinese have yet developed is that for the
automobile industry, particularly passenger cars. But the essence of the
policy is to attract foreign investment and concentrate it in a limited
number of large-scale producers. Already today 68 percent of Chinese
passenger car production comes from FIEs, and the impact of Chinese
industrial policy will certainly be to increase that number. More generally, most of what is commonly labeled as Chinese "industrial policy"
actually consists of simple tough bargaining with foreign investors,
trying to get them to transfer as much technology and production as
possible to China in exchange for market access. The simple policy
rule is "it is always better to have more technology and more jobs."
These policies resemble Malaysia today more than Japan during its
high growth era.

China is indeed trying to strengthen domestic enterprises into "national champions," primarily through the encouragement given to "enterprise groups." Such policies may in the future create a number of
Chinese companies capable of competing on an international scale. But
they are extremely unlikely to create a large number of international
competitive champions. The whole project is simply too entwined with
corruption and government favoritism to be very promising on a large
scale. One notes in particular the almost complete absence of the kind
of external pressures and standards that were placed on Korean
chaebol during their formative period, in which despite egregious favoritism and corruption, success in the international marketplace was
still used as the ultimate standard to determine which firms would
receive government favors and support. This is not true in China. Nor
is it likely to be in the foreseeable future.

This brings us to the third major difference, which is simply China's
enormous size. China's size means that its domestic market will always be large relative to the world market. For individual firms, no
matter how big, it will never be a matter of "export or die." From the

incentive standpoint, the domestic market will exert a pull that at least equals the export market. For the same reason, when national economic policymakers make critical decisions—such as those affecting interest rates and money supply—they are unlikely to give primacy to foreign trade over domestic economic objectives. Thus, national policy-making will not be as single-mindedly focused on maintaining export competitiveness as was the case in the forerunner export powers. Relatedly, size also has an impact on the *capabilities* for national economic management as well. Japan, Korea, and Taiwan were all in a position to maintain currency values at relatively stable, low levels. They were able to do this first because they established tough and consistent domestic macroeconomic policies that generally kept inflation low and because they restricted foreign capital inflows and maintained direct control of many trade transactions. China, on the other hand, has had several inflationary cycles during the course of economic reform, and is likely to experience at least moderately high and variable inflation over the coming years. Indeed, most observers feel that China's financial system is one of the least reformed parts of the economy, and the institutions most likely to cause economic problems in the next decade. Thus, the mix of incentives and capabilities was such that the governments of Japan, Korea, and Taiwan were all able to maintain focused and stable economic policies that gave domestic firms consistent, strong incentives to export. China lacks both the incentives and the capabilities to maintain such policies and is highly unlikely to reproduce a similar incentive environment for domestic firms.

China is so large that coordination problems are very different than in the East Asian NIEs. Different industries are developing at different paces in different regions of the country. It is not clear that a given set of exchange rate or industrial policies will be advantageous for the national economic interest at any given time. Indeed, it was precisely for these reasons that China's dualistic trade policy, with an almost completely separate export promotion sector, was introduced in the first place. Moreover, with a large domestic market and large, basically uncontrollable flows of capital, China is unlikely to maintain extremely stable real exchange rates at any level. The real exchange rate appreciated more than 35 percent between January 1, 1994, and January 1, 1996. Such a policy would make no sense for a neomercantilist power, but it might make sense for a large continental power struggling to reform the domestic economy and control inflation.

In a more general sense, understanding the dual foreign trade regime in China should lead us to understand another fundamental fact about China. It is economically pluralistic. There are different regions and sectors with substantial differences in interests, and now with significant autonomy. The national government is not capable of operating an integrated economic policy that somehow balances all these competing interests. Someday, it will recognize this fact. China will emerge as a major world power, but almost certainly not on the basis of neomercantilist policies. Rather, China will continue to integrate into the world economy in approximately the same uneven way that it has begun its integration. Different regions, different sectors, and different companies will continue to move forward at different paces.

China and the World Trade Organization (WTO)

A particular focus of contention between China and the United States recently has been the terms under which China would enter the World Trade Organization. WTO entry terms have assumed importance in part because they represent a displacement to a multilateral arena of the issues affecting bilateral relations. Initially, it appeared that it might be much easier to make progress on economic issues in a multilateral forum, where they would be insulated from the noneconomic issues (such as human rights and nuclear proliferation) that were bedeviling the bilateral relationship. In fact, the previous discussion should help to explain why China's entry into the WTO has also been contentious and the process of finding common ground difficult. Three factors appear destined to slow the process. These are first, the disproportion between China's economic importance and its status as a developing country; second, the relative unimportance of tariffs in regulating China's trade, and the problem of nontariff barriers; and third, the uncertain status of law in regulating China's foreign economic transactions, and the way in which foreign and domestic actors are treated.

Because China's trade is already important, and China has decisively proven its capability to dramatically further expand that trade, every decision with respect to the terms of China's accession to the WTO is extremely important, and therefore sensitive. Indeed, as Don Clarke notes:

> Variance from GATT norms was not a problem with the occasional small nonmarket economies like Romania or Poland, which could be let

into the GATT primarily for Cold War reasons without any fear of disruption of the system. But it is ironically China's presence in international markets which, while seeming to make it a natural candidate for membership, at the same time makes the current GATT members very nervous about its potential for disruption.[22]

But to add to the paradox, we have already seen that China's trade growth has come largely from an export-promotion sector of the economy that is significantly walled off from the rest of the economy. Thus, China's increased trade makes WTO membership more important and more contentious, without *necessarily* reflecting an improvement in the basic institutional conditions governing the Chinese economy. China has managed to become an export power while still retaining the inefficient and protected industrial system typical of a developing country.

Developing countries had special status in the GATT (the General Agreement on Trade and Tariffs), the forerunner of the WTO. They were given much more leeway to protect infant industries, to restrict imports for balance of payments purposes, and to adopt "flexible" provisions to regulate trade. Countries such as India, Pakistan, and Brazil became GATT members in 1948, and are founding members of the WTO. Yet none of them has a trading regime that can be called open by any stretch of the imagination. In this sense, developing countries, particularly those that are already members, are under much less pressure to conform to the principles of WTO membership than are developed countries. China has repeatedly insisted that it is a developing country and that it ought to be admitted into the WTO under terms appropriate to a developing economy.

It is unquestionably true that China is a developing country, since it is a low-income country with limited infrastructure and urbanization, and substantial widespread poverty. However, it is not entirely clear exactly what difference this should make for China's WTO accession. WTO does not have a formal status for developing countries, only a set of targets and timetables that are somewhat more relaxed than those for developed countries. For example, developed countries commit to lowering their average tariffs to 3.5 percent, while developing countries commit only to lowering them below 10 percent. Any country entering the WTO must negotiate a protocol of entry that is acceptable to all existing WTO members. The United States has taken the lead in insisting on a large number of relatively short timetables for specific industries, and China has refused to accept these timetables, insisting that more lenient treatment is appropriate.

This dispute seems counterproductive. In fact, China is making substantial progress in reducing its overall level of tariffs. Tariff reductions undertaken on April 1, 1996, following its commitment at Osaka in November 1995, reduced the average tariff from 36 percent to 23 percent. During 1997, additional tariff cuts were announced, and China committed itself to the goal of an average 10 percent tariff rate. Moreover, these steps should be seen in the context of the remarkable improvements in currency policy that occurred in the wake of January 1, 1994, when the Chinese renminbi was unified and devalued. Since that time, the currency has remained stable (in nominal terms) and current account convertibility has been gradually and successfully phased in. Viewed in these (traditional) terms, China is doing quite well in achieving trade-related convertibility with substantially lower tariffs, and it is hard to see why the United States should insist on especially stringent requirements for the next round of tariff reductions.

However, problems are more evident when we examine the second main problem bedeviling the WTO negotiations. This is the question of reliance on tariffs as opposed to administrative controls over imports. WTO members are supposed to quickly phase out quantitative restrictions and rely on tariffs to regulate imports. WTO provisions for tariff reductions attract a lot of attention, but they are actually less important than the general principle that tariffs are to be uniformly preferred to administrative controls and that recourse to administrative controls should be rare and exceptional. Tariffs are preferred in part because they are deemed more transparent, affecting all parties equally and making explicit the real level (and cost) of trade barriers. But in this area, the Chinese system falls far short of WTO standards. In the first place, tariffs cannot really be the instrument regulating imports because we saw earlier that China only collects import duties on a sixth of its imports! According to one source, in 1995, not including processing trade (which is entirely exempt from tariffs), China exempted a total of 100 billion renminbi of import duties, of which 44 percent was for foreign investor investment goods, 22 percent was for state-run investment project investment goods, and 18 percent was for policies implemented by Special Economic Zones and other development zones (*China Economic News*, April 21, 1997, p. 15). Clearly, the crucial consideration for many imports is not the level of tariffs, but rather the availability of tariff exemptions. And tariff exemptions depend on who you are, and what contacts you have, rather than on the price and quality of your imported goods.

Inconsistent application of tariffs strongly reinforces the distortions imposed by nontariff barriers. As described earlier, the number of overt nontariff barriers has also been reduced in recent years. But one critical barrier remains basically unmodified: that is the restriction of trading rights predominantly to state-owned foreign trade corporations. As long as the power to import is given only to a limited number of state-owned companies, and as long as those companies have some monopoly power and are dependent on continued government approval to enjoy their trading rights, the objective of full and fair impartial access by all to the trading system cannot be realized. Unequal access to tariff exemptions, significant nontariff barriers, and restriction of trading rights to state-owned companies together create a substantial barrier to adoption of the impartial and transparent, tariff-based system of trade that WTO principles call for. It is reasonable for the United States and other countries to insist that China substantially dismantles this system as a condition for WTO membership.

These issues are widely recognized within China. The discussion of them often focuses on one requirement of WTO membership, the commitment to "national treatment." National treatment requires that governments treat foreign-owned corporations at least as well as domestic corporations: they may not discriminate against companies because of foreign ownership. Of course, it is true, and ironic, that in many cases China discriminates *in favor* of foreign companies, because they have privileged access to the liberal export processing regime. It is even true that technically China could join WTO and continue to give foreign companies special privileges in some areas. But realistically, China will have to move toward a system in which foreign companies receive fewer privileges but also are less restricted in other ways. The only way for China to come into compliance would be by creating a true level playing field. Again, China has recognized this necessity and has promised to adopt "national treatment" by the year 2000 (Zhu Linan 1996). But in order to accomplish this objective, China will need to fundamentally dismantle the dualistic system that exists now. It is extremely doubtful that China will be able to achieve national treatment in such a short time without a major new commitment and acceleration of reform.

Some recent progress has been made. China allowed the establishment of three joint venture (i.e., foreign invested) foreign trading companies in 1996, beginning in Shanghai. Similarly, China now allows foreign invested retail operations in China to directly import up to one third of the value of their retail sales. As of now, these experiments are limited both geographically and in terms of the number of cases allowed. China has clearly selected foreign partners for the trading companies who can be expected to cooperate with Chinese formal and informal guidance.

The issue of national treatment naturally brings us to the final issue of judicial oversight and transparency. A fundamental presumption of the WTO is that there exists a system of judicial oversight that can regulate the behavior of traders. In China, the judiciary does not have real independence. China's legal order is essentially administrative, which most laws best characterized as commands running from superiors to inferiors. The public, and especially the foreign public, cannot attend legal proceedings without special permission, and transcripts of legal proceedings may not be released to the public without special permission. Many laws and regulations remain secret, and any independent publication of laws and regulations is a punishable offense. While China has pledged to make all laws and regulations that are specifically binding on the foreign trade system publicly available, this will not be enough unless there is an independent judicial system available to which recourse can be had.

One recent issue that disrupted China's progress toward the WTO was the question of intellectual property rights (IPR). Many analysts felt that the United States gave undue importance to IPR and treated China unfairly, given that disrespect for IPR is common in many developing countries. A central part of the dispute hinged on a commitment that China made to close during 1995 factories in southern China that produced pirated compact discs (CDs). China took tentative steps to close down these factories in early 1995. However, as U.S.-China relations deteriorated during 1995, in response to issues relating to Taiwan, China abandoned attempts to enforce the IPR agreement. During 1996, the issue reached a peak, and China narrowly avoided unilateral sanctions threatened by the United States in June 1996. Since that time, China has begun to make a serious effort to close down CD pirates, with some success. By the end of summer 1997, many Chinese producers had been shut down, and pirates had fled to the comparative safety of Macao and some Southeast Asian countries (Ferranti 1997; Warner 1997). In the long run, China's commitment to enforcement probably did not have much effect on the volume of CD piracy in Asia overall, and eventually China fell in line with its previous commitments. What then was the impact of the incident?

In retrospect, the incident represented a serious missed opportunity for China. The U.S. insistence on Chinese action with respect to a handful of already identified CD factories gave China the opportunity to signal its intentions at relatively low cost. By moving decisively to close down a few violators identified by the United States, China would have been able to unambiguously demonstrate its commitment to enforce its own laws. In fact, China eventually did this anyway. But China missed the opportunity to take prompt decisive action that would have had immediate impact as a signaling device. This could have been achieved at modest cost and would have implicitly demonstrated the Chinese intention to move gradually to a system of full enforcement, as resources permitted. Instead, by reneging on a promise—albeit temporarily—China missed an opportunity to demonstrate its commitment to gradually strengthen a rule-based system.

The IPR dispute thus needs to be seen within the context of the broader issues of judicial transparency and oversight. China's formal legal framework with regard to IPR is evolving rapidly and, notwithstanding a few egregious problems, is already fairly sound given China's stage in the development process (Schlesinger 1995). In this, it resembles much of the Chinese legal system, in that there is a discrepancy between formal legal institutions and actual practice that is difficult for outsiders to understand. These discrepancies are susceptible to many different interpretations. They may be due to the inherent weakness of formal and legal institutions in a developing country, and the limits on the government's enforcement ability. But they may also be due to an unwillingness on the part of the government to actually abide by or enforce such institutions. Even with strong political will, it is not easy to universalize the rule of law, and China would doubtless need a substantial transitional period before such rules would be judged effective. But that reality only makes it more important that the government signal a real intention to move in the proper direction. A signal in the IPR case would also have provided reassurance that China's nontariff barriers could be gradually eliminated, because it would indicate willingness to have international commitments override convenient (and cozy) domestic institutional arrangements. Instead, by failing to take steps until absolutely necessary, China ended up increasing the mistrust with which her other commitments are viewed by some in the United States.

Surprisingly, given China's current policy with respect to investment and trade, protection of IPR is probably the policy most in accord with China's own economic interest. For a smaller country with limited involvement in world trade, a government policy of intellectual piracy might well be economically rational. But China is seeking to maximize the inflow of advanced technology through the vehicle of foreign investment. Moreover, China has the basic technological resources that would allow it to master relatively advanced technologies quickly. In this policy context, China maximizes its own economic welfare by providing intellectual property rights protection to foreign investors and then bargaining as hard as possible over the distribution of revenues from the resulting production. Conversely, inability to protect IPR scares off precisely those foreign investors with proprietary, firm-specific technologies and capabilities that China wants to attract. It seems highly unlikely that China's foot-dragging on the issue corresponds to its own interests, even aside from its impact on WTO membership.

China's accession to WTO is likely to continue to be difficult, notwithstanding recent professions on both sides of the desire to work together to achieve early entry. Accession is difficult because of the coexistence of two different foreign trade economies, one highly protected and similar to other inward-looking developing countries and the other highly open and integrated with dynamic East Asian production networks. That coexistence of regimes makes it difficult for the WTO to determine how China should be treated. In the final analysis, the WTO is all about modifying trade regimes to conform to international principles. But China has two different trade regimes, and they lead to different conclusions about the direction and pace of the required changes. Finally, the specific features of the WTO-endorsed regime are quite different from those of the existing Chinese regimes. With only a bit of exaggeration we can say that the WTO requires a system in which trade is regulated by tariffs overseen by an independent judiciary. The problem with China's accession to WTO is that China does not possess either a fully workable tariff system or an independent judiciary.

Conclusion: Some Observations on Domestic Factors in U.S.-China Trade Relations

The Chinese domestic politics of WTO accession have clearly swung in a new direction. At the outset, China was able to mobilize a remarkably rapid and cohesive determination to rejoin GATT. It is quite remarkable that despite the apparent vulnerability of some of China's crucial industrial sectors—notably petrochemicals, pharmaceuticals, machinery, and automobiles—the leadership was able to achieve consensus on the desirability of China's rejoining GATT. To a certain extent, this was due to the fact that GATT resumption clearly embodied an issue of national interest and prestige. Not only did it appear that GATT membership would defuse recurrent trade frictions over U.S. MFN status, but it was obvious that China's prestige and importance in the world demanded full GATT membership. Moreover, it was clear that GATT membership could be an important force driving the economic reform process forward. For all these reasons, national interest was elevated above sectoral interest groups. The flood of publications in China on the challenge of GATT membership clearly demonstrates the anxiety felt by many sectoral interests but also reflects what they clearly felt was the inevitability of membership and the serious nature of the import competition GATT membership would bring (see, for example, Sun 1992; Zhu 1993).

Although these considerations are still salient, the political environment has shifted. It now seems politically inexpedient to be seen to be yielding too much to U.S. pressure. These attitudes seem to spring partially from a newly found assertiveness and resentment of U.S. pressure and also from a belief that concessions to the United States will simply be followed by additional new demands. From the Chinese perspective, they have taken massive steps in the directions asked by the United States: they have unified their currency, reduced tariffs, cut nontariff barriers, and demonopolized the foreign trade system. They have opened the country wide to foreign investment. During 1997 they launched into a major program of state enterprise divestment and restructuring that can be seen as a response to U.S. demands that the government cease subsidizing state-owned enterprises. And they have begun cautiously and slowly to allow foreign participation in the heretofore completely protected trade and banking sectors. By any standard, these are huge adjustments. Yet the United States seems to want more, and the fear from the Chinese side is that no response will ever be accepted as adequate on the U.S. side.

A very large area of common interest between the Chinese central government and the U.S. government is being overlooked. The Chinese central government has a very strong interest in enhancing its enforcement capability throughout the country, improving its customs service, and unifying and strengthening its revenue collection capability. In general, the United States has an interest in the same things. U.S. external pressure could easily be used by the central government in China to strengthen its hand in consolidating power and building institutions. Perhaps such a consideration is already in the minds of United States Trade Representative (USTR) negotiators. In response to lack of action on IPR, USTR negotiators selected for retaliation sectors—garments and consumer electronics—that are predominantly located in southern China and have a large foreign investor component. Pressure was being directed primarily at provincial leaders and at economic interests involved in the export promotion sector of the Chinese economy.

On the U.S. side, most of the important domestic factors relating to U.S.-China trade can be deduced from the previous sections. First, the existing trade imbalance has not, so far, by itself created a significant political issue in the United States. Since the overwhelming majority of Chinese exports to the United States are labor-intensive consumer goods in which the United States long ago lost any significant comparative advantage, there are no significant trade-competing industries of this type in the United States, and as a result, lobbying activity is minuscule. (See Noland, Chapter 4 in this volume). The exception is the textile industry which is protected (primarily from China) by the Multi-Fiber Arrangement (MFA).[23] This creates the peculiar political outcome in the United States that the deficit with China becomes a political issue primarily in the context of noneconomic criticisms of China. Given human rights abuses, the argument goes, we should exploit the Chinese "vulnerability" to economic sanctions that the trade balance seems to show.

Second, given sustained growth of U.S. exports to China and U.S. investment in China, the business lobby in favor of continued economic ties with China is active, strong, and committed. The most powerful political asset that China has in the United States today is this business lobby. Even though the United States cannot export as much as it wants to China, U.S. businesses are often in a position to profit from the operation of their subsidiaries in China. Perceiving the importance of China's economy in future years, numerous American businesses support a policy of intensified engagement with China. U.S. businesses are an important lobby not only because of their interests but also because of their perceptions of China. Given the magnitude of U.S. investment, many businessmen have now spent time in China. They see that China is a dynamic, rapidly evolving, and increasingly prosperous society. Their positive impressions partially offset the negative impressions of China created by problems relating to human rights, nuclear proliferation, and arms sales.

Third, there is substantial agreement among American businesses, even those most committed to developing ties with China, on the necessity to have China "play by the rules" and to have meaningful requirements imposed on China as part of its entry into WTO. There is broad agreement that accession to the WTO without substantial compliance with its most important principles would be disastrous to the world trading order. Moreover, this view is shared by most of the other major WTO trading nations. Although they are happy to have the United States be out in front in pushing China to obtain greater compliance, they privately support the U.S. effort. Moreover, a U.S. proposal to accept Chinese membership under relatively "soft" conditions would meet with substantial opposition in the U.S. Congress and probably would not be viable. Thus, the political support in the United States and other developed market economies for a tough and meaningful set of conditions on China's entry in the WTO is quite firm.

The analysis in this chapter suggests that the emphasis on having China agree to meaningful commitments as part of WTO membership should not be seen merely as an abstract commitment to government by law. There is no doubt that China will need substantial time before its legal system corresponds to U.S. notions of fairness, if indeed it ever does. But more immediately, China has to make concrete progress in moving from a dualistic trade regime, where imports are restricted by an opaque mass of special trading rights, quotas, and exemptions, to one in which approximately equal privileges and access are available to all comers. This can occur within the context of medium-high tariffs and long (though still time-bounded) phase-in periods. But it is clear that there must be a serious demonstration of commitment to move toward a unified trading regime. Specifically, it is reasonable for the United

States to insist that China extend trading rights significantly beyond domestic state-owned firms as a precondition for WTO membership.

The U.S.-China trading relationship is extremely beneficial to both sides and has a great deal of political support in the United States. Until the present, despite occasional frictions, the economic relationship has fundamentally been a positive element in the relationship, giving both parties an incentive to work through problems caused by conflicts over human rights, missile proliferation, and other areas. This can continue to be true in the future. However, it is important for both sides to be aware of potential problems on the horizon. As China's economy reaches a new level of sophistication, it is even more important than ever that it adopts a set of institutional reforms that will permit more complete coordination with the world economy, for the benefit of both China and her trading partners. Economics is only one among many strands of the relationship between the United States and China and thus cannot possibly explain the full range of the relationship. Yet neither can one even begin to understand the relationship without exploring the complex economic relationship between two dissimilar giants.

Notes

1. This is because imports are an important part of the tax base for most countries (as exports are not), and because the country of origin may affect the tax rates applied to imports, as well as the coverage of import quotas. While there is agreement on the principle, there is no agreement on any particular set of procedures for classifying goods according to country of origin, and this problem is becoming increasingly severe as production chains are increasingly international. (Stephenson and James 1995). An additional set of problems, discussed subsequently, apply to China-U.S. trade.

2. The equivalence is not exact, of course. Most countries measure their exports FOB (free on board), i.e., not including shipping and insurance costs. Most countries measure their imports CIF (cost of insurance and freight), which is larger, typically by about 10 percent. Because of this factor, we would expect U.S. measured imports from China to be larger than the sum of Chinese exports to the United States plus Hong Kong reexports of Chinese goods to the United States. In fact, they are consistently smaller, indicating some continuing double counting of Chinese exports and Hong Kong reexports.

3. According to the International Data Bank at Australian National University (ANU), China's exports consisted of 53.7 percent labor-intensive products in 1994, up from 29 percent in 1980. The ANU data bank classifies commodities into four categories: agricultural, capital, labor, and mineral-intensive goods. See also World Bank 1994: 9.

4. The concept of intraindustry trade is not always treated consistently in the

trade literature. Conceptually, intraindustry includes the strategic rivalry emphasized in this paragraph, as well as cooperation in which different economies specialize in different stages of a single production chain. China is beginning to engage in the latter form of intraindustry trade with the United States, for example in electronics. U.S. firms ship technologically advanced components to China, where low-wage assembly operations package them into finished and semifinished products. While clearly a form of intraindustry trade, these flows simultaneously accord strongly with the comparative advantage, or factor endowment principle, discussed here. In Chapter 4 in this volume, Noland argues that intraindustry trade in general is associated with a lesser incidence of trade disputes: that would be because the second kind of intraindustry trade encourages cooperative relations.

5. The 1995 trade deficit of $60 billion with Japan and $40 billion with Greater China constitute the majority of the U.S.'s overall trade deficit of $174 billion. The United States also ran large deficits with Canada ($20 B.), Mexico ($16 B.), and Germany ($15 B.).

6. The reason the share of ordinary trade in imports is so much lower is that the large share of imports are brought in duty-free as part of foreign investment projects (see Table 5.3).

7. *Customs Yearbook for 1993*, pp. 150–151, 157. The largest importers in 1993 were the Metal & Ores Corp. ($3 B.); Chemicals Corp. ($2.5 B.), Technology ($1.4 B.), Cearoils ($0.88 B.), Aviation Materials ($0.82 B.) and Baoli Corp. ($0.5 B.).

8. These exports show up as state-owned enterprise (SOE) exports in Table 5.3, because the FTCs that do the actual exporting are virtually all state-owned. *TVE Yearbook 1996*, pp. 122–123.

9. World Bank (1994), esp. pp. 63–67; 82–84. Thirty-two percent of imports were subject to "canalization," which thus had quantitatively the largest coverage. Canalization refers to the requirement that a given import be handled only by specific FTCs designated by the central government: this could be a monopolist ("single desk") or a larger number.

10. "China Adjusts Catalogue of Import Licensing," *China Economic News,* 1996, Supplement No. 7 (August 19), pp. 1–16.

11. For example, Dickson (1996) describes the system of "automatic registration" for steel imports that in 1994 replaced the canceled system of import licensing. He explains that automatic registration appears to be less than automatic in most cases, and suggests that the system plausibly explains at least a part of the 54 percent decline in steel imports between 1993 and 1995. Pei (1996) describes registration for machinery commodities, and describes it as a "transitional form" in NTBs and free trade.

12. World Bank, *China: Foreign Trade Reform*, Washington, DC: World Bank, 1994, pp. 48–63. The 1992 tariff structure analyzed reflected the reduction in tariffs on 225 categories on January 1, 1992, and the abolition in March 1992 of the Import Regulatory Duty. Thus, prevailing nominal tariffs in 1991 were probably higher than the 1992 tariffs analyzed, making the discrepancy between actual and nominal tariffs larger.

13. Estimate cited in Huang Weiting, *Zhongguo Yinxing Jingji [China's Hidden Economy]*, Beijing: Zhongguo Shangye, p. 39.

14. Ibid., pp. 36, 38.

15. "Trade with Mainland Grows," *Free China Journal*, September 2, 1994.

16. This number shows the imported input contribution to these exports is *high*, but not necessarily as high as 80 percent. Some inputs are imported duty-free but diverted to other uses. Moreover, the value of exports leaving China is understated because of widespread underinvoicing, caused by the desire to transfer profits to Hong Kong to enjoy lower tax rates and move capital out of China. Finally, production is growing rapidly, and this year's inputs are partially for next year's production and export, which will be much larger than this year.

17. In this case, the fact that trade is growing steadily makes the comparison even more surprising. Much of the 1995 reexport of PRC goods from Hong Kong will have been of goods imported into Hong Kong in 1994, when the total amount of such imports was 15 percent smaller than in 1995.

18. As a thought experiment, consider the case if the value of the commodities exported from China to Hong Kong is set at 100 and the value of components and materials imported from Hong Kong or Taiwan is estimated at 70 percent of the output value. In turn, conservatively assume that an additional 25 percent of total value is added by downstream businesses, primarily in Hong Kong. Then ($100 - 70)/125$ or 24 percent of the value of "Made in China" imports would actually represent value-added in China.

19. Directorate-General of the Budget, Accounting and Statistics, Executive Yuan, Republic of China, *Monthly Bulletin of Statistics of the Republic of China*, February 1996, p. 35.

20. In turn, some argue that Taiwan has a structural deficit with Japan. Taiwan's deficit with Japan was $17 billion in 1995.

21. Clyde Prestowitz was quoted to this effect on "Marketplace," American Public Radio, May 19, 1996.

22. Donald Clarke, "GATT Membership for China?" *University of Puget Sound Law Review* 17:3 (Spring 1994), p. 518.

23. The MFA will be phased out over the next ten years under the recently concluded Uruguay Round (though if China does not become a member of WTO it could conceivably be left inside the MFA), but it currently sets a tight and binding restraint on China's textile exports to the United States. U.S. imports of Chinese textiles will increase only 1 percent per year in 1995 and 1996. There are a few other exceptions, but even these prove the rule: for example, the U.S. bicycle industry brought antidumping accusations against China this year (Reuters, April 5, 1995).

References

CEN. China Economic News [Zhongguo Jingji Xinxi]. Hong Kong weekly.

Ferranti, Marc. 1997. "U.S.TR Puts China at Top of Copyright Watch List," *IDG China Market News,* April 30. At http://www.IDGChina.com/NEWS/may97/U.S.TR.htm.

Fung, K.C., and Lawrence Lau. 1996, "How Large Is the U.S. Deficit with China?" Stanford University Asia Pacific Research Center, Working Paper, April.

Huang Weiting. 1993. *Zhongguo Yinxing Jingji [China's Hidden Economy]*. Beijing: Zhongguo Shangye.

Lardy, Nicholas. 1992. *Foreign Trade and Economic Reform in China, 1978–1990*. New York: Cambridge University Press.

————. 1995. "The Role of Foreign Trade and Investment in China's Economic Transformation," *The China Quarterly*, No. 144, December, pp. 1065–1082.

Ledeen, Michael. 1996. "Take Our Technology . . . Please! The McDonnell-Douglas Experience in China," *Wall Street Journal*, March 12, 1996, p. A22.

Ma Xiaoye and Zheng Handa. 1996. "China and the United States—'Rules of Origin' and Trade Statistics Discrepancies," *Journal of World Trade*, 30:2 (April), pp. 39–51.

Mastel, Greg. 1995. "Trading with the Middle Kingdom," Washington, DC: Economic Strategy Institute.

Naughton, Barry (ed.). 1997. *The China Circle: Economics and Technology in the PRC, Taiwan, and Hong Kong*. Washington, DC: The Brookings Institution.

Noland, Marcus. 1996. "U.S.-China Economic Relations," Asia Pacific Economic Cooperation Working Paper 96-6, Institute for International Economics, Washington, DC.

Schlesinger, Michael N. 1995. "A Sleeping Giant Awakens: the Development of Intellectual Property Law in China," *Journal of Chinese Law*, Vol. 9: No. 1, pp. 93–140.

Seki, Mitsuhiro. 1994. *Beyond the Full-Set Industrial Structure: Japanese Industry in the New Age of East Asia*, Tokyo: LTCB International Library Foundation.

Smith, Craig. 1996. "Smugglers Stoke B.A.T.'s Cigarette Sales in China: Company Condemns Illicit Trade, but Churns Out Smokes to Supply It," *Wall Street Journal*, December 18, p. A16.

Stephenson, Sherry M., and William E. James. 1995. "Rules of Origin and the Asia-Pacific Economic Co-operation," *Journal of World Trade*, Volume 29, No. 2, pp. 77–104.

Sun Yanzhun. 1992. *Zhongguo Jiaru Guanmao Zongxieding de Libi ji Duice [Pluses and Minuses of Chinese Entering GATT and Appropriate Responses]*. Beijing: Zhongguo Jingji.

Warner, Fara. 1997. "The War on Pirated CD's Rages on a New Front," *Asian Wall Street Journal*, August 22–23, 1997, pp. 1, 10.

World Bank. 1994. *China: Foreign Trade Reform*, Washington, DC: World Bank.

Zhu Linan. 1996. "Inward foreign investment and national treatment [in Chinese]," *Guoji Maoyi [Intertrade]* 1996:1, pp. 27–29.

Zhu Qingzuo (ed.). 1993. *Ruguan yu Duice—Guangmao Zongxieding yu Zhongguo [Re-entering GATT and Appropriate Responses: the GATT and China]*. Shanghai: Zhongguo Dabaike Quanshu, Shanghai Fenshe.

Zweig, David. 1995. "'Developmental Communities' on China's Coast: The Impact of Trade, Investment, and Transnational Alliances," *Comparative Politics*, April, pp. 253–74.

About the Contributors

Robert S. Ross is Professor of Political Science, Boston College, and Associate of the John King Fairbank Center for East Asian Research, Harvard University. His most recent books are *Great Wall and Empty Fortress: China's Search for Security* (co-author, W.W. Norton) and *Negotiating Cooperation: U.S.-China Relations, 1969–1989* (Stanford University Press). He is the author of articles on Chinese security policy and U.S.-China relations in various scholarly and policy journals.

Barry Naughton was named So Kuanlok Professor of Chinese and International Affairs at the Graduate School of International Relations and Pacific Studies of the University of California, San Diego in 1998. His first book, *Growing Out of the Plan: Chinese Economic Reform, 1978–1993*, received the Ohira Memorial Prize; most recently, he edited *The China Circle: Economics and Technology in the PRC, Taiwan, and Hong Kong* (1997). Naughton is completing a study of provincial economic growth in China.

Marcus Noland is currently a Senior Fellow at the Institute for International Economics. He has held positions at the Johns Hopkins University, Tokyo University, the Council of Economic Advisers in the Executive Office of the President of the United States, the Korea Development Institute, the University of Southern California, and Saitama University. His most recent book is *Global Economic Effects of the Asian Currency Devaluations* published by the Institute for International Economics.

Robert Sutter has specialized in Asian and Pacific affairs and U.S. foreign policy with the Congressional Research Service of the Library of Congress since 1977. He is currently the Senior Specialist in International Politics with the Congressional Research Service. In his government service of over thirty years, Dr. Sutter has held a variety of analytical and supervisory positions with the Central Intelligence Agency, the Department of State, the Senate Foreign Relations Committee, and the Congressional Research Service. He received a Ph.D. in History and East Asian languages from Harvard University. He teaches regularly at Georgetown, George Washington, and Johns Hopkins universities. He has published eleven books and numerous articles dealing with contemporary East Asian countries and their relations with the United States.

Steven Teles is Research Assistant Professor at the Institute on Race and Social Division at Boston University, and has held appointments at Harvard University, Holy Cross, and Hamilton Colleges. He has written extensively on American public policy-making, including his book *Whose Welfare: AFDC and Elite Politics* (1996, University Press of Kansas). He is currently at work on a book examining the politics of pensions reform in the United States and the United Kingdom.

Index